VOICES AND THE SOUND OF DRUMS

VOICES AND THE SOUND OF DRUMS

An Irish Autobiography

Patrick Shea

Blackstaff Press

Published by Blackstaff Press Limited, 3 Galway Park, Dundonald, Belfast BT16 0AN
with the assistance of the Arts Council of Northern Ireland

ISBN 0 85640 228 1 (Hardback)
      0 85640 247 8 (Paperback)

Printed and bound in Great Britain by Billing and Sons Limited, Guildford, London,
Oxford, Worcester

The Publishers would like to thank the Ulster Museum for permission to photograph the
Still Life on the cover from part of their Collection.

Cover photograph by Dermott Dunbar

One

My father was born on a small farm on a steep mountainside in County Kerry. The fields behind the house went straight up into the sky. From the front door the ground fell down into a deep valley, the floor of which was a patchwork of little fields stitched together by low stone walls. The cultivated plots had been worked by patient men using hand implements; in the untilled land small black cows grazed. On the far side of the valley the ground rose steeply in shades of green and brown and black, overlaid by a high peak of bare grey rock that touched the clouds and looked as though some mighty force had thrust it through the surface of the earth. Over the growing face of the mountain and in the dark cracks up in the high rock, sheep clung like lice. This peak was known as Cnoc na Uaigness, the Hill of Loneliness.

When we went on a visit to Kerry, which was not very often for it was a whole day's journey by train, Uncle Dan would meet us in Kenmare with the horse and trap and we would cross the wide river by the suspension bridge which quivered to the trotting of the horse, along the road by Kenmare Bay, through wooded glens and up into the mountains where the trees were fewer and the air sharp. Up here Irish was the spoken language. During our stay the conversation would be in English until we had gone to bed; then we could hear Father and all of the others in the crowded kitchen conversing in Gaelic.

Father told us a lot about his youth in Kerry, about the local school in which the use of the Irish language was a punishable offence. As a result, although he was bilingual, he had never been taught to read or write in Irish. He told us about his grandparents' account of the great famine when the countryside was almost

1

depopulated by death and emigration and the family that owned a cow had to guard it by night and day against those who wandered the roads in search of food, and he showed us the road that had been made by hungry men whose wages had been meal; it was known locally as 'Bóthar na Mine', the 'Road of the Meal'. We went to the fair in the local village in a cavalcade of carts laden with squat tubs of butter covered with white cloths and when the selling and the buying had been done we stood outside the village public house and saw the men drinking porter from overflowing tumblers.

The farms in the Kerry mountains were too small to sustain large households so that in almost every home, as the children grew up, some had to look elsewhere for a living. Eighty years ago the normal outlets for ambitious children of small farmers were the Catholic priesthood, America and the Royal Irish Constabulary. One of my father's brothers and a sister emigrated to the United States. He joined the Royal Irish Constabulary. In the dark of a winter's morning in 1895 his father harnessed the horse and cart and together they drove the twelve miles into Kenmare where he took the train for Dublin to start his new life in the training depot in Phoenix Park. There he spent six months learning to be a policeman.

His first posting was to Newcastle in County Down, a holiday town where the Mountains of Mourne really 'sweep down to the sea'. This was about as far from his home as he could have been sent but he loved the tidy, fertile hills of Down and the smooth Mournes, so different from the wild Kerry landscape. For the rest of his life he never missed a chance to revisit Newcastle. He would stand in the main street and tell us that it was there he had learned to ride a bicycle and that from the sands along the promenade he had had his first bathe in the sea.

From Newcastle he went to nearby Saintfield where police duties seem to have been concerned mainly with the behaviour of gangs of workmen making the tunnel which was to bring water from the Silent Valley in the middle of the Mournes, thirty miles or so to Belfast. His next station was Newry, then, as now, a town rich in the variety of its citizens.

It was during my father's time in Newry that Jimmy Gill was captured. Gill, a steeplejack, had failed to answer a summons in connection with some minor crime and when the police went to arrest him he ran from his home to the mill chimney where he was doing repairs and, getting into his steeple-jack's chair, hoisted

2

himself to the top. There he stayed whilst the police stood below, by day and night, waiting for him to come back to earth and grudgingly sending up food whenever he lowered his billycan. Being informed in the ways of the law, Mr Gill knew that the warrant which bore his name could not be enforced on a Sunday. Each Saturday night, as the clocks struck midnight, he came swinging down to a hero's welcome, to spend Sunday enjoying the company of his friends and the hospitality of the newspapermen who had come to the town to report his vigil. And just before midnight, to the cheers of his assembled fans and the chagrin of the police force, he returned to the mill chimney, got into his chair and hoisted himself back to the sanctuary of his high perch. But one Sunday evening no-one in the party noticed that at the height of the revelry some dirty dog had tampered with the clock on the mantelpiece. The hands indicated that it was not yet midnight when two constables came to break the news that it was, in fact, Monday morning and take the fugitive away. His exploits had been so widely reported that, when he had answered for his sins against society, he was engaged to tour the music halls and tell the story of how he had placed himself beyond the reach of the long arm of the law.

My parents met and were married in Newry and, in accordance with a rule which barred a member of the force from serving in a district in which he had close family ties, a transfer to Mullingar, the county town of Westmeath, followed at once. After a couple of years there, during which my brother Jack was born, came a move to the nearby village of Delvin where, on 27 April 1908, I, their second son, arrived.

In those days policemen did not like service in the midlands. The country, generally, was peaceful; the Land Acts had given most of the tenant farmers ownership of their holdings, the violent movements of the nineteenth century had been left behind and the campaign for self-government was in the hands of the constitutional party. But in the midland counties embers of the land agitation still smouldered. It was an area of small tillage farms clinging to the perimeters of extensive grazing ranches and the small farmers, struggling to win a living from their minute holdings, were resentful of the prosperity of their erstwhile landlords whose wealth came, not from ploughing the land, but from the raising of fat cattle, a type of farming which provided little employment. The farmers wanted more land to till, and their anger periodically exploded into lawlessness in the form of organised 'cattle-driving'. They would enter a grazing ranch, throw down the fences, drive the cattle on to the roads and if time and the absence of the police permitted, plough the land. My father's time in Mullingar and Delvin coincided with a period of cattle-driving in that area. Being the son of a small farmer, like most members of the force, he had no enthusiasm for the role of protector of the property of landlords. It was with a feeling of relief that he received the news of his transfer to the lively town of Athlone, right in the centre of Ireland.

I was then six months old. The first home I remember was the Royal Irish Constabulary barracks at Fry Place, Athlone.

The earliest fragment in my rag-bag of memories is of sitting in the Convent School classroom and writing, and with a glow of achievement, understanding, the date. Until then the words and numbers which I had learned to make represented objects chosen by the teacher. For the future each day would bring a new date, a new headline to be drawn from my own small store of knowledge, to be written down by me without instruction or help.

I cannot remember the day or the month of that momentous happening but the figures of the year, 1912, I see as clearly as if I had written them yesterday. I have sometimes wondered if the indelible impression left by that moment of discovery came from recognition, at the age of four, of the beginning of independence.

I remember being wakened by my father in a dark bedroom, being brought into the brightly-lit kitchen and told to hurry and get dressed for going out. Jack was already there urgently struggling into his clothes. Mother was at the table buttering slices of bread and protesting at the foolishness of bringing children out of their warm beds in the middle of the night. Father smiled defensively. This was a great occasion, he urged, something the boys would remember all of their lives. Despite his impatience to be off, she insisted that we must take cups of cocoa and bread and butter to protect us against the cold night air.

As we hurried along empty streets, dimly lit by flickering gas lamps, past silent, shuttered shops and dark doorways, Jack and I had to run to keep up with Father's long strides. The appearance of the town at this late hour was new and a little frightening to me. I kept a tight grip on Father's hand. He made no mention of where we were going or what we were being brought to see.

4

At the top of Connaught Street, where the gas lamps ended, we turned into the Batteries, a sort of town common, an area of deep valleys and grassy mounds scarred with stone-lined trenches and emplacements, the remains of the habitation of a garrison of long ago. Here in the daytime children gathered for noisy games and the townspeople took the air and golf was played, but at night it was unlit and silent and small boys who were seldom out of doors after tea-time would never have ventured into the darkness beyond the big, crumbling gateposts.

We clung closer to Father as he led us across the dewy ground, down the steep slope of a grassy trough which in the darkness seemed twice as deep as it ever did in daylight, and up the opposite side, heading, I then knew, for a high plateau which was a favourite spot for picnickers and pitch-and-toss schools and men who exercised greyhounds. As we went up the far slope, leaning forward into the hard, rising ground, we began to hear the dull beating of a drum and the murmuring sound of many voices. Then quite suddenly we were at the top, out of breath and at the end of our journey. In the centre of the wide, grassy arena an enormous fire was burning and around it a great crowd of people was gathered; a boisterous, cheering, talking, laughing assembly of all ages and conditions. Somewhere a brass band was playing an Irish air.

We went in through the crowd, Father now and then speaking to someone he knew, until the press of bodies brought us to a halt; then he lifted us up, one on each arm, so that we were suddenly confronted with the violence of the scene around the fire which was no more than twenty or thirty yards away. Our sudden exposure to the bright, warm glare brought tears to our eyes. Not even the big fire in the bakery had been anything like this. Men and women and boys leaped and danced dangerously close to the high tower of flame from which smoke and sparks roared up into the black sky. Surely there had never before been a fire like this or such a gathering of noisy, disorderly people.

As we watched, exhilarated and a little frightened, the discordant noises of the crowd began to respond to the rhythm of the band buried somewhere amongst them and suddenly everyone was singing; singing with fervour and passion and joy.

> When boyhood's fire was in my blood
> I dreamt of ancient freemen,

5

Of Greece and Rome who bravely stood,
Three hundred men and three men.
And then I prayed I yet might see
Our fetters rent in twain,
And Ireland, long a province, be
A nation once again.

A nation once again.
A nation once again.
And Ireland, long a province, be
A nation once again.

They sang many verses and each chorus rang through the night air with a roar of joy and triumph. The song ended with cheering and hand-shaking and back-slapping.

In obedience to Mother's instructions, we did not stay long watching the bonfire and on the way home Father told us that the reason for the celebrations was the passing of the Home Rule Bill in the British Parliament. This was a very special happening, he said; Ireland would have its own government for the first time since Henry Grattan's Parliament had been closed, more than a hundred years before.

We returned by the way we had come; along Connaught Street and Bastion Street, down the narrow, unlit street which led to Fry Place and through the gateway into the police barrack.

Next morning we were up early. We told Tim, our younger brother, about our midnight visit to the Batteries and undertook to bring him to see the bonfire on our way to school.

A few people were moving about as we went through the streets, milk was being delivered from wooden churns sitting high in small carts drawn by donkeys, shops were being opened. It was surprising to find that after the excitement of the night before, the town was wakening to a normal day.

Inside the Batteries gate we started to run, down into the valley and up the other side so that we were out of breath when we climbed expectantly to the top of the far slope.

The place which we had last seen crowded with noisy people was now silent and deserted. Where the great fire had been there was only a ring of blackened stones surrounding a low mound of grey ashes from which a thin wisp of blue smoke rose idly into the quiet air. The trampled grass bore witness to the gathering of towns-people we had seen but of the sights and sounds which had excited and thrilled us, nothing remained.

There were no sounds coming up from the town. As we turned to make our way to school I could feel my feet wet from the dewy grass.

The date must have been 26 May 1914. On the previous day the Bill to give Home Rule to Ireland had passed its final stage in the British Parliament.

Two

The police barrack in Athlone was built around a large rectangular yard which served as a barrack square and, for the children of the residents and their friends, a playground. As you went in through the arched gateway at one of the short ends of the rectangle, the living accommodation was to the left. To the right there were redundant horse-stalls and haylofts and harness rooms in which we played on wet days. What had been a carriage house was occupied by the District Inspector's Ford car with its brass carbide lamps shining and polished leather straps stretched between the hood and the front mudguards. Here the District Inspector's civilian chauffeur seemed to be forever washing and polishing the car as he sang Fenian songs in a shrill voice from which there was no escaping. The remainder of the yard was bounded by a high wall beyond which there were the gardens of private houses. On a summer's evening you could hear from Parson Watson's lawn the laughter of women and the sound of croquet balls being struck. Those of us agile enough would climb the wall to have an envious peep at the party. In the wall opposite the main gate a door opened on to the riverside where barges and pleasure boats tied up. The river locks were just outside the doorway and the roar of the water tumbling down the weir which ran from the locks to the other side of the river was in our ears all the time.

The staff of the barrack comprised the District Inspector, who did not live on the premises, a Head Constable, three or four sergeants, of whom my father was one, and perhaps a dozen or fifteen constables. The single men and two or three married men whose wives were living on the family farm slept in a large dormitory on the first floor. The married quarters were two flats: one was occupied by the

8

Head Constable and his large family and the other by my parents and, at the point at which my memory begins, their four sons.

Every morning as we got ready for school the police would be parading in the yard with their carbines, forming fours and marching and countermarching so that when the District Inspector took the parade once a month and when the County Inspector came on his quarterly visit, they could be seen to be a diligent, presentable and well-disciplined body of men. When the morning parade ended the carbines were hung up in the dayroom and for the rest of the day the big yard became a place of recreation. Handball was played against one of the old buildings, the yard was a practice ground for runners and jumpers and weight-throwers practising for the police sports in Dublin and for local sports meetings. There were tug-of-war matches with men from neighbouring barracks and with soldiers from the military barrack. Our activities duplicated those of the adults and we missed nothing of what was going on. If some of the men were going swimming along the Shannon they tied their towels to the crossbars of their bicycles so that we could ride with them. They taught us to swim, organised our games, brought us fishing on the river and were our guardians when our parents were out. We had our favourites amongst them. One I particularly remember was a gentle, smiling man who told us magical stories of the fairies and giants and witches who inhabited his native County Mayo. When my younger brother, Tim, a brown-eyed, curly-haired, rather frail boy would protest at being called in for bed earlier than the rest of us, this man would take him on his knee, tell him stories until he fell asleep and then carry him gently along the yard and hand him in to my mother. That kind man was destined to die violently, the victim of an anonymous fellow-Irishman.

We saw everything that went on in the barrack and we were participants in much that did not meet with Mother's approval. Once a year, on a summer's day, the men went out to target practice and we went with them, knowing that we would get firing a few shots. The barrels of the guns were fitted with special tubes so that only .22 ammunition could be used for target practice. Each man had to fire twenty-one shots, seven from each of three different positions and the used targets were retained for inspection. We saw indifferent marksmen manufacturing evidence of competence by putting their cardboard targets on the soft ground and piercing them with the front end of a bullet so as to produce results which the sergeant in charge of the party could sign and confidently place amongst the district archives.

We enjoyed our exclusive spectatorship of much that was unusual. Youths who had deserted from the army and were being held for return to their regiments were allowed to join in our games; they told us how they had been trapped into taking the King's shilling and it seemed to us sad and unreasonable that they should be torn away from their families. We watched violent madmen, roped hand and foot, being brought in and, after committal by a magistrate, taken off to the lunatic asylum at Mullingar. We saw the hand of the law on pickpockets and thieves and fighting drunks.

The arrest of Bosh Hopkins was always a special occasion. He was an old soldier whose face bore the marks of countless brawls and whose record of convictions for being 'drunk and disorderly' placed him in a class alone. The climax of every one of Bosh's drinking bouts was flying missiles in a public house or a minor riot in the main street. But however fierce the altercation, the moment the hand of a policeman touched him he came smartly to attention and marched with a soldierly swagger alongside his escort to the barrack. Once inside the door, however, war was declared. Unless he was seized immediately, his boots, which came off in a flash, and everything portable in the room, were used to bombard his captors. There would be groans and angry words and loud laughter and, in the end, large, dishevelled, breathless men, lying on the floor, holding down the old warrior who, although overcome by superior numbers, made no truce with his captors. On our perches on the outside windowsill of the dayroom we had ringside seats.

In the big barrack yard, bounded by the grey buildings and the high wall, we felt somewhat cut off from the town but life in this adult world was full of excitement and novelty and sometimes great entertainment. Lying in bed we could hear the angry profanities of prisoners in the cells which were below our bedroom windows; on Saturday nights the entertainment was specially good.

Mother was sure that we saw and heard too much of the seamy side of life for our own good. She had known policemen's children who had gone to the bad, and no wonder.

The River Shannon cuts the town of Athlone in two so that one part of it is in the province of Connaught and the other in Leinster; the two parts being joined by a bridge near the spot where an immortal

10

episode in Irish history took place.

During the summer the river and its banks were our playground. We had learned to swim when we were very young. We went on family picnics by rowboat to the islands in Lough Ree. We fished for perch and roach and bream from the bank and went out in boats to troll for pike. On Sunday mornings when the river bailiff was at church we 'snatched' in the locks. Every time a boat went through the locks dozens of fish went out at the upstream end to be replaced by more coming in downstream so that between the gates there was always a shoal of trapped fish swimming around, close to the pier walls, vainly looking for a way out. At one point they passed over a flat, yellow stone and it was there our weighted treble hooks lay whilst we sat up above on the edge of the pier, holding our lines, waiting to snatch the hooks up through the passing shoal. This was illegal fishing but the bailiff's house was across the river and his boat was very easy to observe from our side.

From the outer pier of the locks the weir runs in a long arc across to the Leinster side. If the flow of water coming over the wall was not too strong I would cross by the lock gate to the far pier, slide down an iron beam to the top of the weir and, carrying my fishing rod and with my shoes hanging by their laces from around my neck, walk along the top of the submerged weir wall to the middle of the river where I would cast my line into the white surf below the sloping fall of water. There I would stand whilst the sun shone, the swift, smooth stream being split against the calves of my bare legs, watching the line being tossed about in the tumbling foam, exhilarated by the roar of the falling water which shut out all other sound. And if I climbed back on to the pier with a wriggling trout in my pocket, I felt as good a man as the Resident Magistrate fishing salmon from his varnished boat.

Athlone was a busy town, the venue of a horse fair that on a January day each year filled every street with restless horses and every public house with dealing men speaking in the strange, hard accents of the northern counties. At the weekly market in the square, farmers sold potatoes and poultry and suckling pigs (called 'bonnabs') from a gathering of orange-painted carts. Over in the shelter of the castle there would be flat boxes of eels which were sold by the pound and if the purchaser so wished, skinned before being wrapped, still wriggling, in sheets of newspaper. Beside the bridge, sitting on a flat stone, would be blind Dinny Delaney, the last of the bards, playing his Uilleann pipes.

The Royal Field Artillery, at a time when army life was all parades and route marches and moving to the sound of a bugle, were in the big barrack which opened on to the square. The annual mobilisation of the Connaught Rangers Militia in a camp near the town brought a fortnight of fighting and drunk men in the streets and full, noisy cells in the police barrack. At the edge of the town, on the Leinster side, there was a permanent colony of tinkers, amongst them Davy Joyce, the King of the Tinkers, who went about sedately in a frock coat and top hat, carrying a bundle of tin saucepans hanging from a loop of wire. The town's most celebrated sons were T.P. O'Connor who represented a Liverpool constituency in the House of Commons and John McCormack whose performances as an operatic tenor had already brought him fame. I remember hearing a gramophone played for the first time; a group of people had gathered in a friend's house to hear John McCormack's rendering of 'Dark Rosaleen'.

Athlone was a town of farmers and soldiers and shopkeepers and vagrants and country 'gentry' moving about in their shiny horse-drawn carriages. On special days, such as the King's Birthday, the Artillery would bring out their field guns, three pairs of horses drawing each gun, the gun teams sitting stiffly erect, mounted officers leading, and clatter through the streets to the King's Meadow, down by the river where they would fire a salute of many shots, sending small clouds of black smoke skimming over the surface of the water. On St Patrick's Day the Irish National Foresters put on their plumed hats and tail coats and lace ruffles and walked sedately in procession through the town. When the hunt met, the Colonel of the Regiment rode out in his hunting coach which would come through the military barrack gate axle-deep in hounds with their tails in the air, to the blare of bugles from the red-coated army bandboys on the upper deck. On St Stephen's Day and New Year's Day the Wren Boys came around the houses collecting pennies; eight or nine men wrapped in sacking, with blackened faces, their leader carrying a long cane from which hung an inflated pig's bladder with which to belabour unwilling contributors. Their song began:

> The wren, the wren, the king of the birds
> On St Stephen's Day was caught in the furze.

12

There was always something to be seen. Band parades and soldiers' funerals with the regimental band playing a solemn funeral march on the way to the cemetery and, coming back, a lively tune (which we were told was 'We'll Get Another Soldier for a Bob'), regattas and sports meetings and swimming galas and a race meeting twice a year which brought to the town the Dublin hawkers with their three-wheeled barrows and sharp tongues. And everywhere there were donkeys harnessed to small carts carrying shawled women or wooden milk churns or small pigs or stacked high with rectangular sods of brown turf.

Going to and from school we passed the mineral water works where the father of one of our school friends was the bottler, to us the most desirable occupation imaginable. Occasionally our friend would bring us through the works gateway to the door into the bare white-walled warehouse where we could watch his father, a large gauze mask covering his face, supervising the filling of long lines of bottles in which exquisitely coloured liquids sparkled tantalisingly.

Mineral water bottles were then sealed by a glass marble which lodged in a bulbous neck so that when the bottle was fully charged the pressure of the gas held it rigidly against the upper part of the bulb. In an empty bottle the marble rattled about freely in the wide neck. One of my most vivid memories of those years is the sound of the four-wheeled iron-shod dray, drawn by a tired old horse, having spent the day in the delivery of lemonade and all the other 'ades', returning in the dark evenings, candles flickering dimly in its small square lamps as it clattered over the uneven roadway causing the marbles to tinkle in a gay chorus in the empty bottles which filled the stack of wooden crates built high up over the driver's head. Through the dark, shabby streets around Fry Place every evening the homing mineral water van brought a sound like the music of a thousand fairy bells.

Our first school was St Clare's Convent which was near the barrack. At the age of seven the boys had to leave it and enrol in the national school. From the fields behind the convent we could see the all-male establishment in which our educational future lay. We saw an open door high in a grey gable and from the darkness beyond we could hear the angry roars of the Principal, a sound that carried a chilling threat across the meadows as the time for the change approached.

Deerpark National School for boys was in the upper floor of a very

13

old, two-storeyed stone building, the ground floor of which had long since been abandoned as habitable accommodation and become the resting place of an accumulation of domestic jetsam through which tall, rank weeds reached out towards the gaping holes where windows had once been. Entrance to the school was by way of an iron-balustraded, stone staircase to a door up in the gable which opened into one large rectangular room. That room was the school; there six classes, a total of perhaps eighty or ninety boys, were under the care of three men teachers.

Along one side of the room, set at right angles to the wall, were long desks bearing the inkstains and the scraped initials of many generations. Here sat half of the boys, whilst the others stood in three semi-circular classes, one at each end of the room and one around the open turf fire which was midway along one of the longer walls. Each teacher had two classes; one sitting doing written work and one standing 'being taught'.

In Deerpark National School silence, even for one moment, was unknown. All through the day the teachers explained, ranted, interrogated, swung their canes; boys shouted out answers, read set pieces or recited prayers. Every half hour the sitting and the standing classes exchanged places with a shuffle and a clatter that made the floor quiver. In winter the heat was fairly shared, each class having one period each day around the fire (which was only just and fair since periodically the pupils were required to bring tuppence each for the purchase of a load of turf). The wall decorations consisted of a tonic-solfa chart, two maps of Ireland, on one of which the place names were in Irish, and a chart giving the Ten Commandments and endorsed with the approval of the Commissioners of National Education. At the back of the school building, through a wasteland of nettles, a muddy path led to the malodorous 'toilets', the creation of some long-forgotten handyman whose skills did not include plumbing.

Even by the Spartan standards of sixty years ago, this must have been one of the worst-provided schools in Ireland. Yet the three teachers who spent their days trying to cultivate the seeds of knowledge in such an unpromising garden managed, in their different ways, to achieve the seemingly impossible, for Deerpark School had a reputation for scholarship that ridiculed its appearance.

The junior teacher was a small, bespectacled, fretful man with receding, fuzzy hair and a neglected, underslept appearance. He

14

was a visionary and his vision was a free Ireland cleansed of everything that had come from England, including its language. From him we heard that taxes raised in Ireland kept the English in sinful luxury, that in a free, independent Ireland there would be little or no need for taxation. I have a particular reason for remembering him. He it was who, shortly after I had started at Deerpark School, took me out in front of the class to belabour me until his yellow cane had stung half of my body into throbbing agony, sending me home crying bitter tears, humiliated and angry and full of despair. That evening Father sat down with me and, patiently taking me through my schoolbooks, persuaded me that the tasks which I was being set were not beyond my capabilities. For the rest of my time in that man's class I never got a sum wrong or gave an incorrect answer or failed in any test he set me and as the months passed my response to his signs of growing respect was unsmiling, silent and wholly-satisfying enmity. My inspiration was not the pursuit of knowledge; I was punishing my torturer with weapons against which he had no defence. Such excellence was not to be the pattern of my later studies but when I went on from him to higher things I was a grim, triumphant eight-year-old.

The other assistant was a tall, pale, very thin, monosyllabic hurley player who conveyed his message with an economy of words and threatening solemnity. He never smiled, he taught well and he used his cane with chilling accuracy; he well knew that a sharp stroke delivered on the end finger joints sent a shudder of pain right to his victim's toes. For lesser misdemeanours the offender might find himself virtually suspended from a tuft of his short neck hairs clamped between the teacher's thumb and forefinger. He took singing; two classes combined for one hour once a week during which we fairly belted out 'The Minstrel Boy', 'Let Erin Remember', 'A Nation Once Again' and, out of respect for the Principal's native county, 'The Bells of Shandon'. He also presided over the weekly science lesson at which, after a lunchtime of preparation and with the aid of equipment consisting of a basin, a few test tubes, a tiny spirit heater, some pieces of glass tubing and a zinc bucket with water drawn from the roadside pump, he demonstrated by experiment such mysterious phenomena as atmospheric pressure, the distillation of water and the working of the thermometer. It was an hour of magical interest.

The terror and the inspiration of that crowded room was the

Principal, a stocky, pugnacious Corkman with a bushy black moustache, short curly hair sitting on a rectangular forehead, lively brown eyes peering from beneath thick black eyebrows, the body of an oriental wrestler and the supple knees and light step of an athlete. He dressed in a navy blue serge suit that shone when he moved. From the watchchain that stretched across his wide waist-coat two silver medals hung; it was said that they were trophies of the boxing ring and that could well have been true. He had a ferocious temper, a liberal mind, the talents of a circus clown and a vast knowledge of greyhound coursing, horse-racing and boxing. His place in the room was beside the door where he sat in a wooden armchair behind a deal table with his 'Standing' class gathered around him. On the wall behind him hung a large rectangular display card with, on one side, in heavy black letters, the words 'SECULAR INSTRUCTION' and on the other 'RELIGIOUS INSTRUCTION'. The finger-worn stains on the bottom corners of the card bore witness to his punctiliousness in ensuring that, as required by the rules of the Commissioners of National Education, the exposed side truly conveyed what was going on in the school.

The Master (as the Principal was known to the townspeople) lived on the Leinster side of the town and every morning he walked to school reading his *Irish Independent*. Pupils dallying along the way knew that they must be in school before him; on his morning journey, every time he came into a street he must have seen a scurrying of small boys disappearing around the corner at the other end. If a mother had a son whose objection to education had reached the point of rebellion, the rebel was pushed on to the footpath ahead of the oncoming walker and his day was made. On most mornings the Master arrived at the school with two or three unwilling scholars trotting fearfully in front of him.

If it was learned that a pupil was 'mitching' he was sought and invariably found in Kelly's Wood which was beside the school. The Master would bring out a dozen of the bigger boys and deploy them at strategic points around the wood. At a word of command the search would begin and when the maverick had been run to earth the search party would be gathered around him for the march back to school, the Master leading, carrying the school broom over his shoulder and the whole company singing 'The Minstrel Boy to the Wood Has Gone'. The fate of mitchers, none of whom, it seemed, ever escaped detection, planted in my mind at that early age the belief that life is hard for those who don't conform.

For those in the Master's class the most dreaded time of the day was the first period in the morning when he called for the results of the previous night's homework. The boys stood in a semi-circle around his table and when the moment came to exhibit the harvest of their toil, copy books had to be held up, face high, pages outward, for scrutiny by the Master. He would begin at the top of the class and walk slowly from boy to boy, hands clasped behind his back, cane switching against his trouser-leg, commenting pungently on what he beheld. If the results were below his expectations the exposed knuckles of the exhibitor might get a sharp rap of the cane or the Master might bring his large hand down on the book, sending it crashing into the face behind it. If the symbols on the page before him were disfigured by blots or clumsily executed alterations he might bring his arm swinging up from his side and with the back of his hand send the copy-book flying to the ceiling with a roar of, 'Take it away before I vomit'. The Master's inspection began at the end of the class at which the best pupils stood (continuous competition for privileged places being a feature of every class) and as he moved purposefully along in descending order of merit his judgements grew louder and more violent, he called upon the Almighty to bear witness to his unproductive labours and the veins stood out on his strong forehead as the whole performance ended in a riotous tirade of anger and abuse and self-pity. Countless must have been the heartbeats I missed when, having listened in terror to the approaching storm, I saw below the bottom of my open book that the shiny, black boots had stopped opposite me and I knew that my uncertain efforts were under the scrutiny of those black, angry eyes.

The Master was the most respected man in the town, feared alike by his pupils and their parents. His appearance in the noisiest street brought immediate silence. Most of his pupils came from very poor homes and he was determined to make something of them whether or not they liked it. Those who had no ideas about how they would one day earn a living were told what their careers would be and if the normal curriculum did not cater for their particular needs, he organised tuition in whatever subjects were necessary for entry to their chosen occupations. He knew what was good for them and even if it meant teaching by terror, they got it.

But life in Deerpark National School was not all violence and anger. The Master was a superb entertainer. In the midst of the most passionate outburst his anger could suddenly subside and the face of the clown appear. His stories were the best we had ever heard, he could mimic complaining parents, the other teachers, the school inspector, even the Parish Priest. If he encountered a travelling musician or a juggler or a man with performing animals he would engage him to entertain us. We would bring a penny each for the visiting artiste and for a whole afternoon the desks would be pushed to the end of the room and we would be treated to professional entertainment which the Master presided over like a proud ringmaster. If he got tired teaching he would gather us close around the table and tell us about great boxers and horses and running dogs. We shared his admiration for Jack Dempsey and Georges Carpentier and we heard from him about the short-tailed greyhound that won the Waterloo Cup. He was a comedian and a scholar and a holy terror and he was the best teacher I have ever known.

On Sundays we went to Mass in St Peter's Church, a building which must have been as old as our school. It had three galleries; one was reserved at the late Mass for the soldiers of the garrison, in another the congregation was farmers in their suits of dark cloth and the third, which contained the private pew of 'Turney Kelly', was where the more prosperous townspeople came to pray. The galleries were known, respectively, as the Military Gallery, the Bogmen's Gallery and the Grand Gallery.

I was first made aware of political conflict on the morning on which Jack and Tim and I were set upon and beaten by our fellow-pupils at Deerpark School. We had delivered our youngest brother, Tommy at the Convent and were on our way along the narrow road that led to our school when we were suddenly attacked by a howling crowd of boys who knocked us down and beat and kicked us, calling us 'traitors' and 'English spies'. We fought back all the more furiously because we knew of no reason why we should be the victims of such fierce anger. When the row was over we learned that during the previous night the police had raided a number of houses in search of arms or other evidence of rebellious intent.

Although we missed nothing of the day-to-day comings and goings in the barrack, we knew very little of those aspects of police duties which did not produce noisy voices in the cells beneath our bedroom windows. Political issues did not seriously agitate my parents. They believed in the proposition that Ireland should have Home Rule and in so far as they had any political views, they were, like most people at that time, supporters of the Irish Parliamentary Party, then under the leadership of John Redmond, which was pledged to a constitutional campaign for Home Rule. That party had succeeded in persuading the British Government to sponsor the Bill of 1914. On the night on which Jack and I were brought out to watch the celebration of the passing of that Bill my father was no less moved than anyone in the crowd.

I was too young to have more than a fragmentary understanding of what had impeded the operation of the 1914 Act. I had heard my parents talking about opposition up in the north. The name Carson had been mentioned and his place in the controversy was clarified in a song being sung in the streets:

> His face is fat and warty
> Of pimples he has forty
> And ribbons in his hat, red, white and blue.

I remember the outbreak of the 1914-1918 War and I knew that Home Rule had then been postponed. There were crowds at the station saying good-bye to men going off to the Army. 'Big-Head' who used to serve behind the counter in the grocer's shop, appeared in khaki uniform and went off, to be killed a few months later. Families all over the town talked about the welfare of husbands and sons at the front, we heard of 'separation allowances', there were recruiting meetings addressed by bemedalled Irish officers (including Michael O'Leary VC) and farewell parties; there were sugar ration cards and high prices which brought prosperity to the farmers who began again to look at the broad acres of the ranchers and there were occasional outbreaks of cattle-driving.

As the war went on more and more soldiers came into the town. They were young men and in the evenings some of them would come walking along the river bank to watch us fishing. They would ask to hold our fishing-rods and we were surprised to find that grown men didn't know a perch from a trout and had to be taught to put a worm on a hook. Some of them became very keen anglers and they and we would fish together and they would tell us about their homes in England. Then one day they would be gone and new men would arrive and a little later we would hear that some of those with whom we had become friendly had been killed in France. Every now and then the body of a young soldier would be found in the river, some, no doubt, because they chose suicide rather than face the trenches.

The soldiers mixed freely with the townspeople, many of them married local girls, there were soldiers in the town football team. New arrivals soon accepted 'crubeens' as the next best thing to fish and chips or tripe and onions and on Saturday nights the 'eating houses' would be crowded with soldiers sitting around large bowls of steaming pigs' feet.

I have a clear memory of the Easter Week Rebellion of 1916. Mother had gone to Dublin for a surgical operation and on the day on which news of the Rising reached us Father told us that he was going off to try and see her because she was very ill. From what we overheard of his conversation with people who called to enquire about her we knew that he had been told that she was critically ill. I remember his distracted face as he left his four sons, the eldest less than nine years of age, to stay with friends and the sick feeling that came over me when I overheard a passer-by on the street referring to us as the 'poor little orphans'. Fortunately Mother recovered and lived to a great age.

During that Easter week, when there was no news either of Father's whereabouts or Mother's condition, we went to the Square every day and watched the lorries carrying armed soldiers and policemen racing through on their way to Dublin. The townspeople cheered them as they passed and, when a lorry stopped for a few minutes, brought them refreshments. In that week Yeats's 'terrible beauty' was born but its birth was not celebrated by the people of Ireland. There was only anger at the wild, foolhardy men who had been responsible for many deaths and the destruction of much property in Dublin.

When Mother came home she told us of returning to consciousness to the sound of a machine-gun operating from the roof of the hospital, of seeing from her window horse-drawn breadvans being set upon by crowds of hungry people and emptied of their loads in seconds. We had a visit from a big ruddy-complexioned sergeant in the police whose brother, also a policeman, had been killed at Ashbourne where a party of police reinforcements had been attacked. I had to leave the room because he was crying and the sight of an adult shedding tears was too much for me.

After the execution of the leaders of the Rising, pictures of them and ballads about their exploits began to appear but only one or two shops in Athlone stocked them. But opinion was changing. Sympathy for the dead leaders was growing as people began to learn more about the kind of men they were; the idea of a republic rather than the 1914 propositon of a subordinate Irish parliament was being thought about. But this was still a minority movement; the revolutionary implications of republicanism were unwelcome to God-fearing people who were making money as never before. Besides, Athlone had long been a garrison town, the young men of the district had gone to the war in large numbers and the big army training camp which had been established early in the war had brought new business to the town and new diversions for the townspeople. From most of them the appeal to participation in a hazardous form of extreme patriotism met with little response.

There was a fierce earnestness about those who were preaching the doctrine of complete separation. Their flag, the green, white and orange tricolour, began to be seen more often. They organised public meetings which were addressed by articulate young men from Dublin and fiery old men who had taken part in the land agitation of the nineteenth century. Every Sunday afternoon they gathered in Mardyke Street and if the meeting was to be held in a neighbouring village they went off in horse-drawn brakes with a tricolour hoisted over the leading vehicle. Police were required to attend the meetings and at first they went in the brakes with the organisers but this handy arrangement came to an end when the letters 'IRA' began to appear on the flags, for the Irish Republican Army, of which people had first heard in 1916, was a proscribed organisation.

Early in 1918 the announcement of the British Government's intention to impose military conscription on Ireland sent the temperature of the country soaring. It aroused anger and dismay everywhere; mass meetings and petitions were organised, resolutions of protest were passed by public bodies, cries of condemnation came from the press and the pulpit, men wore green, white and orange badges inscribed 'Death Before Conscription'. Although the Parliamentary Party's members at Westminster bitterly opposed the proposal to conscript Irishmen, the Government's declaration came powerfully to the aid of those who had been crying out about the futility of trying to achieve anything by negotiation with England

21

and advocating abstention from the British Parliament. Reasonable people thought the Government's announcement was an ungracious affront to a country which had contributed so many thousands of volunteers to fight in the British forces. The Constitutional party, with the promise of Home Rule when peace came, had, at least until the 1916 Rising hardened many British hearts, collaborated with the Government in the prosecution of the war effort. Now they were discredited. The separatists reminded their listeners that the men who died in the Rising had declared an Irish Republic and sanctified the declaration with their blood. If further Irish blood was to be shed, let it be for Ireland, they said.

In the face of opposition both in Great Britain and in Ireland, the conscription proposal was dropped. But a body blow had been dealt the Irish Parliamentary Party. John Redmond, its leader, had urged his followers to join in the fight for the freedom of small nations; he had lost his brother at the battle of the Somme. The conscription threat had brushed aside the helping hand of the parliamentarians and the Sinn Fein party had benefited enormously. Sinn Fein leaders had taken a prominent part in the expression of the people's anger and when the argument was over their weekly gatherings were seen to gather larger crowds than ever before. The newspapers gave more space to what they had to say and in parts of the country meetings ended in clashes with the police who were under instructions to seize flags bearing the letters 'IRA'.

My brothers and I were in the crowds watching the parades and the torchlight processions and we went to the open-air meetings. We saw Maud Gonne MacBride, Countess Markiewicz and red-bearded Darrel Figgis; de Valera, Harry Boland, Father O'Flanagan, then the leading orator of the movement, Laurence Ginnell and many others. Like the military displays and the picnics on the river and the pilgrimages to Clonmacnoise, it was all part of a very busy boyhood; there was no feeling of involvement in the controversy in which so many earnest words were being used. But on the morning on which we were first attacked by our schoolmates, everything changed; whether or not we wished it, we were involved in a conflict of loyalties and we were on the side that, although not yet a minority, was losing support. The beatings were to continue but we were sturdy and not excessively put out by our experiences. The Master was on our side and if danger threatened he made an excuse to walk home with us. But these juvenile outbursts were spasmodic. For much of the time our relations with the other pupils were, with one or two exceptions, normal.

The possibility of violence was being talked about; there were convictions of men who had publicly called for the use of arms against the oppressor, it was known that young men were acquiring arms. The police had some knowledge of what was going on and it became their duty to seek out and enforce the law against those found with arms or other evidence of association with seditious intentions.

My first sight of political prisoners was when half a dozen young men, most of them farmers' sons, were brought into Fry Place Barrack. They were cheerful, friendly men and during their four or five days in the barrack they sang Irish songs, played handball or sat about in the yard talking with the police. On one night a ceilidh was held; musicians were brought in, girl friends of the arrested men were invited and the young constables and their prisoners danced Irish dances in the big, tiled kitchen.

In the more southerly parts of the country there were occasional skirmishes between the police and Sinn Fein supporters; stones were thrown and batons were drawn. It was a time of great emotional verbiage. There was talk of the resumption of the fight for freedom, of throwing off the yoke of England; Thomas Francis Meagher's 'Stigmatise the sword' speech was the text of many an oration; Patrick Pearse, the executed 1916 leader, was much quoted: 'Ireland unfree can never be at peace'. There were new patriotic songs. 'Who Fears to Speak of Easter Week' was a re-write of a song about the 'Ninety-Eight' but the 'Soldiers' Song' was new and stirring and quickly became the theme song of Republicanism. The oddest composition for a Republican movement must have been 'We'll Crown de Valera King of Ireland'. The clergy were divided. Some of the priests spoke out against the violent implications of Sinn Fein, others used their pulpits to rouse their parishioners to support of the ideals of the militant Republicans. And Father Michael O'Flanagan was addressing meetings here there and everywhere so that people wondered if his parishioners ever saw him at all.

On 11 November 1918 as I crossed the town Square, the big gates of the military barrack swung open and the entire garrison came running out in one great, disorderly crowd. The war in Europe had ended. For the rest of the day there was drinking and music and dancing. There was a sports meeting and band parade in the field in which the Gaelic Football team played. Many of the townspeople put red, white and blue ribbons in their buttonholes; everyone was out celebrating.

In December 1918 there was a General Election. Except in the northern counties the Sinn Fein party had a big victory. It won seventy-three seats and the once great Parliamentary Party's representation shrank to six members. Some said that a good many voters had changed their allegiance through fear of the young men in trench coats who were on the move wherever political arguments arose but there could be no doubt that public opinion had changed dramatically. The men who had died in 1916 were becoming the inspiration of the new generation.

The Sinn Fein candidates had taken a pledge not to claim their seats in the British Parliament. The Irish Republican Army was being talked about in school. In secret, it was swearing in new members whose oath, it was said, bound them to pursue the ideal of a free Irish Republic even at the risk of their lives. Arms and explosives and books on military training and operations were being acquired and by unseen means distributed to the underground army. The St Patrick's Day parade of the Irish National Foresters became a small procession of old men in fancy dress.

There were more and more police raids, arrests and prison sentences, more meetings and angry, defiant words, seizures of privately-owned arms and explosive materials by groups of masked men, the burning of houses regarded as possible accommodation for Crown Forces.

The political atmosphere was tense; the Sinn Fein party, triumphant at the polls, was becoming increasingly defiant; the existence of an armed organisation was undeniable; magistrates concerned with the trials of political prisoners were getting threatening letters; men sent to gaol for preaching sedition were the heroes of the hour. The question on many minds was whether all the threats and the secret plotting and the wild words would lead to bloodshed. A repeat of the 1916 Rising was improbable; the precaution of locking up possible leaders of a rebellion had been taken. Nevertheless, the frequency of lawless acts was on the increase, the shooting of the enforcers of British law had openly been advocated by some of the more fanatical leaders. But one was reassured by the thought that Ireland was a Catholic country with a long Christian tradition and although its history contained many instances of hot-blooded violence under the stress of oppressive laws, peace-loving people felt that, in the conditions then prevailing, a planned campaign of calculated killing was, despite what was being said by the hotheads, unlikely.

Three

On the morning of 21 January 1919, in the town of Tipperary, a supply of dynamite was loaded on to a horse-drawn cart for delivery to the quarry at Soloheadbeg which was about three miles away. For some time, because of thefts of explosives by armed raiders, assumed to be the IRA, it had been usual for deliveries of this sort to be sent under armed police escort. The party going to Soloheadbeg on that morning was two County Council employees and two constables with their carbines slung over their shoulders.

Behind a hedge along the narrow road leading to the quarry eight masked men with an assortment of firearms lay in wait. A cyclist who had watched the cart and its escort leaving the town had brought to the waiting men news of the approach of the slow-moving convoy. As the cart turned into the road leading to the quarry, the two constables walking behind it knew nothing of the danger that lay ahead. A few minutes later their dead bodies lay on the roadway and their attackers had disappeared, taking with them the box of dynamite and the policemen's guns.

The accounts of what happened on that quiet road differ in some details. One of the civilians who was with the constables said that there had been a shout of 'Hands up' followed immediately by a fusillade of shots. Some of those who took part in the attack said that on hearing the command from the hidden men, the constables reached for their carbines; some said that they reacted as though they thought they were victims of a prank. One fact has never been disputed. The two men who died that morning had been quiet, harmless men; one of them, the head of a large family, was within a few months of retiring age.

The ambush at Soloheadbeg was the first deliberate killing in

26

what is now known as the War of Independence. But on the morning of that day, and for many a day, it was not given the dignity of an act of war. The newspapers called it 'brutal murder' and 'murder' was the word used by priests and politicians, the same word was heard in the shops and in the streets; it was even spoken by some of those who had subscribed to the same patriotic pledge which bound the eight masked men who had waited and killed and disappeared without trace.

Amongst the community in the barrack in which we lived there was incredulity and fear and horror, and there were angry words. There was talk about the dead constables who were known to some of the men and there was nervous speculation about what the future might hold. My father was silent and grim; Mother could not conceal her anxiety. What had happened was for us a sign of approaching danger.

The ambush at Soloheadbeg was planned and carried out by a small group of men who, having been provided with arms, decided to use them. It now seems that their higher command was unaware of the plan and actually expressed disapproval, although the presence today of a memorial commemorating the killing indicates at least retrospective blessing of the enterprise.

On the day of the shooting those elected Sinn Fein Members of Parliament who were still at liberty, for many of them had been arrested and imprisoned, were meeting in Dublin formally to declare their non-recognition of the British Government in Ireland and call for the support and the allegiance of the Irish people. This new assembly took the name Dáil Éireann, the Parliament of the Irish Republic. For the future, Dáil Éireann's declaration was to give those who were so minded a licence to regard employees of the British Administration in Ireland, whether they were British or Irish born, as intruders. The possessors of hidden arms had no longer to wrestle with their consciences; killing had ceased to be murder.

What was happening in Dublin or what was being argued in the inner councils of the Republican organisation meant nothing to me. I was eleven years of age. My father's occupation had become a dangerous one; the fiery speeches had led to the killing of two men who had done no wrong. I was filled with a fierce anger towards everyone associated with the new patriotism.

27

Soloheadbeg was followed by further shootings. Unarmed policemen were shot in the streets, or from behind ditches as they walked or cycled along country roads. If Father was late coming home we lay awake and listened for the sound of his step. He became the centre of all our thoughts; we were frightened and sorry for him. We knew that he was not made of the stuff of fighting men but we also knew that he was not likely to come to any sort of compromise with what he believed to be wrong.

At the beginning of the twentieth century Ireland was at peace; the turmoil of the land agitation had come to an end and the campaign for Home Rule, which had the support of the great majority of the people, was being conducted constitutionally. Violence, it seemed, had at last disappeared from the Irish political scene. There was no resentment towards Irishmen who took employment under the British Crown. Ireland had for many years been a fruitful recruiting ground for the Army and now, with improved educational opportunities, more and more young men were going into the British Civil Service and the Government Departments in Ireland were staffed almost entirely by Irishmen. The Royal Irish Constabulary was a native police force under the British Crown, a force of Irishmen with the duty of maintaining peace and order in their homeland. Government policy was settled in London but the administration of the country was virtually in the hands of its own sons and those who took up Government employment did so with no feeling of disloyalty towards the land of their birth or the aspirations of their fellow-countrymen. They had, they knew, the backing of their clergy for those were years in which influential voices in the Catholic Church were urging their people to co-operate with the Government. The men who were killed at Soloheadbeg were of that generation, a generation which was caught in the rising tide of militant Republicanism. But whilst civilians in the Government service were exempted from accusations of disloyalty (and Patrick Pearse, the author of many quotable assertions about the infamy of British rule, had founded his school for young Republicans with the aid of a loan of £500 from a British Government Department), the men of the Royal Irish Constabulary, being the direct instruments of the enforcement of law, were condemned by the Republicans as enemies of their country.

Republican apologists have made much of the point that the RIC

28

was a semi-military force. It was, it is true, organised on military lines, its hierarchy was comparable with a military unit, many of its officers were recruited in a cadet class and its members were trained in the use of arms with which they maintained familiarity by firing twenty-one shots at a target once a year. But police and military duties are very different and any military indoctrination received during training in the police depot was lost in the day-to-day job of being a policeman. They sometimes carried arms on ceremonial occasions and but for the IRA campaign, a contemporary of the Soloheadbeg victims could have gone through all of his service without ever being armed on duty.

In the week in which the Soloheadbeg ambush took place, the *Irish Independent*, a paper with nationalist sympathies, was calling for improved conditions for the force, complaining that too few senior posts were open to the rank and file. This was a continuing grievance; the majority of the officers were recruited as cadets and were the sort of men who, had they the means then necessary for aspirants to officer rank in the Army, would probably have chosen soldiering. This system produced, perhaps it was meant to produce, the sort of rigid social barrier between officers and men which is found in most armies. One other result was, as the *Independent* pointed out, that the majority of the officers were Protestants of the 'ascendancy' class and almost all of the 'other ranks' were Catholics.

Although its members were not without grievances, they really believed that the Royal Irish Constabulary was an exceptionally good force and they bitterly resented allegations that they were oppressors in their own country. They were of the people; they were, almost to a man, believers in Home Rule for Ireland. When they had disappeared from the scene and the Irish Free State had been established, Kevin O'Higgins, a member of the new Irish Government, said of the RIC, 'Let us not forget that it was the height of the ambition of most young fellows who happened to be five foot nine or thereabouts'. In his declining years Dan Breen, whose adventures as a guerilla fighter included the Soloheadbeg ambush, said, 'The RIC were as good Irishmen as we were.'

My father was a tall, pale-complexioned, lean man. He was not robust and although he was never ill, Mother was forever concerned about his well-being. He had the ambition for success which was characteristic of those of his generation who had escaped from the

29

insecurity of life on a small farm. He was intelligent with a lively, logical mind which fought against the inadequacy of his education. His great interest was legal processes and I believe that, given suitable educational opportunities, he could have been a very good lawyer. He drank little, he liked to go fishing, he was a better than average chess player and he enjoyed a day at the races where he would have the odd shilling bet.

He was self-contained and thoughtful and shy; he could be moody and quickly roused to anger but his anger was expressed in silences. I never heard him speak affectionately to anyone but he had all sorts of simple mannerisms which conveyed to those about him his warm, sentimental nature. This inarticulateness at times of emotional stress drew his family very close to him and caused us to respond quickly to his moods.

My mother was small and dark and the busiest person I have ever known. She had a good singing voice and in those early years all the hours of her days were spent moving about the house from one chore to another, usually singing a popular song. I can remember 'Dark Rosaleen', 'The Low Backed Car', 'Who Were You With Last Night?' and of course 'I Hear You Calling Me' which was then John McCormack's contribution to popular music. She had the northerner's impatience of deviousness and when she had opinions she expressed them whether or not they were likely to be well received. She had no capacity for neutrality and there were always some whose company she shunned.

In the years in which I was first conscious of political argument the advocates of separation from Britain were calling for more spectacular sacrifices than were within the thinking of hardworking breadwinners. The unconverted were being told where their duty lay, they were being invited to tread a path laid out for them by a small group of passionate idealists who seemed little concerned with the cold facts of life for the head of a family with a small income.

My father was intelligent, he was capable of objective judgement and he was a good Christian. I am certain that, without feeling any less a true Irishman than those in the new movement, he could not find any sympathy for the course which young men were being urged to follow. He was not a West Briton. I had heard him speak angrily of Britain's passive attitude towards those in the north who had threatened armed resistance to Home Rule in 1914, of her failure adequately to acknowledge the south's contribution to the wartime forces, of the crass blunder of the conscription proposal, all of which had fanned the flames of resentment in those who wished for an Irish Government in Ireland. But his answer was not the answer of the extremists. He was sure that what they were advocating was sinful and wrong. But it would be less than just to say that if the possibility of quitting the force ever came into his mind, as indeed it must have, his decision was influenced any more by ideological considerations than by the practical problems of a middle-aged, kindly man with a young family and no alternative occupation.

I had no knowledge of my father's dilemma. The possibility that he might give up his job was never in my mind. I was at the age when the props of life are permanent and unchanging; my father was a member of the Royal Irish Constabulary and, for better or worse, that was that.

After the Soloheadbeg ambush people hoped that there would be no more shooting, that the killing of the two constables was an isolated act of folly by a few wild men. But their hopes were vain. Soloheadbeg had only drawn the headline. Policemen were shot in the streets, in their homes, going to Mass, doing messages for their wives, having a drink in a pub. The shots which killed them were fired from behind ditches, from alley-ways, sometimes in busy thoroughfares; those who looked on and were disposed to disapprove were too fearful of the consequences of giving information. In places where there had been shooting, policemen began to carry arms on duty.

Small police barracks in remote southern villages were being attacked at night and we saw photographs in the Dublin newspapers of garrisons who had repelled the raiders. Mother, her Ulster blood roused by the whole sad business, was full of admiration for the men who had refused to be terrorised. Father was silent.

There had been no shooting in Athlone and despite the fear that danger was spreading we were too young for continuous anxiety. We went to school and although there were occasional bouts of hostility we were not unhappy. We went to the pictures in the Father Matthew Hall to see Pearl White in weekly danger, we caught fish and cooked them over wood fires along the river bank, we watched football matches between the town team and the regiment and one Sunday afternoon we listened to the soldiers' goalkeeper telling spectators gathered around his goalposts about

31

his trade in rifles which, he said, he was able to smuggle out of the barrack and sell for three pounds apiece. When Father was going into the country on weights and measures inspections he would hire a sidecar and take us with him through Oliver Goldsmith's country where, on one visit, we were presented with wine glasses bearing the crest of the Three Jolly Pigeons Inn. When the winter floods froze we skated for miles through the tops of the hedges. In summer we went south of the town, into the Bog of Allen, and got wild honey in the heather banks. We watched otters frolicking in a reedy bay. My youngest brother Tommy had a special facility for collecting unwanted animals and if he went out into the country to visit one of his schoolfriends he was liable to come home with a dog or a cat or a young goat but as animals were not allowed on the barrack premises the disposal of his livestock was a recurring problem.

One summer's day, as we sat at the edge of a broad meadow with a crop of high, standing hay, we watched a skylark coming down, step by step, singing in the dazzling sunshine and go to ground somewhere in the middle of the field. Tommy announced that he would pick the bird off its nest and, crawling on his hands and knees, he disappeared into the long grass. For five minutes there was no sign or sound from him and then we saw the top of his head as he came towards us from the middle of the field, the skylark in his small hand. He was then no more than five years old. More than forty years ago, at the age of twenty-one, he died. That scene is my most vivid memory of him.

There were plenty of diversions in the barrack. Because of the increasing frequency of attacks on remote barracks, some of those in the smaller villages were closed and the men transferred to the towns. There were new faces and new voices singing in the wash-house in the mornings and the handball alley was in use all day long. After what appeared an unconscionably long delay the British Government decided that the attacks on policemen were more than sporadic acts of local disaffection and that something must be done to help them protect themselves. The obsolete arms were gradually replaced by more recent makes of rifles and revolvers; sandbags were being provided for the protection of barracks which, for the most part, were rented houses hopelessly vulnerable against organised attack. Ford touring cars and Crossley tenders which could hold ten men sitting back to back were supplied to garrisons in the more troubled counties so that the chance of getting a shot at an unwary man cycling along a country road would, at last, be lessened. The Government could not yet rise to supplying motor transport to places like Athlone where no-one had yet been killed – it seemed that entitlement was measured in dead men – but we were on one of the main roads to the south and west and the new vehicles, driven by dust-covered men wearing goggles, who told us about their journeying, often stopped for a few hours at Fry Place.

More and more our activities in the big yard were subordinated to the needs of the bigger, busier garrison, the coming and going of vehicles, official occasions of many kinds. Once we were sent indoors whilst an identification parade was being held. From an upstairs window we saw eight or nine rough-looking men being arranged in a line, then a small, anaemic-looking man came from the dayroom and, accompanied by a sergeant and a constable, he walked slowly towards the line of waiting men. He was a country-man who had been beaten and left tied hand and foot at a roadside because of having, in some way, brought upon himself the dis-pleasure of the Sinn Feiners. His head was bandaged and we could see the black bruises on his wrists as he shuffled along the line of motionless men. He trembled visibly as he looked at one expres-sionless face after another. When he got to the end of the line he turned to the sergeant and shook his head. He was brought back into the barrack and the men who had been lined up for his inspection went out through the big gate.

It was at about this time that Fry Place Barrack had one of its more distinguished prisoners.

Laurence Ginnell came of 'rancher' stock but his political views differed considerably from those normally expected of one of his class. He was a hot-headed, eccentric Republican and he made his extreme opinions known in writings and in speeches at meetings up and down the country. He came to stay in our barrack because he had been arrested for preaching sedition at a local meeting. During the days when he was with us awaiting trial the big gates were kept shut and within the walls he was free to move about as he wished. He was a stocky, white-bearded man splendidly dressed in frock coat and top hat and he spent his time walking about the yard reading a book. He scorned fraternisation with the police but occasionally he watched our games and talked to us. One day when

33

the gates were left open whilst coal was being delivered this old man suddenly and to our great surprise, made a dash for freedom and was only grabbed by the coat-tails as he was disappearing around the corner of the gateway. We were sorry he hadn't succeeded for he had become a friend of ours and the agility of the old 'toff' was a revelation to us.

When the day of Laurence Ginnell's trial came Jack and I persuaded Father to smuggle us into a corner of the Courthouse. As soon as the prisoner appeared in the dock he clapped his top hat on his head to assert his non-recognition of an alien court. The hat was removed by a constable but Laurence put it on again and for several minutes, to the delight of the crowded courtroom, prisoner and policeman kept the hat moving between the wooden bench in the dock and the white head of its indignant owner until the performance was brought to an end when the Magistrate ordered the hat's removal out of the prisoner's reach.

It was at this time that the barrack yard ceased to be a place of recreation for all and sundry. The instruction which brought to an end the admission of outsiders applied to young and old. We could no longer bring in our friends to make up two teams for football; our friendships ended at the gate. A little later, when the big gates were closed and barred by night and day and anyone coming or going had to call the constable who was the 'guard' from his place of rest before the dayroom fire, our freedom was very much restricted. The back door leading to the river bank was padlocked and bolted and workmen arrived to brick up windows in the outbuildings which looked on to the streets. The feeling of an approaching siege grew; as security tightened we became more isolated from the townspeople. Men went on duty in twos after dark. One winter's night I saw my father going out with a revolver in a holster on his belt and I felt very sorry for him.

There was talk of Republican policemen and Republican courts and it seemed that in some parts of the country there were, in fact, the elements of a state within a state but the new civil organisation was, like the armed one, operating under cover and we saw nothing of it. Disaffection was greatest in the counties of Tipperary, Cork, Kerry and Clare and in the City of Dublin where detectives of the Metropolitan Police were shot down with regularity. In Athlone day-to-day police work went on as usual but there was always the consciousness that armed men were about and that the shooting might start any day.

Each week brought a new list of policemen killed 'by a person or persons unknown', as the Coroner's courts put it, with no apparent casualties amongst those who were killing them, no identification of the men who went about their daily work and only picked up a gun when a man in uniform was marked down for death or an attack was to be made on a patrol or a small barrack. As the debit balance of killing grew there were those in the police force who thought that the only realistic way of correcting it was by reprisals. Some of the new recruits had served in the Great War, most of the new officers were ex-servicemen, men who had fewer scruples about seeking out and identifying their enemies than those whose lives had been spent quietly in Irish villages and small towns; they were not prepared to be sitting targets at a time and place chosen by a hidden man with a gun. The police had ample information about the membership of the IRA, but desperately lacked proof of participation in crime. The power to intern without trial had been widely used but the shootings went on.

In the opinion of men like my father the police force was not trained or equipped or organised to deal with the situation then developing. Sooner or later the Army must take over. Reprisals and all that would be involved in arbitrary retribution were outside his thinking; policemen were trained to work within the rule of law, the Royal Irish Constabulary was a proud force, its traditions must be upheld with dignity despite the malevolence of the gunmen and the optimistic inactivity of the British Government. The man with a gun was a self-appointed accuser, judge and executioner; the adoption of reprisals would place the policeman in the same unjustifiable role.

On 19 March 1920, Alderman Thomas MacCurtain, the Lord Mayor of Cork, was shot dead in his home. In spite of loud denials from Government sources, there seemed no doubt that the night raiders who killed him in the presence of his family were members of the Royal Irish Constabulary. He held high rank in the Irish Republican Army and his killing was, it appeared, a reprisal for the killing of policemen in circumstances which had been no more merciful than his end. Public sorrow and anger left me unmoved. The initiative was no longer on one side only; the sitting targets had struck back. I did not see that this deed was the beginning of anarchy, the beginning of the end of a great police force.

Four

The British Government decided that the time had come to take off its coat to the Irish. A new Chief Secretary was appointed and one of his first acts was to announce the opening up of recruitment to the Royal Irish Constabulary so that men from any part of the British Isles could join. In addition, an Auxiliary Police Force, to be composed of men who had held commissions in the Army, was created; their role was to be that of shock troops, free to act independently of the Constabulary. Sir Joseph Byrne, the Inspector General of the RIC, resigned; he saw, more clearly than most, what the future had in store for the force over which he had presided with distinction. All over England and Scotland and Wales, we read, men were flocking to the recruiting offices to take advantage of these new opportunities for adventure.

It would be some time before we would have an opportunity for a close look at the new policemen. To make room for the larger garrisons that were planned and at the same time remove women and children from the danger of being involved in attacks on barracks, as had happened in a number of cases, it was decreed that families must move out of married quarters. We were under orders to leave the only home I had known.

Father had no sooner begun his search for a house than he was told that he was to go on transfer to Rathfriland in County Down. This unexpected news brought joy to our home. Mother had never liked the flat midlands, so different from the coastal strip around the mountains of south Down where, up to her marriage, her home had been. We were going to safety for County Down was a stronghold of loyalty to the British Crown.

We left Athlone in June 1920. Jack was then thirteen years of age;

he was strong and courageous, then and for many a day he was my prop and my shelter. Tim was not yet ten, small and lithe and good at games. Tom was an imaginative, lively five-year-old. We had a baby sister, Dorothy, born a few months before we left. At the age of twelve I was full of hatred towards my fellow-countrymen. I did not know that the Republican movement included many who were not in sympathy with those who had decided to shoot their way to freedom. I made no distinction between those who killed and the gentle Arthur Griffith, the father of Sinn Fein, who had advocated passive resistance until his voice was drowned in the noise of violence. To me every Republican was a gunman and the guns were pointed towards those I loved. Those on the other side were my enemies and I hated every one of them. I was an uncompromising, unapologetic West Briton.

A few days before we left Athlone I saw one of the new English recruits. He wore khaki trousers and cap and the dark green jacket of the Royal Irish Constabulary. He was wheeling a bicycle along Barrack Street and he was very drunk. Within weeks the name 'Black and Tans' was given to these imported reinforcements.

Our journey to the north took one whole day. Father had had to leave some weeks earlier and had quickly found a house for us in Rathfriland. Before leaving he had made arrangements for the transfer of the furniture and settled our travel arrangements. He coached Mother and Jack in the details of the journey. We could have gone by Dublin but it was decided that, encumbered with a pile of luggage and five young children, the problem of crossing the city from the Great Southern Railway terminus to catch a train to the north at Amiens Street Station would be too much for Mother, so we started out on the Midland Great Western line. We travelled up through the middle of the country, by Mullingar and Cavan and Clones, then across to Dundalk and into Newry. We had five changes of train and at each change we were all busy. Mother looked after the baby and her associated paraphernalia; Jack, Tim and I kept an eye on Tommy and supervised the transfer of the luggage.

Once we got to Cavan we were in the north. On the journey across to Dundalk the dark top of Slieve Gullion told us that we were skirting the border of County Armagh. As we changed trains at Dundalk we felt the sharp air blowing in from the bay; the next train took us north-west, along the lower slopes of the Camlough hills and at Goraghwood we turned towards the east again and downhill to Newry beyond which we could see the curve of Carlingford Lough shining between the Mourne and Carlingford Mountains. It had been a long adventurous day.

We stayed in Newry, with Mother's parents, for a few days before going by hired car the last ten miles to our new home.

Rathfriland is said to be the highest town in Ireland. It sits on a high mound with a town square on the summit and the streets spilling down the steep slopes. It looks over a rolling countryside of small fertile fields, well-tended hedges and neat, white houses; to the east a meandering road runs off into the heart of the Mourne Mountains. This was very different from the flat, grazing fields and the broken boglands of the midlands.

There were many differences. Rathfriland was no more than a large village; Athlone had been a moderately big town. There was no river in Rathfriland so that there would be no more fishing or boating or swimming or skating over frozen floods in winter. We had difficulty in understanding the northern speech and our accent amused the townspeople. It was a clean, tidy town, well dusted by strong winds. The nearest railway station was several miles away and Sam Peters' long sidecar, drawn by two horses, went down to meet each train. It carried perhaps a dozen passengers sitting back to back and on the return journey, when it came to the foot of the hill, the men had to dismount and walk up to the Square. Hughie Downey's long car went to Newry twice a week.

If you were a Catholic in Rathfriland you belonged to the 'Nationalist' minority, whether you liked it or not, for the Protestants treated the Union Jack as their exclusive property. They regarded the Pope as an active Irish Nationalist and the Catholics, for their part, were fairly sure he was. A Catholic claiming to be for King and Empire, as I indeed did, met with disbelief from both sides. Politics and religion were inseparably bound together and you were either one of *us* or one of *them*, depending on where you went to church; that was accepted as a fundamental fact of life and nobody wanted to hear of any eccentric exceptions. The majority in Athlone had been Catholics but the number of Protestants in the town had not been insignificant. Some had lived near us and we had associated with them; we thought their religion a bit odd and some of the boys in the town had a rhyme which began:

The Prods the Prods against the wall
A pint of piss would drown yez all.

But that had nothing to do with politics. We had known at least one Protestant Republican family and there were a good many Catholics in Athlone who supported the union with Britain. In Rathfriland the line of demarcation was clear and simple and final.

We were not long in our new town when the Twelfth of July celebrations came along. We had heard of the Twelfth of July. Every year a number of policemen in Athlone had gone on temporary duty to the north at this time and I had seen trains with numbers of policemen in uniform passing through on their way to the north for 'The Twelfth'. I then knew that it was some sort of festival but I had never thought about its particular significance; it had not occurred to me that policemen were gathered in hundreds from all over the country on this day each year for the purpose of keeping the Protestants and the Catholics in the north from doing violence to one another. I had heard about the Orange Order and had assumed that it was something like the Irish National Foresters whose members in Athlone had been a not very numerous group of benevolent, middle-aged gentlemen who liked to dress up for occasional parades.

I was twelve years of age when I saw my first Twelfth of July Demonstration. The Orangemen had come to Rathfriland from all over the south of County Down and for several hours they moved in procession past our door, walking four abreast, all of them dressed in navy blue suits, with bowler hats and ornate sashes of orange decorated with metal trinkets representing five-cornered stars and Jacob's ladders and Masonic symbols. At the head of each lodge the principal officers, highly ornamented with sashes and large matching cuffs and tasselated aprons and carrying Bibles or gavels or ceremonial swords as symbols of their distinguished positions, bore themselves with solemn dignity. There were bands by the dozen and large painted banners, held aloft by waltzing men, depicting in a hundred different themes the benefits which Protestantism and Britain had brought to mankind. Over the caption 'The Secret of England's Greatness' one banner showed a portly Queen Victoria handing a Bible to a black man; another showed the burning of Latimer and Laud at the stake; we saw Martin Luther nailing a wad of papers to an iron-studded door, Jacob's vision, Britannia holding her trident proudly in front of a Union Jack, Queen Victoria sitting on a Union Jack, a Bible sitting on a Union Jack; John Bull, Bible in hand, out with his bulldog; unsophisticated paintings of local squires, of aged clergymen, of Joseph Chamberlain, of Sir Edward Carson and other heroes of the Orange movement. Each lodge had a number and a fanciful title emblazoned on its banner. There were 'True Blues', 'Chosen Few', 'Loyal Sons', 'Boyne Defenders' and 'Purple Stars'. Nearly every lodge had its drumming party made up of six or more sweating shirt-sleeved men lashing big drums with canes, making an ear-shattering noise with a sort of primitive rhythm. Each party of drummers was led by a man blowing a yellow cane flute from which an occasional squeal could be heard over the thunder of the drums.

The procession went through the streets in the morning to the place of assembly, a field outside the town, and came back by the same route in the late afternoon by which time the surfaces of the drums flowed with blood from the chafed knuckles of the drummers. The marchers were still solemn and unsmiling, there was nothing lighthearted about this gathering of men in their Sunday suits.

My brothers and I watched all through the day. We had taken part in religious processions, had seen political celebrities marched through Athlone with bands playing and torchlights blazing but this had neither the devotional fervour of one or the immediate enthusiasm of the other. This was secular Protestantism soberly commemorating the Battle of the Boyne which was fought in 1690 and demonstrating with all those fantastic trimmings its support for the Protestant succession to the English throne which did not seem to me to be in any danger. My first impression, at that early age, was that whatever was to be said about the need to show an attitude to the Reformation and the Throne, this was a very primitive way of doing it. But the whole Protestant community was involved. Amazed, I had seen them all, merchants and farmers, shop-assistants and labourers, masters and men, marching four abreast with grim faces behind the bands and the thundering drums and the painted images of their 'betters'.

We were probably the only Catholics in the town to show any interest in the events of the day. Our co-religionists, to whom the procession was no novelty, were withdrawn and sullen. They pointed out to us that most of the music of the bands had been the airs of songs which were very offensive to Catholics. Later, when we learned the words of some of the Orange songs, we saw that this was not an unreasonable complaint.

The next morning's newspapers brought further enlightenment about the Orange Order. We read the resolutions which had been passed by the brethren and the speeches of their leaders from which it might have been inferred that the forces of Popery were about to seize the Crown of England.

But the residents of Rathfriland, despite the religious barriers which divided them, were not inhospitable. We, with our strange accents, aroused as much curiosity as if we had come from some distant, foreign country. We very quickly got to know many of the townspeople, amongst whom we were surprised to find more than a few who had prospered without the aid of the skills of reading and writing.

Our favourite rendezvous in the evenings was the home of an elderly spinster and her two middle-aged unmarried brothers. The men were dealers in cattle and they had a blacksmith's forge and, at the bottom of the hill, a farm. They lived a comfortable, leisurely life in their well-kept, bright house. We bought milk from them and in the evenings when we called for the day's supply we had a standing invitation to read the daily paper for the household. The day's work had ended, a big, bright fire would be burning, the kitchen floor swept and around the large, brightly-scrubbed deal table, wooden chairs would be placed. On the table opposite each chair there would be a soup plate of flat, steaming, yellow-meal porridge with a large mug of fresh cream beside it. The place at the head of the table was reserved for the reader who was expected to read every word of news in the paper. Never had a performer a more attentive audience. The news was more and more about the worsening situation in the southern counties.

On our last morning in Athlone one of the sergeants in the barrack came to help Mother get her family and her possessions on to the train. He was a rather stern, aloof man and as he was not one of those who took part in the recreational activities in the barrack yard we were a little surprised that he should be the one to come and help us on our way. But his home was in the north and on that morning he wanted to wish us luck and tell us something about the place to which we were going. On the way to the station he talked about the Ulster counties, he told us to look out for the blue blossoms on the flax, he described the small hills of County Down – 'like a basket of eggs' he said – and the way the sea washed the foothills of the Mountains of Mourne. He stayed talking to us until the train moved out.

Shortly after we arrived in Rathfriland we read in the paper that the sergeant who had seen us off had been shot dead. He was going home, unarmed, late at night, when eight bullets were fired into him from the shelter of a dark entry. Later we read of the death of a merry little man who had been one of the organisers of our games in the yard; he died a slow death from a bullet wound in the stomach. Then Charlie was killed. He was a young constable who used to cycle into Athlone barrack with despatches from some country station. The bicycle he rode was always bright and shining and it had every fitting imaginable. Every time he came into the yard we would get him to lift us, each in his turn, on to the saddle and walk us around the yard, all the time chattering nonsense in his County Clare accent. Riding along a country road on his shining bicycle, Charlie was shot down, and the news saddened four small boys in Rathfriland.

From the papers we learned that the Black and Tans and the Auxiliaries were coming into the country in large numbers and being posted to districts where trouble was likely. Their arrival aroused hostility and there was a growing clamour of complaints and protests, for the new policemen were making it known that they would not be inhibited by the precept that a man is presumed to be innocent until proved guilty; they treated the whole populace as hostile. I was secretly pleased that the burden of fear was spreading.

Tommy Moran was sentenced to death. He was the boy who had delivered milk to us from his parents' farm outside Athlone until one morning, dressed in the black suit of a clerical student, he had come to say goodbye before leaving, at the age of fourteen or fifteen, to enrol in a college for the training of candidates for one of the religious orders of Brothers. Some time later his mother brought him again into our kitchen in Athlone, this time to display him in the uniform of a private in the Connaught Rangers. In his new suit of khaki cloth with shining brass buttons and badges, he was still only a boy with a bright smile and his mother was sad because he was going overseas and she might not see him again for

42

several years.

Tommy was one of a group of Connaught Rangers who, on a parade ground in India, expressed their disapproval of Britain's handling of Irish affairs by refusing to obey their officers. Fourteen of the leaders of the mutiny, including Tommy Moran, were sentenced to death. One man, James Daley, died before a firing squad and Tommy was one of the remainder whose ultimate sentence was life imprisonment.

The police force in Rathfriland was my father and four or five constables. Duties were very much as they had been before the emergence of militant Republicanism. The people of the neighbourhood were predominantly Unionist and for my father and mother remoteness from violence must have been a welcome change. The religious-political gamesmanship must have been an irritant at times but it was not a call to battle. Life was leisurely and secure and free from the menace of the gunmen.

No more than a few months after our arrival in Rathfriland we suddenly got the news that Father was to go on transfer to Templemore in County Tipperary. He was being promoted to the rank of Head Constable but the news of his advancement, instead of being a matter for congratulations, filled us with fear. The shooting had started in Tipperary and had continued without mercy so that it had become the most lawless county in the whole country. Every week brought news of more ambushes and shootings in the streets and burning and wrecking; the Black and Tans were there in numbers and their unconventional ideas on retaliation were adding chaos to terror.

Late into the night Mother and Father talked about what lay ahead. They decided to make no plans to move house again; he would go off to his new station and we would stay where we were until better times. Everyone in the force had now to do a spell of duty in the 'troubled counties' but for men with families it was usually not a long one. With luck, they hoped, we might be united again within the year.

My recollection of the period of separation is of Mother writing letters late into the night, of her anxiety if three days should pass without a letter from Father, of looking in the morning papers fearfully for the mention of Templemore, of prayers every night for my father's safety.

By now there were members of the IRA devoting their whole

43

time to the guerilla campaign. These were, almost all of them, men wanted by the police, who had gone 'on the run' and formed themselves into 'flying columns' based on districts where the residents were prepared to shelter them. The flying columns were usually available to join with their part-time associates for special assignments. But both the whole-time and the occasional combatants still went about in civilian clothes, sometimes under assumed names, ready to strike when a favourable opportunity came their way. Their hostility to the RIC was sharpened by the possibility of being recognised by men who had served in their home districts; they were without mercy on informers and the finding on roadsides of bodies labelled 'Spies and Informers Beware' deterred association with the Crown Forces. The Black and Tans and Auxiliaries and the Military had neither the knowledge nor the patience to distinguish between the actively hostile and the innocent. The Government seemed to have approved reprisals as a deterrent. Irrespective of political loyalties, every man, woman and child in the troubled areas was in danger.

We read in the paper that the District Inspector in Templemore had been assassinated. The new sergeant in Rathfriland came to tell us that he had had a telephone message saying that Father was all right. For a fuller account of what happened then and later we had to wait until our next meeting with him.

The majority of the men in Templemore police barrack were Black and Tans and to my father they were an eye-opener. They had all seen service in the Great War and had come back to Lloyd George's 'Land fit for Heroes' to find a great shortage of jobs. Most of those who responded to the invitation to join the Irish police probably came from the unemployed, some had been in dead-end jobs of which they had quickly tired after years in the battlefields of France. They had had all sorts of occupations; there were lapsed motor mechanics and cooks and retired professional boxers, over-weight jockeys, ex-commercial travellers, unsuccessful university students, unskilled labourers, tinkers and tailors and candlestick makers; there were confidence men, petty crooks, congenital loafers, card sharpers and gun-happy adventurers. There were decent men and scoundrels, adventurers and frightened youths, domesticated family men and fugitives from deserted wives; there were English and Scottish and Welsh, Jew and Gentile. They came

44

in all sizes and for all sorts of reasons, the most unlikely of which was, probably, to do a policeman's job. Once they passed an elementary test in reading and writing they were in without, apparently, much inquiry about character or background or much thought about suitability for police duties. But no-one, least of all those who conceived the idea of bringing them over, thought for one moment that they would serve their time as guardians of the peace. This was an emergency operation; the British Government had decided to 'take murder by the throat'. In the words of the song:

> Said Lloyd George to Macpherson, 'I'll give you the sack.
> For to govern Ireland you have not the knack.
> I'll send over Greenwood, a much stronger man
> And he'll do my work with the bold Black and Tan.'

The decision to recruit this motley band of reinforcements was made at a time when it was clear that something needed to be done to relieve and sustain the Royal Irish Constabulary. The sponsors of violence had expected resignations in large numbers; the fear of death, they thought, would render the force ineffective. That had not happened. A small number had resigned but the majority remained, angry and frustrated and fiercely resentful of the out-pourings of the Republican propagandists. But by temperament and training they were quite unfit for the shoot-or-be-shot situation then developing in many parts of the south. If they were to survive they needed help but never was a relieving force so dissimilar to those to whose aid they came. Irish policemen, by and large, were unsophisticated, untravelled countrymen who said their prayers and did their duty as they saw it. The newcomers, they found, had neither religion or morals, they used foul language, they had the old soldier's talent for dodging and scrounging, they spoke in strange accents, called the Irish 'natives', associated with low company, stole from one another, sneered at the customs of the country, drank to excess and put sugar on their porridge. To the men of the Royal Irish Constabulary they were a revelation and a plague and a Godsend. They brought help but they frightened even those they had come to help.

My father found the people of Templemore, for the most part, civil; some of them were very kind to him. But life was very different from anything he had previously known; he was now a member of a garrison in a hostile area. In the barrack steel shutters and sandbags shut out the light, wire mesh was fixed over every exposed pane of glass, guards were posted by day and night, men went on duty in numbers, heavily armed, cars and lorries were provided for patrolling the rural areas.

Although Templemore was in the most trouble-torn county in Ireland, the town had not been the scene of any very serious incidents. All over the county IRA men were 'on the run', the organisation of the secret army was strong; attacks and reprisals, deaths and the destruction of property had stirred those involved in the conflict to anger and hatred and fear and desperation. Police and soldiers patrolled the countryside in convoys of lorries, knowing that any wall or ditch or rocky slope might shelter armed men lying in wait for them.

On one day each week Father had to attend a conference at the county headquarters in Thurles. The journey was done by car and on his return to Templemore he would call at the house of the District Inspector, who was the senior police officer for the area, and together they would walk through the town to the barrack. The fact that this was a weekly routine suggests a sad failure to recognise a fairly obvious hazard.

On one of his weekly visits to Thurles Father agreed to take an urgent message to police at a station a long way off his direct route and, as a result, he got back to Templemore much later than usual. He found the District Inspector lying dead on the footpath in the main street. Having waited for my Father to call and possibly fearing that there had been some mishap, he had started out alone for the barrack and as he walked along the street a bullet was fired into the back of his head. When he fell dead his right hand still held the revolver in his greatcoat pocket.

There was terror in Templemore that night. The Black and Tans and soldiers broke out of barrack and set fire to property. In the burning of the town hall an officer and a young soldier lost their lives. The wrecking was brought to an end when the police, amongst them some Black and Tans, sent the soldiers back to their barrack. But the shooting and the wrecking was not the end of the strange happenings in Templemore. For a reason that had no connection with political strife the name of the town was to stay in the headlines a little longer.

Five

The funeral of a shot policeman in County Tipperary in 1920 was symbolic of the condition of the country. Along the route shopkeepers closed their shops, some out of respect for the dead, others because in the presence of a display of arms conformity was prudent. The funeral procession was made up of policemen in their bottle-green uniforms, soldiers in khaki, a few civilian relatives of the dead man and almost no-one else, for even the friendly and the uncommitted were slow to join in a public expression of sympathy which might have exposed them to the suspicion of collaboration with the Crown Forces. No-one wanted to end up in a ditch with a 'Spies and Informers' label in his buttonhole.

As the District Inspector's funeral passed along the deserted streets of Templemore, past the blackened gables of burnt-out buildings, townspeople listening in the half-light behind drawn blinds heard the impatient clatter of the hooves of the restrained horses drawing the hearse and the slow tread of the marching men and they waited in silence until the sounds disappeared into the next street. Then the blinds were raised again, the shutters came off, doors were opened and daylight came back into front rooms; the coming and going of people was resumed.

Mr Dwan lived above his newsagent's shop. He and his family must have had little sleep during the previous night and when the wild shooting had stopped and the light from the burning buildings had begun to fade, he must have felt relieved that his premises had not suffered in the night's reckless destruction. He did not know that his humble home would soon be heard of all over Ireland.

Young James Welsh, a seventeen-year-old farm labourer from

47

the townland of Curraheen at the foot of the mountains, was a visitor to Mr Dwan's house that day. When the funeral of the District Inspector had passed, Welsh announced to Mr Dwan that the time had come to give his message to the world.

Welsh was no ordinary youth. He was frail and gentle and much given to talking about spiritual things; it was said that he had at one time been a student for the priesthood but his health had interfered with his studies. In 1920 he was employed as a farm labourer by Mr Dwan's sister. Dwan had befriended him, had listened to his earnest words about the sins of the world and when the young man came into the town had given him the hospitality of his home. In recent weeks Welsh had confided in him about the apparitions which he had had. The Blessed Virgin had appeared to him and told him of her displeasure at the sinful happenings in Ireland; she had asked him to let the people know of her disapproval. At her request he had scraped a small hole in the earthen floor of his cottage at the foot of the mountain that is known as the Devil's Bit; the hole had filled with water and become a clear, running spring well. After each vision a statue in his house had started to bleed. He had entrusted the care of the bleeding statues to Mr Dwan.

After the night of terror in Templemore the Blessed Virgin had come again to Welsh and had told him that through her intervention the fire-raising soldiers and Black and Tans had been brought under control and most of the town saved from destruction. She had announced that the time was come to make known her communications with him.

Welsh and Dwan put a small table, covered with a white cloth, in the yard behind the stationery shop. On it they placed three statues of the Blessed Virgin on each of which a dark stain of shining blood ran from the face down over the blue and white mantle of the Virgin.

Late that afternoon my father, hearing of crowds gathering in the town, went out to see what was the cause of the excitement. In the main street he saw, coming towards him, a great crowd of people and out in front of them a wild-eyed, hysterical man, dancing and leaping in the air, laughing and crying out his thanks to God, calling on all present to witness the miracle of the banishment of his disability. My Father had seen this man dragging himself about the streets on crutches, he was known to everyone in the town; as long as most of them could remember he had been a cripple, a man

48

apparently destined to go through life dragging his twisted legs between wooden crutches. But there he was before a laughing, weeping, praying, hysterical crowd, his body made normal, leaping about, as my father said, 'like a circus tumbler'. He had been out to Welsh's house, had partaken of water from the well in the earthen floor of the kitchen and, going outside, had thrown his crutches from him. Templemore was seeing its first miracle.

Next morning the newspapers told the story of the bleeding statues, the holy well and the straightened cripple. All over the country the story brought wonder and hope to homes where there was illness or infirmity. From neighbouring towns people set out for Templemore, relatives bringing the disabled, the deformed and the sick; sad, praying people coming hopefully to seek relief at the new shrine of the Virgin Mary. With each day the converging crowds got bigger, the journeys longer. Returning pilgrims brought home news of new cures. In every corner of Ireland charitable people were making arrangements so that afflicted neighbours could make the journey to Templemore.

At the centre of this bewildering migration the business of shooting and pillaging was forgotten; the pursued and their pursuers, it seemed, paused briefly to look on in wonder. There was no point in trying to enforce the regulation which prohibited motorists from travelling more than twenty miles without a permit; that restriction had been imposed so as to hamper the movements of the IRA, but was now ignored by the hurrying pilgrims and by the police. During every hour of the day and night pilgrims were arriving, visiting the statues in Mr Dwan's yard, going out to Welsh's home and waiting for hour after hour in the great crowd, hoping to get close enough to touch the water of the holy well. There came stretcher cases, babies in arms, invalids in wheel chairs, the mentally ill, the blind led along by loving friends, the deformed supported on the strong arms of brothers and sisters. And outside the little cottage the pile of discarded crutches got bigger. The town was full of dust-covered vehicles of every sort, the streets crowded with tired people, sustained by hope and unquestioning faith, whose conversation was about journeys and attempts to get close to the objects of devotion, and the latest miracles. Because of the sudden gathering of many thousands, food was almost unobtainable.

A policeman in Templemore barrack had bought a statue of the Blessed Virgin in Dwan's shop. The black iron-bound box supplied to him for the safe-keeping of his belongings was opened and his statue taken out. It was red-stained. Word went around that a Black and Tan had a bleeding statue and the crowds came and stood silently in the street in front of the police barrack, a drab building made even more ugly by its defensive armour. The silent watchers must have been conscious of being scrutinised by the bemused occupants behind the dark peep-holes in the fortifications. A more unlikely place of pilgrimage could hardly be imagined.

The older priests were non-committal; they urged their flock to suspend judgement on what was happening but some of the younger clergy accepted the phenomena as Divine manifestations and went out to help and pray with the pilgrims. The townspeople were full of fear and astonishment. All over Ireland people read of each day's events with growing belief that something special had happened in Templemore. Nor was the significance of these happenings confined to those who said their prayers regularly. Black and Tans began to think of their immortal souls, British soldiers went to the Parochial House in Templemore and asked to be instructed in the Catholic faith. A young private told of having seen a 'beautiful Lydy' dressed in blue, who had appeared before him in the town square. It was thereupon decided to erect a statue of the Blessed Virgin at the spot where he had had his vision.

On the Sunday following the revelation of the bleeding statues, special reinforcements of troops had to be brought into the town to assist in dealing with the avalanche of vehicles. During the afternoon, my father was in the police barrack when a woman with a baby in her arms came to the door. She had travelled from Donegal, she said, and having spent many hours in the long queue at the Welsh home, had had to give up all hope of getting to the holy well; she had tried to get into Dwan's yard so that she could pray at the bleeding statues but there also the crowd was so great that she had failed. She had been on the road all night, the purpose of her journey being to seek Divine aid for her deformed child; it was dreadfully misshapen and had not grown since birth. She pleaded to be allowed to pray at the bleeding statue in the barrack. The woman from Donegal was brought in, the constable's statue was placed on a table in a small room and she and her baby were left alone. After a little while she came out, tears of thankfulness in her eyes. Father went to the door with her to find that a great crowd, having heard that a pilgrim had been admitted to the fortified barrack, was

50

clamouring to be let in. They also had been unable to get near the scenes of the other manifestations and had brought their sick and disabled to make their pilgrimage in the Royal Irish Constabulary barrack. My harrassed father was trying to explain why he could not help them when, with a blare of horns, a convoy made up of a large staff car and its escorting vehicles came nosing through the crowd. The Divisional Commissioner for Munster, the head of all of the forces in the province, had come on a visit of inspection. When he heard of my father's dilemma, the visiting dignitary took charge of the situation. He instructed the members of his escorting party to arrange the assembled pilgrims in an orderly line and asked for the statue. For an hour he stood in front of the barrack reverently holding the constable's statue until all of the suppliants had moved slowly past him, each one stopping for a moment to kneel and say a prayer. The Commissioner's armed retinue of Auxiliaries and Black and Tans stood silently around.

Despite the words of warning from the older clergy, the cause of young Welsh and his bleeding statues was taken up with enthusiasm. We read of his being brought to Dublin where the crowds which had gathered at the railway station knelt in the street as he passed. He accepted an invitation to visit the Bishop of the Diocese and next day came the news that when he crossed the threshold of the Bishop's palace all of the statues in the house had started to bleed. This was immediately denied.

Suddenly, almost as suddenly as the whole thing had started, the bleeding statues of Templemore ceased to be news. The newspapers mentioned them no more, the flow of pilgrims ceased, work on the erection of the statue to commemorate the young soldier's vision was stopped, there were no more miracles. When it was over it was hard to believe that all of the strange happenings in Templemore had been crowded into, at most, two weeks.

It has since been acknowledged that the confusion caused by these events was put to good use by the guerilla forces of the Irish Republican Army. Men 'on the run' were moved to new hiding places, the disposition of active service groups was rearranged and conditions were found to be favourable for the distribution of new supplies of arms and munitions.

Six

At the other end of the country, in Rathfriland 'on the hill', we followed the news of the happenings in Templemore and in Father's letters we got first-hand accounts of some bizarre episodes. His letters gave no indication of his own views about the bleeding statues and the miraculous well and the fantastic claims of people freed of lifelong disabilities. But there was no doubt that he had been moved by the fervour of the pilgrims and the sight of so much infirmity. I was quite sure that God had chosen the shooting of the District Inspector as the occasion to show his disapproval of the sins of the gunmen and it was, to me, significant that the hand of God had manifested itself in the county in which the first killing had taken place.

Rathfriland sent pilgrims to Templemore. In the town there were two small boys who walked with the aid of crutches; one of them was at our school and the other was a Protestant, the youngest son in a large family of Orangemen. When the papers were full of accounts of miraculous cures at Templemore the parents of the Protestant boy provided a motor car and a small party with the two afflicted boys set out early one morning to travel the two hundred miles of dusty roads to County Tipperary. Rathfriland was sleeping when they got home. Next morning the Catholic boy appeared making his way to school without his crutches although he walked with a limp. The condition of the young Protestant had not improved but even those who saw understandable discrimination in the distribution of the Lord's favours, were obliged to acknowledge that of the two pilgrims the young Protestant's disability had always been the more serious.

Life in Rathfriland was very close to the land. The town was small, gathered together on top of a steep, gusty hill at the foot of which the farms began. Everyone who owned anything owned land; practically every householder, whatever his occupation, spent part of his time down in the fields. At milking time, morning and evening, cows ambled slowly up the steep streets. When flax was being pulled or corn cut or hay saved the able-bodied deserted the town to spend the daylight hours in the fields and in the evening they would come climbing wearily up the hill in the fading light. During our stay there we learned a lot about the round of events on a County Down farm. At flax-pulling time we were taught to make rush bands for tying the newly-pulled flax and as the line of stooping pullers stripped the field of its crop, we joined the women and boys following in their wake to bind the bundles of green, blue-blossomed stalks. We walked behind mowing machines as they cut down the ripe hay and corn, sending frightened corncrakes scuttling for shelter into the ditches. In autumn or early winter the blue smoke of a steam traction engine told us that corn was being threshed and we gathered all the mongrels in the countryside to chase the rats that came racing out of the bottom of the stack. There was a market once a week and a monthly fair, there was horse-shoeing at the bottom of our street, there was always someone wanting a cow or a pony brought up from the fields and there were several houses in which, possibly because of the novelty of our strange southern accents, we were in demand as readers of the newspapers. When the winter frosts put a shine on the roads every imaginable sort of home-made sleigh was brought out, the trees along the Banbridge Road were decked with lanterns and laughing, screaming parties went skimming down the hill into the darkness.

The principal of our school was a timid man who rarely raised his voice; it was said of him that he used his cane only in self-defence. The programme of instruction was unadventurous and its presentation was, compared with our former school, tame indeed. After my rumbustious apprenticeship in the Deerpark School I quickly made up my mind that I had nothing to fear from the knicker-bockered, pipe-smoking, slow-moving man in whose care I had been placed. My schooling in Rathfriland was, therefore, a time of carefree idleness except for the history lesson in which I plagued the teacher with questions about his interpretation of the history of Ireland. Whatever the Protestants and the Catholics of Rathfriland might think was my proper place under their local rules, I would not remain a silent listener to opinions which bore the taint of Sinn Fein and I was not going to be brainwashed by a schoolmaster with no capacity for inspiring or even frightening his pupils.

One day Mother sent me off to Newry to do some messages for her. It was a summer's morning, very early, when I went to the square and climbed on to Hughie Downey's long car. The driver tucked the rugs around the knees of the dozen or so travellers, six on each side facing outwards, settled himself in his high 'Dickey' seat, whipped up his horses and off we went down Newry Street and out into the country at an easy trot, perched over the tops of the hedges, waving back to people working in the fields, stopping to pick up or set down passengers, to collect or deliver parcels, to let the horses drink at wayside wells. For two hours we travelled on, pleasantly lulled by the rhythm of the horses' trotting hooves as the sun rose higher in the morning sky, and finally downhill into Newry where my aunt was waiting to supervise my shopping, then lunch at my grandmother's home and the drive back along the undulating, winding road lined with green hedges all the way to Rathfriland. I sat deep amongst the row of adult passengers, watching the passing countryside and listening to their talk about prices and absent friends and sick relations. At the foot of Newry Street the long car stopped and I got off with the men and walked with them up the hill to the Square where Mother was waiting for me. It had been a whole day of the sort of pure joy that can never be repeated.

It was while we were in Rathfriland that the state of Northern Ireland was established. I now know that that event was brought about by the passing of the Government of Ireland Act of 1920 which divided the country in two and gave to each part a Government subordinate to Westminster but with delegated powers in certain internal matters. The sponsors of the Act hoped that it would bring peace to Ireland but their hopes were not fulfilled. The twenty-six southern counties decided to have none of it but in the remaining six counties the Government of Northern Ireland was established.

In Rathfriland, as the birth of the new government was celebrated, legislative processes meant nothing to me. Men gathered in the town carrying a variety of weapons which, it was said, had been amongst those illegally imported when Carson was arming his Ulster Volunteers to resist the Home Rule proposals of 1914. As

54

darkness fell the crowds roamed the streets firing shots in the air. Mother gathered her children into a back room and there we cowered far into the night, listening to the shooting and the carousing and the singing of anti-Popery songs and the whine of bullets. Whatever might be my thoughts about the benefit of British rule, the path we took to church on Sundays placed us in the 'minority' which, from the beginning, was assumed to be engaged in a deep plot to overthrow the new state in the north. Next morning all was quiet but the Catholics had had a very uneasy night. It was my second experience of Home Rule celebrations.

The establishment of the state of Northern Ireland was followed by outbreaks of sectarian rioting in the north, chiefly in Belfast. Catholic employees were chased out of the Belfast shipyards, a development which brought to an end my ambition, on which my mother had smiled, to become an engineer and take part in the building of great ships. The Irish Republican Army took a hand in the northern troubles; there were shootings of policemen and politicians and innocent people; there was gang warfare, there were riots and reprisals and the wholesale burning and sacking of Catholic homes and places of business.

The Government, faced with the possibility of the new state distintegrating in anarchy, its fanatical supporters being no less a menace than its opponents, established a special force whose full-time members wore uniform similar to that of the Royal Irish Constabulary. There were three categories of Special Constables – 'A' Specials who were recruited for full-time duty, 'B' Specials who were called up for service when there was a need to reinforce the full-time men and 'C' Specials who did occasional duties, and when on duty wore armbands and their everyday civilian clothes. The members of the old Constabulary thought very little of this miscellaneous collection of amateur policemen who had emerged, as had the Black and Tans, out of conditions very different from those in which the traditions of the Royal Irish Constabulary had been created.

The news that Father's spell in the troubled zone was over came as a joyful surprise. His letter said that he was to be transferred on permanent duty to Clones in County Monaghan, that he would be home on leave for a few days following which he would take up duty in his new station and find a house with all possible speed so that we would all be together again.

55

On the day on which he was due home Jack, Tim, Tommy and I went out along the Newry Road to meet him, for he had said that he would travel by train to Newry and cycle to Rathfriland. About a mile from the town, from the top of a high roadside bank, we saw his tall dark figure in the distance, appearing and disappearing as he rode his bicycle over the wavy, white road. He was quite near before he saw us. He jumped off his bicycle and stood laughing down at us, asking how we were and how were Mother and Dorothy. He laughed and rubbed his eyes and laughed again; then he got on his bicycle and we ran after him all the way back to the town.

There were no heartbreaks about leaving Rathfriland. Our stay there had not been a long one; we had made no enduring friendships, we had experienced neither warm hospitality nor unfriendliness and for myself, I was still bewildered at the sort of community into which we had been injected. I had come to Rathfriland full of prejudice against Irishism, eager for the protection of the north's bulwark against disloyalty but increasingly I had found myself out of harmony with those with whom I had come prepared to make common cause. I was unable to identify myself with a political creed whose outward symbols and expressions of loyalty were hostile to my religious beliefs; I could not understand or accept the association between the spiritual and the temporal which was everywhere evident and was symbolised in the flying of the Union Jack from the tower of the Church of Ireland in the square on all of the days of July in commemoration of the Battle of the Boyne. I felt no bond with people who gathered at the call of their landlords to hear speeches about the Divine Right of the institutions of the Reformed Church to manage the affairs of the British Empire, I had no respect for employees who put on their best suits to march respectfully behind their employers on the Twelfth of July, I just could not understand how an adult could appear before his children decked out in the ridiculous regalia of the Orange Order. Compared with Athlone where the air was full of argument and challenge and disrespect for traditional attitudes, living in Rathfriland was like being in a remote place where the tribal customs of a bygone age had survived.

I did not allow the tribal feudalism of the hill-dwellers of County Down to tarnish my Britishism. Be damned to them all! At the age of thirteen, after a year living in Rathfriland, I was a political 'loner'.

Seven

It was early afternoon on a sunless, cold day as the train carrying my mother and her five children climbed the gradual slope along the side of the Camlough hills with the grey town of Newry slipping away in the valley below us. Our itinerary was back over part of the route we had taken on our previous migration – change of train at Goraghwood and Dundalk, along by the southern side of Slieve Gullion, through the flat lands of Louth and Monaghan and after a couple of hours in a slow train which would stop at every station, into the wide, busy station at Clones.

At Dundalk we got into a compartment already occupied by two middle-aged women. As Jack and Tim and I watched the thinning down of movement indicating that all was ready for departure, a small group of laughing men came walking along the platform. There were five or six large men who looked like farmers, grouped around a small man wearing a brown trilby hat and a grey tweed overcoat almost down to his toes. As they came towards us we could see that the small man was the entertainer of the group; he talked unceasingly and what he had to say was obviously highly entertaining to his companions.

The men stopped at the compartment next to ours. The small man got in, closed the door, let down the window and resumed the cheerful conversation with his laughing friends gathered on the platform in front of him. He spoke with an English accent; his listeners were local men and it was clear that they had all been drinking.

The guard sounded his whistle, the noisy group shouted their farewells and good-lucks and safe-homes to their departing friend and he called back to them saying how much he had enjoyed their merry meeting and just as the train started to move, he pulled out a large revolver, the biggest I had ever seen, and with deliberation and whoops of delight, he fired shot after shot into the roof of the station. His erstwhile companions dived in panic for doorways that were not there and as we slid along the platform to the thunder of the little man's revolver, men and women and children were throwing themselves in all directions. In the train women were screaming; the two ladies in our compartment were down on the floor and Mother was vainly trying to bring her brood within her protecting embrace.

We realised that the man in the next carriage must be a Black and Tan. My brothers and I, far from feeling the possibility of danger, were delighted and exhilarated at the Wild West performance at which we had a ringside seat. As the train moved out of the town we could hear him in the next compartment singing at the top of his voice. The women in our compartment were almost in a state of collapse; only a thin partition separated us from a drunk man with a large revolver. Jack and Tim and I sat close to the window so as to miss nothing of our neighbour's antics. Every now and then as the train chugged through the fields, the revolver would appear, right beside us, and he would take a shot at a tree or a rock or a telegraph pole and up and down the train the cries of frightened females could be heard. The train stopped at every small station and each time it stopped the little Englishman would call out to people standing on the platform, engage them in bantering conversation and as we moved on send them scattering in panic with bullets screaming over their heads. What must have been for many people, my mother included, a truly frightening experience was for us boys great entertainment and we were disappointed when, at Ballybay, which was near the end of our journey, the man in the next carriage got off the train and soberly walked away with the dozen or so departing passengers.

Clones station was deserted. When the train stopped people opened carriage doors and got out but there was no-one there to receive them. Father appeared from the doorway of the station-master's office, then policemen carrying rifles and revolvers came out of every nook and corner around the big station. Looking very pale, Father came hurrying to us, wanting to know what had happened during the journey. He had had a number of messages saying that Black and Tans and IRA men were engaged in a running battle on the train in which he knew his family was travelling. We told him about the performance of the man in the next carriage and when we had described the little Englishman with the gun, he burst out, 'It's that bastard Fitz!'

He told us that Fitz was a Black and Tan who, much to his relief, had just been transferred from Clones to Ballybay. When they had first met, Father asked Fitz where he had served.

'Maynooth.'

'That's a fairly quiet place,' commented my father.

'Not on your life,' said Fitz. 'Maynooth has the biggest Sin Fin college in Ireland.'

Athlone was still the basis of all my comparisons and the first thing to be said about Clones was that it was a smaller town than Athlone. It was, however, a busy, thriving town with electric lights hanging over the middle of the streets, the first public electric lighting I had seen. And nearly all of the children as well as a good many grown-ups wore clogs which were made by a family of red-haired sons working in a black wooden building on the Monaghan Road. Outside their workshop the shaped, wooden clog soles were built into a rectangular pile that looked like a stack of yellow turf. Clogs were very much cheaper than shoes or boots and you could call at the workshop and have a pair made while you waited. The men working in the fields, most of the children of the town, messenger boys, yardmen, all wore clogs and in the early morning and late at night the clatter of hurrying iron-shod feet was a new sound to us.

The business of the town was based mainly on farming. There were dealers in livestock and agricultural produce of every sort and a great deal of the trade of the shops had to do with supplying the needs of the farming community. There was a great interest in horses. Three or four horse-dealers whose business took them to fairs all over Ireland had their stables in and about the town and every morning and evening strings of horses were led through the streets going to or coming from the railway station. Everyone seemed to be in some way concerned with horses and in the town the buying and selling and appraisal of horses went on all the time.

In the evenings the pump in the Diamond was the gathering place of the young people. It was beside 'Peter's Box', a wooden hut in which blind Peter Reilly sold newspapers and magazines and Westerns and paperback Nat Gould racing novels. He was always there in his box and in the evenings a regular panel of retired men read Buffalo Bill stories to him. He was, in fact, very well read and something of an authority on the history and folklore of the district. But to us he was a garrulous old man and if the company around the pump was short of diversion, a sturdy kick on the wall of Peter's wooden hut always produced a stream of profane invective from within. He was no respecter of persons and anyone so foolish as to question his judgement or disagree with his opinion was very quickly sent about his business.

The border which had been drawn around the six counties of Northern Ireland ran close to the northern edge of the town. Five minutes walk from the Diamond was a border road-post manned by members of the Ulster Special Constabulary, some of whom were Clones men. Six miles away, in the village of Newtownbutler, there was a large garrison of 'Specials' who patrolled in their lorries the northern roads right to where the town ended. Amongst the 'Nationally-minded' in Clones there was probably more hostility felt towards them than towards the regular police.

Our new home was a large terrace house at a corner of the Diamond, as the open space in the centre of the town is called. It was a big, rambling house with sufficient rooms for our needs on the ground and first floors, above which there were numerous attics to which we were banished on wet days.

When we arrived in Clones our parents decided that the time had come for Jack and me to attend secondary school. But the nearest Catholic secondary school was in Monaghan town; it was not possible to travel there and back daily and as Father's income could not have borne the cost of boarding two of us he decided to have us enrolled in Clones High School which was a Protestant school. He went to tell the Parish Priest, hoping to get his acquiescence and came home smarting from the angry words he had brought about his ears. But we were enrolled in the High School and our religious education was continued every Sunday when we attended Sunday School in the Catholic Church. I think Father's resolution on the school question was strengthened by his indignation at being lectured about his religious duties at a time when many of his own clergy were openly hostile to the force to which he belonged. Because he did not expect too much of the clergy he was not unduly put out by their strictures; his personal relationship with them was not relevant to his attitude to the Church of which, all his life, he was a devout member. During our attendance at the Protestant school he would take no excuse for our failure to attend Sunday School.

The Parish Priest was not a politician. He preached peace and goodwill and was, indeed, a kindly old man who kept a good horse. The highlight of the ecclesiastical year was a sermon, delivered in the early autumn, on the sin of theft with particular reference to the evil of fruit-stealing from one's neighbour's orchard, much of the fire of which was lost on his listeners who knew well of his special interest in his own well-provided, beautifully arranged but rather vulnerable fruit garden. One of his curates was a fanatical, outspoken Republican with whom my father had some terrible row after which no word passed between them. The other curate was a cheerful, kind man with whom we became very friendly.

The police garrison in Clones was, perhaps, twenty men of whom about half were Black and Tans who had by then been supplied with standard uniform and had shed the two-tone ensemble after which they had been named. They were distinguishable only by their English (or Scottish or Welsh) accents and in many cases by a lack of inches compared with those who had joined when physical standards were important.

One night the men in the barrack were awakened by the sound of rapid shooting at the back of the building. Down in the kitchen they found the night guard, a recently-arrived Black and Tan, bleeding from a bullet wound in his forearm. The small window showed a number of bullet holes but no raiders were found. The wounded man was taken to hospital and from his hospital bed he made a claim for a large sum by way of compensation for malicious injury. Some months later I saw my father before a military court, the civilian courts having been suspended, demonstrating with the help of a schoolboy's magnifying glass, how he had come to the conclusion that all of the holes in the window panes had been caused by bullets fired from inside the room. The Black and Tan was sent to gaol.

At Castlesaunderson, a stately home some miles from the town, there was a company of Auxiliaries, the corps of ex-officers (the rank and file were called 'temporary cadets') who had been involved in some bloody escapades in the southern counties. Their uniform was different from the regular force. They wore glengarry hats, riding breeches and leggings and many of them carried revolvers slung, cowboy style, from their hips. Their reputation for

61

ruthlessness was well-known but when they came to the Clones district they let it be known that so long as peace reigned they would make no trouble; and they were as good as their word. On summer evenings they would drive into the town and sit in their Crossley tenders in the Diamond singing and drinking beer carried out to them by the Boots of the Lennard Arms Hotel. Before starting on a wild drive back to their quarters they would pick up more supplies at Peter Carron's pub in Cara Street.

A short time after our arrival a detachment of the King's Royal Rifles came to Clones. The advance party drove up to the Workhouse and a few hours later their lorries came back through the town laden with paupers who waved cheerfully to the townspeople as they were borne off on the most exciting journey of their lives to the Workhouse in Monaghan. In a few days the remainder of the soldiers came and occupied the Workhouse. They had a good football team and an excellent band which on Sunday afternoons played in the Diamond under the baton of the elegant Bandmaster Dunne. Chairs were provided for the townspeople and the alfresco concerts, which at first were received rather coolly, became very popular.

The police barrack was at the opposite side of the Diamond from our house. It was a three-storeyed building with a porch of sandbags inside the front door. As you went in you could see a man with a gun at the ready watching through a small opening in the sandbags. All of the windows were fitted with steel shutters in each of which there was a small loophole. From the hole in the shutter of one of the top windows the muzzle of a machine-gun could be seen, pointing across the Diamond at a shop whose owner was known to be an important man in the Sinn Fein movement.

The police had by now been supplied with more modern arms and equipment and in Clones there were two 'Tin Lizzie' Ford cars and two police drivers, one of whom was so incompetent that we wondered how he had ever come to be given charge of a car. Father was now required to live in barrack. He came home for breakfast every morning and each night, just before ten o'clock, he had to leave. After supper Mother would go to the door with him and on dark nights she would stand in the light of the open doorway until he disappeared into the unlit area in the middle of the Diamond, then she would remain still, listening to the sound of his receding footsteps until the distant thud of the barrack door closing told her that he was safe for the night. And in the bedrooms above, her sons also listened in silence for the comforting sound of the closing door.

Although it was claimed that the Irish Republican Army was well organised in County Monaghan, conditions there were much less disturbed than in many other parts of the country. There had been occasional incidents; farmhouses had been raided for arms, police had been fired on and in Ballybay several men had been killed. More than once the police had surprised and captured men carrying arms in Clones and it was known that out in the country ambushes had been laid for patrols which, either because of good luck or good information, had failed to turn up. One of the leaders of the IRA for the area was Eoin O'Duffy, later to become a General in the Army of the Irish Free State and head of its police force. Although he eluded many attempts to capture him he had then no great reputation as a guerilla leader. On gateways and gable walls there were fading election posters bearing a picture of a bespectacled, unsmiling man and the injunction 'VOTE FOR THE MAN IN GAOL'. The man in gaol was Ernest Blythe at whose fireside, almost half a century later, I was to learn something about the tribulations of a political revolutionary.

The gunfight in Clones took place a short time before we left Rathfriland.

One morning, in the very early hours, every man in the police barrack was awakened by loud, continuous, frantic knocking on the front door. When it was opened a frightened man, clad in a long nightshirt, dashed past the guard and into the dayroom. He was a well-known publican, a big man, known in the town as 'Black Jack' because of his shock of jet black hair with large moustache and stubbled chin to match. His story was that the IRA were raiding his pub down at the foot of Fermanagh Street and were robbing him of everything of value, including his stock. From his bachelor room above the shop he had escaped and run barefoot, in his long nightshirt, to the police. He was very distressed and kept calling for retribution on the raiders.

The police were organised in groups which quickly cut off the raiders' lines of retreat. Those going down the main street could see a lorry outside Black Jack's pub and men carrying the stock out to it. Then the shooting started. The police approaching the premises through the back garden called on the raiders to surrender and were immediately fired upon. The besieged and the besiegers set about one another and the noise of the shooting wakened the whole town.

One policeman standing beside my father in the main street got bullets through his cap and overcoat (and was thereafter known in the town as 'Bullets'). After some minutes the besieged men called out that they wished to surrender. Gingerly the encircling force closed in on them to find that they had been engaging a party of Special Constabulary from Northern Ireland who had slipped across the border on a looting expedition. One of the Specials was dead and one severely wounded.

Next morning's paper, which we read in Rathfriland, said that the townspeople had been awakened by the sounds of battle in which the police had surprised and attacked a party of IRA. The truth soon came out. The captured Specials were taken back to Northern Ireland, brought to trial and almost all of them given terms of imprisonment.

Mention of this incident used to make Father angry. In protecting property, which is part of a policeman's job, men's lives had been put in danger. The thwarting of the lawbreakers, which should have brought some sort of commendation to those who had faced danger, brought only an embarrassed silence.

The Republican movement was more than bands of civilian raiders intermittently shooting at policemen and soldiers, attacking rural barracks by night and setting fire to coastguard stations. The number of men in possession of arms was probably comparatively small and there were many firm believers in the doctrine of separatism who took no pride in the violent deeds of the IRA. When Dáil Éireann was established in 1919 a Cabinet was appointed with Ministers nominally responsible for the public services. This, at the time, was regarded as no more than a gesture – in any case some of the new Ministers were in gaol – but in time the existence of this structure of government gave non-combatant sympathisers opportunities for giving service to the Cause. Republican policemen, distinguished by armbands, appeared at gatherings such as race-meetings, Republican courts were set up and the people were invited to seek justice under the tricolour and to turn their backs on British institutions. Jurymen called to serve in British courts were threatened with dire punishment if they obeyed and in some areas it became virtually impossible to muster juries. This led to the replacement of civil courts by military tribunals, a step which probably influenced some people who turned for justice to the native arbitrators. But the extent to which the public co-operated in a boycott of British institutions has been exaggerated. Except in three or four counties the civil agencies of the Republic had probably little to do. The families of policemen were not, as some have said, treated as outcasts by their neighbours; they bought their groceries and sent their children to school and made friends in spite of the advice of the extremists. One was, of course, conscious of conflicting loyalties, of some of the elements of a state within a state, of the presence everywhere of those with knowledge, if not experience, of a revolutionary organisation. Our next-door neighbour in Clones was a Republican judge.

County Monaghan was probably fairly typical of a great part of the country. The IRA had a County organisation, apparently under Dan Hogan, and from time to time it surfaced. But except for occasional acts of violence, conditions for the law-abiding were very much as they had always been. True, some felt obliged to make use of the administrative services of the Republic; there were solicitors who appeared in both the Republican and the British courts. But the boycott of British institutions was far from all-embracing. Some years were to pass before 'War of Independence' became the acceptable designation of the happenings of those times.

Although the IRA in County Monaghan asserted itself only occasionally the Government forces were obliged to be ready for whatever initiatives it might undertake. As well as attending to their non-political duties, they patrolled the countryside in armed parties, sometimes with military reinforcements, the houses of suspected people were searched and they were always on the look out for men who had gone 'on the run'. But many who were reputed to be deeply involved in the violence moved about the town openly and there must have been a great deal of speculation about who was and who was not connected with the revolutionary organisation. It was rather like being present at a great poker game.

Davy Levinson, brother-in-law of Mr Litvinoff who was to become Foreign Minister under Josef Stalin, had cars for hire in his garage in the Diamond. One morning the police called and removed a vital part from each car; it was assumed that Davy or one of his drivers had been making transport available for IRA activities. He was a tubby, excitable little man and after the police raid he would stand at the entrance to his premises which were almost next-door to the barrack, protesting his innocence and indignantly drawing attention to his immobilised hackney cars.

One dark night a message came to the barrack that some sort of fracas was going on about a mile out from the town; Father took a party of men to investigate. Having walked for some time and hearing no sound, he began to suspect that the message had been a bogus one intended to lead them into a trap. They turned back. Next morning he learned that they had turned not fifty yards from where a party of men lay in hiding, waiting to shoot them down. Years after the fighting had ended Father was on a visit to a southern town when the local head of the Civic Guards called at his hotel 'to shake hands with the man who had been "in charge of the RIC in Clones" ' and during an evening's conversation revealed that he had been one of the party lying in ambush that night.

The social life of Clones was lively and when the people of the town were set upon entertaining themselves, political loyalties were overlooked. The regimental band played in the Diamond every Sunday and there were dances and concerts and sporting events. The Regiment had a team in the Summer Football League, a Black and Tan played for the town team and the league championship was won by the Cavan Police team, all of its members Black and Tans, who travelled to matches in their armoured lorries. The division between Catholics and Protestants had none of the tight-lipped sharpness we had experienced in Rathfriland. Politically the alignment was more or less the same but they all enjoyed themselves together. When the Orangemen marched on the Twelfth of July it was a day out for the whole town.

Attendance at a Protestant school was in harmony with my political thinking. My fellow-pupils were the sons and daughters of Unionists, our history books were about British history, we were not taught Irish, the allegiance of our teachers was unshakably to the British Constitution. I was secure in my belief that the British Government of Ireland was in the best interests of all concerned, including the Sinn Feiners.

Tim and Tommy went to the National School where the principal, a frail, querulous man and a fervent Republican, adopted an attitude of non-intervention when they were molested by boys who felt obliged to inflict punishment on the two young representatives of British oppression. One afternoon I went into the school yard as the boys came out and in the presence of the protesting principal and his pupils I horsewhipped the chief aggressor with the leather-thonged whip which I had learned to handle with more than average skill. In the unaccountable way that the affairs of boys are regulated, my victim and I were later to become good friends.

My father had always been very indulgent towards his sons and we were able to persuade him to allow us all sorts of forbidden experiences. If the police had recovered interesting booty from a burglary we would be let into the office to see it. We were often found a place in court, out of sight of the bench, if the proceedings were likely to be unusual. Despite Mother's fears about the moral dangers of familiarity with crime and punishment, by the time I was fourteen I had seen instances of death by misadventure, I knew more than a little about the ways of petty criminals and I had been a spectator at a murder trial.

The two Ford cars in the Clones barrack attracted our attention and we soon wore down Father's resistance to our pleas to take us on some of his trips, for in those days a drive in a car, except for a privileged few, was a notable experience. Occasionally, if there was a short errand of a non-political nature, one or two of us would be squeezed into the car, with Father, the driver and two constables carrying rifles. One evening Jack and I were passengers when the car, rounding a bend, suddenly came to a stop a few feet short of a trench which had been dug in the road. We were instantly pushed down to the floor and made to lie there whilst the car was hurriedly turned. (I can remember that the trench was cut in the shape of a letter H.) I could hear the metallic click of rifles being got ready. But there were no shots. During the journey back to the town Father sat pale and silent. Whether the men who dug the trench had abandoned their post or the presence of two small boys saved the lives of four men, I will never know. But that was our last joyride in the police car.

Our next-door neighbour got his livelihood from a shop, an insurance agency and a small farm. He was also a Republican judge. Republican courts were, of course, outlawed and those taking part in their proceedings were liable to arrest. They were referred to as 'Arbitration Courts' presumably because, with no facilities for the enforcement of punishment, they were available in the main for settling disputes in what are known as civil cases. If our neighbour's court sat at all it sat in secret, probably in some quiet place in the country. The whole town knew about his illegal judicial office; the police knew about it but there was no proof.

There was no contact whatsoever between us and the people next door; each family went about its business as if the other did not exist. But the Republican judge personified everything I hated and feared for I did not distinguish between men who carried guns and those whose services to the freedom movement were in a non-violent role. I saw all of them as collaborators in a campaign of murder and I was on the side of their chosen victims. The Republican judge was my nearest enemy and I found a way of placing him on my own arbitrary scales of justice.

Father came in from the barrack early every morning and by the time we were getting ready for school, he had shaved and was downstairs having breakfast. It was his practice to leave his uniform jacket hanging behind the bathroom door and one morning I discovered that he carried a small automatic pistol in his breast pocket. From that moment our neighbour was a marked man. I found that, standing on the seat of the toilet, I could look through the small bathroom window into his yard and watch him, a small, limping man with a collie dog always at his heels, attending to his cows which were housed at the far end of the yard. Morning after morning, as he went about his routine jobs in the yard, moving slowly between the byre and the fodder store and the milk house, I was at the open window, my elbows set firmly on the deep sill, following his every move over the sights of the loaded pistol. I had resolved that if my father came to any harm I would shoot the Republican judge. But I would not use the small gun; my weapon would be the big Luger pistol with ten bullets in its magazine which my brothers and I had found under a floorboard in the attic. It had been handed to Father by a parent who had come to him (as a good many did) with the problem of disengaging a son from the IRA without incurring the penalties attached to official cognisance of his membership.

I was resolved beyond any doubt that if vengeance was called for I would take the life of the man next door. I told no-one – not even my brothers – about my plan.

Eight

By the autumn of 1920 the whole country was in turmoil. There were few places in which there had not been some sort of violent lawlessness. In Dublin and in the counties of Cork, Kerry, Clare and Tipperary shootings and reprisals, terrorisation and the destruction of property were everyday happenings. Both sides were now better equipped, more alert and better organised. The enormous increase in the Crown Forces through the introduction of the Black and Tans and Auxiliaries, and the transfer to Ireland of large military reinforcements, gave the Government forces a considerable numerical advantage; there were fewer opportunities for killing unsuspecting policemen and there were no longer remote, ill-equipped, small barracks to be attacked by night. But it is probable that because of the fierce vengeance being taken by some of the Crown Forces, many who had disapproved of violence found their sympathy drawn towards the fugitive army. They were not days for outspoken expressions of support for one side or the other but the ever-present consciousness of hidden danger and the ruthless methods of the protagonists swept away neutrality.

I remember 'Bloody Sunday'. On that morning eleven British Army officers were shot dead in their lodgings in Dublin, some in the presence of their wives. In the afternoon the Black and Tans went out in lorries to a Gaelic Football match at Croke Park and fired on the crowd, killing twelve people and causing injuries to many. It was claimed that the murdered officers were Secret Service men and some of them undoubtedly were. It was said that their lady companions who were witnesses of the slaughter were not wives. In a country in which unchastity is almost the only sin for which justification cannot be argued, this information was a great salver of consciences. But it was untrue.

Kevin Barry, a student, was captured in an ambush in which several young soldiers collecting the regimental groceries at a Dublin shop were killed. He was tried before a military court, sentenced to death and hanged. There was no doubt about his participation in the attack but he was young and popular (he had been a notably good rugby player), and his death aroused sympathy and anger throughout the country. Lying in bed at night I could hear boys and girls at the street corner singing the ballad about his death:

> In Mountjoy Gaol, one Monday morning
> High upon the gallows tree,
> Kevin Barry gave his young life
> For the cause of liberty.

It was the best-known song of the day and it still survives.

Clashes between the IRA and the British Forces were now on a bigger scale. Ambushes were no longer brief encounters; they were minor battles, sometimes developing into cross-country pursuits. And the casualties were no longer all on one side. Patrolling soldiers travelled in armoured cars, police moved through the countryside in 'cage' lorries with high steel sides and wire-netting drawn across the top so that hand grenades could not be tossed in amongst the occupants.

The word 'atrocities' was used a good deal. The Crown Forces were accused of ill-treating prisoners, of using 'shot when trying to escape' as the explanation of many a killing. The burning of a co-operative creamery was a way of punishing a hostile rural community. Both sides were guilty of roadside shootings. It was said that in County Kerry two Black and Tans were disposed of in the gasworks furnace, the body of a Resident Magistrate was found in circumstances which indicated that he had been taken to the seashore, rendered immobile and left to drown in the rising tide. A priest was shot dead, magistrates who had been concerned in the trials of political prisoners were killed, girls who associated with policemen or soldiers were liable to have their hair cut off.

The country had gone mad. As comrades were shot their friends were roused to fierce and deadly anger. The IRA operated in small groups, each man engaged in his own personal war against a hated enemy. In the police force men who sought to do their duty calmly and impartially found the effort an impossible and fruitless one. Those who condemned made no distinction between reasonable and irresponsible men; on each side loyalty was measured by capacity to hate. In the Royal Irish Constabulary the first shootings and the words of the propagandists who condemned the force without scruple had aroused fear and resentment. When a man was shot down the names of those who had done the deed were soon known but proof was not forthcoming; even those who sympathised with the police were understandably afraid to give evidence. Some of the younger men, particularly those who had seen service in the 1914 War, were disposed to retaliate and the arrival of the Black and Tans gave support and encouragement to the idea of inflicting punishment without recourse to the courts. The British Government's approval of reprisals brought the rule of law to an end in what were called the 'troubled counties'.

Over much of the country the imposition of curfew confined people to their homes after dark, the movement of vehicles was restricted, traffic was frequently held up, travellers searched and questioned. And yet the whole unhappy business did not add up to the equivalent of a moderate battle in the European War which had just ended. People followed their occupations as usual, children went to school, there were football matches and coursing meetings and, within the hours permitted by curfew regulations, people played whist and danced and went to their local pubs.

The names of some of the IRA leaders were becoming known. Dan Breen from Tipperary was wanted in connection with more than one ambush, Michael Collins was said to be a ruthless leader, Richard Mulcahy was believed to be the organiser-in-chief (he was, in fact, Chief of Staff of the IRA), Eoin O'Duffy was thought of as a chocolate soldier, there was a ballad about Sean McEoin, the Blacksmith of Ballinalee who was the leader of a flying column. Years after peace had come I found an old notebook of my father's in which there was a long list of names and descriptions of wanted men. Beneath the entry about McEoin he had written, presumably from an official circular: 'Treat with respect. He has shown kindness towards wounded men'.

My views had not changed; there was no room in my heart for compromise or compassion. If the Black and Tans were being rough, if the Republicans were complaining about ruthlessness, as indeed they were, what did they expect? When they had started shooting down unarmed policemen they had planted dragons' teeth and now they were reaping the whirlwind. I saw no reason why they should expect sympathy.

Early in 1921 the pursuit of the underground army took on a new impetus. The pursuing forces were now well-equipped and numerous enough to operate over wide areas. A combined force of police and soldiers would surround a district and search every field and house, bringing all the men they found to one point where they would be questioned to establish their identity. At night the beams of searchlights would suddenly sweep over the countryside in search of men moving in the fields. Life was being made more difficult for the roving columns, the sheltering of men 'on the run' became more hazardous. In roadside encounters the IRA was suffering losses, dumps of arms were being found, important men were being captured. It seemed that the situation was coming under the control of the Government forces and the life of a civilian soldier of the Republic had become a more dangerous calling that it had been at Soloheadbeg. One felt that the revolutionaries could not endure much longer.

Suddenly, it was all over. The British Government had negotiated a truce to enable a settlement to be discussed. How this could have come about was beyond my comprehension. I could not understand how a government which had repeatedly declared that it would have no dealings with men who had blood on their hands could, when the opposition seemed about to collapse, when, as Lloyd George said, they had 'murder by the throat', agree to sit around a table with those very men. But I had no knowledge of the ways of governments, I knew nothing of political decisions, of the feelings of other countries about what had been happening in Ireland. It did not occur to me that even if the IRA and their supporters were growing weary, the government of Ireland could never be the same again. The doctrine of separation which had aroused so little interest in 1916 had now wide acceptance and the events over the previous year had hardened many hearts against British rule. Militant nationalism could never again be suppressed. The peaceful government of Ireland by a British administration had ceased to be a possibility.

Any doubts I had about the politics of the arrangement were soon forgotten. The shooting was over and my father had come through unhurt. I would no longer lie in bed praying for the sound of his footstep or watch the colour leave my mother's face when there was a knock on the door after dark. Whatever the future might hold, fear had been banished. My brothers and I went out into the street to watch the celebrations.

During the negotiations which followed the truce we saw photographs in the papers of the Irish representatives headed by bespectacled Arthur Griffith, there were rumours that the Northern Irish Government would be abolished and the whole country would come under a new government; there was talk about 'Dominion status', the Crown, association with the British Empire.

No-one expected that the negotiations in London would fail; everyone was tired of death and destruction and fear and suspicion. Peace with some form of Home Rule was the hope of most people. Those who expected the delegates to wrest an Irish Republic from a British Government headed by Lloyd George must have been very few.

Although a peaceful outcome was confidently expected the police and military forces were required to maintain their vigilance; the sandbags remained stacked around the barrack door, steel shutters continued to blind the windows and the machine gun in the upper window of Clones barrack still pointed across the Diamond. But continuing vigilance was impossible. Policemen and soldiers went about unarmed, duties were minimal and there was plenty of time for relaxation. Amongst the Black and Tans there were a drummer, a cornetist and a banjo player and their attempts to make music could be heard coming from the barrack every evening. It was rumoured that some members of the IRA who had been 'on the run' had returned to their homes, people talked openly about the whereabouts of fugitives. Some said that if the Treaty negotiations were to fail the police would very quickly be able to lay hands on a good many wanted men.

On 6 December 1921, the Treaty between Great Britain and Ireland was signed in London. It provided for the establishment of the Irish Free State with the status of a Dominion within the British Empire. The new state would consist of that part of Ireland not under the control of the Government of Northern Ireland. Northern Ireland was given the option of maintaining its separate existence and there was to be a commission to 'determine in accordance with the wishes of the inhabitants so far as may be compatible

73

with economic and geographic conditions, the boundaries between Northern Ireland and the rest of Ireland'. The Royal Irish Constabulary was to be disbanded and the British Army would go home. The new state would have its own army and police force.

Once again we went out to see Home Rule celebrations, this time with no feeling of involvement. Those who were putting up decorations, marching behind bands, waving green, white and orange tricolours represented something in which we had no part.

There was no sudden switch from the old order to the new. The first change, which came quite quickly, was the departure of the King's Royal Rifles and the handing over of the old Workhouse to representatives of the new Irish Army which was, in fact, the IRA cleansed of its sins against the British Empire by twelve signatures on a document in London. As uniform dress had not yet been provided for any but a few of the new soldiers it was impossible at first to tell how many Irish Army men there were. Two or three of the officers wore uniform of smooth green serge with riding breeches and polished leggings and when they came into the town people stood in the streets and stared proudly at them, but the majority were still, outwardly, civilians. The rank and file were for the most part country boys who, in the evenings, would stroll past the shop windows in small groups. The new garrison had a miscellaneous assortment of second-hand cars which, we assumed, they had stolen during 'the troubles'.

Disbandment of the Royal Irish Constabulary was to be a slow operation. Each man's pension was to be calculated on his period of service plus twelve years to compensate him for premature retirement. My father's income would be reduced by half and a Black and Tan who had joined days before the signing of the truce would have a life pension of about three pounds a week.

Whilst the administrators were doing their calculations the men remained at their posts without authority or responsibility. Law and order was in the hands of the Irish Army pending the recruitment and training of the new police force which was to be called the Garda Síochána or Civic Guard. The fortifications were removed from the barrack and the machine gun which had pointed menacingly across the Diamond was seen to be a piece of iron spouting. There was no fraternisation between the occupants of the police barrack and the new garrison in the workhouse.

At the monthly sitting of the local court our next-door neighbour sat in the seat which had been vacated by His Majesty's Resident Magistrate.

The next two years were full of interest. There was no longer a threat to the security of my home and although I felt no kinship with the men in whose hands power had been placed, it was not possible to be uninterested in the outward signs of the establishment of a new state. We were witnessing the making of history.

The underground movement, its badge of outlawry removed, was now seen in the light of day. Men who had been on the run and political prisoners released under the Treaty amnesty were in the streets again; some were in the Army, others came back to their old occupations and went about in belted trench-coats, conscious of their part in the victory.

Tommy Moran, whose mutinous protest in India had sent him to life imprisonment, was one of the benificiaries of the amnesty. He returned to a hero's reception in Athlone although Republican purists were disposed to devalue his heroism (which was undeniable) because of his having been in the service of Perfidious Albion. One hoped that his kind mother was there to welcome home her wayward boy.

It was possible now to see the Republican movement as it really was and one found that some who had been thought to hold high rank were, in fact, only minor acolytes whilst others who had shown no connection with revolutionary activities were revealed as persons of considerable importance.

Since coming to Clones we had spent much of our time riding horses in the fields of a farmer whose sons were friends of ours. We had always been treated with great kindness in their home where we had never heard an opinion on politics expressed. After the Treaty it was revealed that this house had been a haven of refuge for political fugitives. The family's place in the new state was obviously going to be a respected one.

It must always be the case that the promoters of a successful enterprise in which danger is involved are embarrassed by the numbers of those who, when the smoke of conflict has cleared, claim association with the victory. In the immediate post-Treaty days there were many who, on the strength of having given minor services, placed themselves in the ranks of the heroes of the hour. In a little while one ceased trying to distinguish between men who had lived dangerously and those whose participation in the revolution had been no more than the passing-on of a message or the casting of a vote. (From post-factum claims it might have been deduced that the organisation had been rather generously provided with 'Intelligence Officers'.)

Murder was being done in Northern Ireland. It had begun with sectarian rioting in Belfast. Catholic workers had been chased out of the shipyards, Catholic houses and places of business had been burned, people were shot in the streets and in their homes, the IRA, bitterly hostile to the Unionist Government since its establishment, had taken a hand in the shooting so that at one time the Northern Ireland administration seemed in danger of collapsing in anarchy. In a field on the outskirts of Clones a long wooden hut was built with funds provided by a charitable body and three or four refugee families from Belfast came to live there.

Because of the nearness of the border Clones had a particular interest in conditions in the North. At the edge of the town the armed forces of the two states faced one another with open hostility.

Up at the Workhouse, on the Scotshouse road, the Free State Army was being put into shape. A local man who had served in the British Army and been about the town during the trouble, appeared in the uniform of an officer and was put in charge of the training of the rank and file. During all the hours of daylight drilling went on in a field not far from our house. Young lads who had never known discipline marched and countermarched, stood to attention, formed fours and learned to manipulate their rifles under the lashing tongue of their new master whose flow of invective brought back memories of wartime Tommies being put through their paces in the King's Meadow at Athlone. But soldiers had then been Englishmen in khaki; these new privates were farmers' sons in civilian tweeds and cloth caps who were being told by their vitriolic instructor that if they'd broken their mothers' hearts they wouldn't break his. The blistering words we heard suggested a somewhat ungracious attitude towards young men whose decision to serve in the new army had probably been inspired more by patriotic fervour than any strong vocation for regular soldiering.

When the rejoicing had died down people began to talk about the future. Clones is at the tip of a bulge of land penetrating into County Fermanagh. Much of the farming area on which the business of the town had been very dependent was in Northern Ireland and if there

76

should be any interference with the cross-border movement of people or goods, the town would suffer severely. There was great expectation that the Commission appointed to examine the line of the border would make adjustments which would remove the fears of the shopkeepers. But there were two opinions about what the solution would be. The former Unionists were sure that the position of the town, cut away from its natural catchment area was one of the first problems the Boundary Commission would tackle. As the function of the Commission was to remove anomalous situations they would surely restore Clones as the market town for a large area of County Fermanagh and bring the boundary comfortably south of the town. The Nationalists were confident that a very different solution was the logical and natural one. Were not adjustments to be made 'in accordance with the wishes of the inhabitants' and had it not been demonstrated at elections that the majority of the inhabitants of County Fermanagh were unwilling citizens of Northern Ireland? If the terms of reference of the Boundary Commission meant anything, they argued, Fermanagh would surely be given an opportunity of opting to join the Free State. This would happen all along the border; two or three counties might opt out of the North. Ireland would soon be one. But older men who knew something about the ways of politicians, quoted the qualifying words, 'so far as may be compatible with economic and geographic conditions' and commented that Lloyd George was no fool. They wondered if the discarded Constitutional Party could not have done as well without any blood-letting.

Feeling between Northern Ireland and the new Free State was bitter. The lawlessness in Belfast aroused sympathetic reaction in the South. There was a boycott of Belfast goods and there were calls for other forms of retaliation which must have appealed to men who had grown used to the handling of arms.

In some border districts of Northern Ireland prominent men on the Unionist side were kidnapped and held for a time as hostages. Southern Irishmen travelling in the North were harrassed and subjected to indignity by the gun-waving Special Constabulary. The border bristled with trouble. I remember going to Mass on a Sunday morning as bullets fired by 'Specials', whose outpost was only a few hundred yards away, thumped into the church tower, sending chips of stone down on the heads of the gathering worshippers.

The Free State Army began to molest men who, although living on the southern side, had been, and in some cases still were, members of the Ulster Special Constabulary. Their homes were raided at night and some of them, in fear of their lives, moved into the North. My father, now without any authority, was persuaded by some townspeople to intervene on behalf of those who were being harrassed. He went to the barrack in the Workhouse and he and the officer in charge had a lively but unproductive confrontation. They were parting, rather coolly, when the officer held out his hand.

'My name is Fitzpatrick,' he said, 'I want to thank you for saving my life.'

Until that moment Father had not realised that the man with whom he had been arguing had once been his prisoner. On a winter's night he had been in charge of a party which had found a wounded man being cared for in a remote farmhouse. It was clear that his injury had been caused by a bullet and it seemed likely that he had been a casualty in a recent skirmish some miles from where he then was. The Black and Tans wanted to shoot their captive but they were sent back to the town for an army ambulance and an escorting party. It was clear that the captured man expected to meet his death on the journey to hospital but my father put an elderly Irish policeman in charge of the escort. Fitzpatrick, for he was the prisoner, arrived safely at Monaghan Infirmary and a guard of soldiers was placed at his bed. Several weeks later, when his wound was almost mended, a new guard which marched in to take over from the old proved to be IRA men in British uniform. The prisoner was well enough to make his way to the waiting car and he disappeared into the hills once more.

Not more than a week after Father's meeting with Commandant Fitzpatrick I stood on the footpath outside our house and watched car after car filled with Free State soldiers race through the centre of the town, their klaxon horns screaming continuously. The men in the cars were all carrying arms; some of them had Thompson machine-guns with circular drums of ammunition shining beneath their short barrels. They were on their way to one of the deadliest encounters in the cross-border skirmishing of those unstable days.

It was possible to travel by rail from Belfast to Enniskillen without leaving Northern Ireland, but an alternative route which passed through part of County Monaghan was a more favoured one because it was quicker. There were as yet no restrictions on the movement of traffic of any sort from one part of the country to the other and travellers arranged their journeys as though there were no border. Nevertheless, it was surprising that, in the conditions then prevailing, those sending a party of Special Constables from Belfast to Enniskillen apparently took no account of the fact that in putting them on the more direct route they were starting them on a journey which would take them through Free State territory. The train would stop at several stations in the Free State, Clones being the last of them. The party of Specials was made up of a sergeant and twelve constables, all of them armed. The soldiers whom I saw being rushed through the town in cars were on their way to meet the train and by the time it had arrived they had cleared the station, set up their machine-guns and taken up their positions.

As soon as the train stopped Commandant Fitzpatrick, who was in charge of the Army contingent, walked, revolver in hand, to the compartment in which the Specials were. He called on them to surrender and come out and was immediately shot dead. Hell was then let loose. Bullets poured into the carriage containing the Specials, passengers cried out in terror, jumped from the train and ran in all directions. It was all over in a few minutes. In the shattered carriage the sergeant and three of the constables lay dead.

One of the Special Constables got out on the 'off' side of the train, intending, possibly, to run the few hundred yards along the track to the Northern Ireland border. But he turned in the wrong direction and found himself at a level crossing which crossed the main street. He discarded his uniform jacket and cap and made his way to the Royal Irish Constabulary barrack where he told the story of the attack on the train. Policemen went to the railway station and brought the bodies of the dead Specials to the barrack.

I remember that night, standing in a dark room, watching the Free State soldiers marching back to their barrack; excited, angry men. When they had passed, the town was deserted and silent. People stayed indoors that night, many sat up listening for the sounds that would tell them that retaliation was on the way. There were considerable forces of Special Constabulary, well armed and equipped, not very far away and it was fully expected that they would come across the border seeking retribution for the deaths in the railway station. But the night passed quietly.

Father did not come home that night. Some hours after the soldiers had returned to their quarters they learned of the fugitive

Special who had been given shelter in the RIC barrack. A party of them came into the town and demanded that he be handed over. This was refused and there was some argument about the rights and wrongs of harbouring the wanted man. Father did not tell us how the Special Constable found his way out of the town that night but it was rumoured next day that he had been taken to the County Fermanagh border in a 'borrowed' delivery van.

On Sunday a large furniture lorry drove into the Diamond and pulled up at the police barrack. Four blanket-covered stretchers were carried out and put in the lorry which went down Fermanagh Street and out over the railway bridge into the North.

At last the time came when the arrangements for the disbandment of the Royal Irish Constabulary were completed. They were to go to the big Depot at Gormanston where each man would be given his discharge and a warrant entitling him to a pension for life.

The Black and Tans were first to go. Seeing them in civilian clothes, carrying their shabby luggage to the station, one was struck by their very ordinariness. The name Black and Tan had aroused fear and hatred throughout the country but, stripped of their uniforms and fearsome trappings, they seemed insignificant little men on their way back to their working-class homes in the industrial towns and cities of Britain. There was a great, curious crowd at the station when the train, which had been gathering unfrocked Black and Tans along its journey, came steaming into the station with its occupants crowding the windows, cheering and singing. From one carriage an Irish tricolour fluttered. I had never seen so many drunk men. They got a boisterous, good-humoured send-off.

A little later the remainder of the force went away and after a few days Father came home. He was now a civilian and the Royal Irish Constabulary was no more.

My judgement of the Royal Irish Constabulary must be a very subjective one. I was thirteen years old when the force was disbanded. Those years which were, more than any time in my life, full of exciting and often entertaining happenings, had been spent in the company of these men. My earliest memories are of endless happy days in the barrack in Athlone with large men in uniform always on hand to help solve the immense problems of childhood, to provide interest and entertainment and friendship and to open doors into the exciting and often eccentric world of adults. When the cold wind of hostility began to blow and the new Republicans tried to brand them as enemies of the Irish people, I wanted to cry out for justice for they were my friends. Throughout the campaign of shooting many influential voices were raised in sympathy with them. When the fierce retaliation of the Black and Tans added a new dimension to terrorism men of courage did not exempt one side more than the other from their expressions of disapproval.

The men of the Royal Irish Constabulary had not the background or the disposition or the training which produces heroes; they were quite unfitted for the part which they were called upon to fill by those who saw a resort to violence as the way to the attainment of the Ireland they wanted. The designers of the campaign of killing thought that once they had claimed a few unwary victims the Royal Irish Constabulary would distintegrate, but they knew nothing of the deep loyalty of those simple men one towards another. Because they believed that they belonged to a unique police force with proud traditions, they grew angry at the vituperation of the extremists and they were sustained by the sympathy of responsible opinion. When shootings, following the unheroic pattern of Soloheadbeg, became daily happenings, a small number left the force but the majority remained to serve not (as Tom Kettle put it) for King or Crown or Empire but out of the comradeship which bound them together. Some to whom the events of those years are part of history may say that they were wrong but I can think of them only as I knew them. It would be idle to pretend that in the heat of the conflict there were no instances of men who behaved unworthily. I knew one such man; I knew also of the contempt in which he was held by his colleagues. But I am quite sure that there were in the Royal Irish Constabulary more good men than my children or my children's children will meet in any company, anywhere.

Nine

The year following the setting up of the Irish Free State was a busy, carefree, eventful time. I can recall an abundance of sunlit summer days, bathing parties to the lakes around the town, horse riding, early morning walks through dewy fields in search of mushrooms, generous fruit harvests of which we had our share without troubling to consult the owners, crouching with a poacher as he shot a distant deer in Colonel Madden's estate, fishing for pike with small frogs as bait, playing football, going out into the fields with a miscellaneous collection of dogs to hunt rabbits and hares without ever catching one.

For the first few months of the new regime there was a police force which had been stripped of its authority; for many months afterwards there was none. The Free State Army was too busy making its men into soldiers to concern itself with any but the most serious and obvious crimes. In a hundred ways laws were being broken every day. We were living in a free society and enjoying it.

With my brothers I watched cockfighting for two whole days. The birds had been brought from as far away as County Down and Armagh and from Fermanagh and Tyrone. The venue was a natural amphitheatre, a gorse-rimmed saucer of land at the edge of a bog, no more than a mile from the town. As there was no danger from the law the performance was open to one and all.

The gambling was an eye-opener. In between the bouts there were half a dozen 'pitch and toss' schools with more notes than coins being wagered on the spin of two copper coins. Before each cock-fight a man would be appointed to hold the sidestakes. The contesting cocks would be referred to by the counties of their origin and those wishing to back their fancy would call out for someone prepared to make a bet on the opposing bird. Together they would go to the stakeholder who would enter the bet in his book and put the money in a canvas bag. It was all very orderly.

There was a referee for each bout. When the ring had been cleared the birds would be brought in by their handlers, the same two men throughout the tournament, who had seen to the fixing of the curved steel spurs. For a little while the handlers would stand a few feet apart, stroking their charges, then they would 'breast' them; that is, the birds would be swept along the ground towards one another, still held by the two men, and snatched apart when they were almost touching. After four or five of these confrontations the feathers on the birds's necks would be standing out and their heads jerking with fierce anger. The men would then retire to opposite corners of the arena and release the contestants.

Fighting cocks are smaller and more gaily coloured than farmyard fowl and there is something incongruous about a circle of grown men crowding on top of one another to watch two small multicoloured creatures engaging in mortal combat.

Fighting cocks do not always rush immediately into the fray. Sometimes they approach one another obliquely, moving warily in a series of arcs, in search of an advantageous jumping-off angle. When the assault comes they rise towards one another, bringing their feet up so that the spurs are pointing outwards and they crash together with a flutter of coloured feathers. The fight consists of a series of assaults and withdrawals until one of the contestants is dead or so badly disabled as to be unable to continue. If a bird is temporarily unable to defend himself the referee, after counting ten, allows the handlers to pick up the birds and refresh them by spraying water or whiskey over their heads; they are then 'breasted' once more and the fight is resumed.

I do not recall being particularly shocked at the sight of birds fighting to the death. I accepted the view that these highly-strung, aggressive creatures were born to fight and, if left together without any additional cutlery or ceremonial matchmaking, would kill each other. But I was surprised that men should have been prepared to travel long distances and, in normal times, risk conflict with the law, for what did not appear to me to be adult entertainment.

I saw a man driven mad over a dog licence. I saw it happen a dozen times.

83

He was a farmer, a tall angular man who, when he came into the town, wore a tan tweed suit and cap with his heavy black boots newly polished. He seemed to take more care about his appearance than most farmers; he looked like a man dressed for going to church. He might have been about fifty years of age.

Once or twice every month he would come walking in the Cavan Road, carrying on his arm a square wicker basket in which to take home the things he had come into the town to buy. He would come along Cara Street walking purposefully, apparently unnoticed. To get to Fermanagh Street where the principal shops were he had to cross the Diamond and he would not have taken a dozen steps out into the open space before a voice from a corner or an entry or an upstairs window would call out:

'Pay for your dog!'

The man would walk on, his eyes fixed straight ahead, his lips now moving angrily. Another voice would be heard, this time louder and from a different direction:

'Pay for your dog!'

By now the victim would be alone in the middle of the Diamond. He would hesitate, then stop and slowly look around, searching the faces of the street-corner loafers, people who had stopped on the footpath, men standing in shop doorways. There would be silence. As soon as the man started to walk again the cry would come from three or four directions:

'Pay for your dog! Pay for your dog!'

Suddenly he would spot one of his tormentors and go racing wildly towards him, his nailed boots clattering awkwardly on the roadway. As he ran there would be a chorus of raucous cries behind him:

'Pay for your dog! Pay for your dog! Pay for your dog!'

The man would stop and turn around and roaring with anger and frustration, dash murderously at the new source of his torment. But again a clamour of voices from behind would pull him back and send him shouting for vengeance at another group of laughing accusers. For perhaps half-an-hour the poor man's tormentors would send him careering, heavy-footed, murderously angry, over and back and across the Diamond like a frantic, trapped animal until physical exhaustion brought his futile pursuit to an end.

It was said that he had once been fined for having an unlicensed dog but no-one could say when or if, indeed, the story was true.

84

There were people who showed disapproval of this degrading performance. Attempts were made to stop it but for too many it was high entertainment.

I am sure I have never seen a human being so cruelly treated.

Two boys who lived near us had a fox terrier called Spot and Spot was the best ratter in the town; he seemed to live for nothing but hunting them out and killing them. We took him out to hunt rats at the dump beside the railway bridge on the Monaghan Road, along the canal bank, in the country lanes and in the undergrowth at the foot of the back gardens that ran down to the Jubilee Road. But the most fruitful hunting ground was a field on the road to Newbliss in which the owner of the sawmill stored felled trees. It was a perfect place for boys with a ratting dog.

The day on which we got into trouble must have been very shortly after the signing of the Treaty.

Jack, Tim and I, with Spot and his two owners, were hurrying along the road to the timber field when the dog, responding to some inner urge to which he had never before given expression, suddenly jumped off the footpath and sank his teeth into the leg of a man on a bicycle. As the victim had come up on us from behind we became aware of his presence only when we heard his angry cry. He raised his wounded leg out of reach of Spot's teeth, causing the bicycle to wobble, but he steadied it and turning his front wheel in our direction, jumped off. Tim and our two friends, followed by Spot, dashed through a hole in the hedge and ran. Jack and I hesitated, the man planted his bicycle in front of us and we were caught.

He was a very tall, thin, pale-faced man wearing a brown suit and soft hat. His trouser bottoms were folded into steel cycle clips.

By the time he spoke the other members of our party were half a field away.

'That dog bit me.'

This statement of an obvious fact prompted no helpful comment so we remained silent. Jack, I knew, was struggling with an urge to laugh.

'Do you own him?'

No, we said, we didn't own him. We didn't know whose dog he was.

The man reached into his inner pocket and brought out first a notebook and then a long pencil. He folded back the blue cover of

85

the notebook which, I could see, was a new one in which no note had yet been written. There were small beads of sweat on his upper lip.

'I am a Republican judge,' he announced, 'and I intend to have that dog destroyed. I want your names and addresses.'

Soberly we gave our names and our address which were written down. The man put his notebook and pencil back in his pocket, remounted his bicycle and went on his way.

Our companions were soon back on the footpath and we told them of the grave turn which events had taken. For some minutes we stood there, saying very little, thinking fretfully of what lay ahead. The Sinn Feiners had killed men; it was unlikely that they would be disposed to be merciful to an offending dog. The chances of the offence being overlooked were likely to be especially remote in our case for, our name being an unusual one in the district, the wounded Republican judge would certainly know that he was dealing with representatives of his former enemies.

I cannot remember who came up with the proposal that gave us hope; that Spot should go 'on the run', that he should be put into hiding until, with the passage of time, the pursuit would be abandoned and the threat to his life removed. Between the five of us (our friends being Protestants) we knew a number of farmers who were Unionists, men who through the turmoil of revolution had remained staunch in their loyalty to the British Crown and Constitution. One of them would surely shelter Spot against the vengeance of the Sinn Feiners.

There was no time to be lost. The first house on our list was just over the next hill. Off we went; five unsmiling boys and a ridiculously carefree dog.

But sanctuary was not as easily found as we had expected. At house after house we told our story – the Sinn Feiners were after our dog; would they mind taking him and hiding him whilst the danger lasted. But at every door we were told of some obstacle to the granting of our request; we heard of delicate children, nervous wives, frightened cats, the mortality rate of hens. No-one was prepared to help us.

Daylight was fading by the time we visited the last of the houses at which we had thought we had only to ask for sympathy in a problem with such clear political implications. Again we failed. We turned for home, tired and depressed, our gloom unrelieved by the frolics of the doomed dog.

We had got quite close to the town when a white gate seemed at the same moment to catch the eyes of all of us. We had not particularly noticed this gate before and were not sure that it led to a house; the driveway turned sharply behind a high bank overhanging the roadway. We went through the entrance and had not gone far along the sandy lane when we saw the house ahead, a square, two-storey, grey house; through its open door we could see the lamplight shining in the kitchen at the back. We ran to the door and knocked.

A tall, red-haired man came out. Once more we told of our misadventure with the Republican judge and of the fate which was in store for our dog at the hands of the Sinn Feiners. Would he hide Spot for us?

He told us to wait. He went back into the brightly-lit kitchen and returning with an oil lantern, told us to follow him. Expectantly we trotted at his heels around the side of the house, through the farmyard, to a big barn. He pulled the iron bolt, swung the door open on its creaking hinges and shining his lantern into the blackness inside, said, 'There you are, boys. The Sinn Feiners will never find him there.'

We could see straw and hay and farm implements in the big barn. Spot was inveigled inside, the big door was closed and bolted. The red haired man said that it would be all right for us to come and visit the fugitive. We thanked him eagerly and hurried home as darkness fell.

For a week or more we went out to see Spot every day, bringing him food and taking him out for walks in the fields. Then, as we had received no summons or writ or edict, we assumed that the bitten judge had had a change of heart and Spot was brought home.

A few weeks later there was great excitement in the town when it was announced that General O'Duffy was coming to review the local contingent of the new Army. The forces of the Revolution would be on parade for the first time before their own people; there would be visitors from all over the county.

When the great day came we decided that Spot must be kept indoors lest he should be recognised by the Republican judge, who was sure to be there. We also decided to keep out of sight.

From behind lace curtains in an upstairs room we looked out at the great crowd which lined the procession route. We heard the sound of distant music and as it got nearer the excitement grew. A great cheer went up as the forces of the Free State, led by a local brass band playing a patriotic air, came marching up Analore Street and into the Diamond. Except for the officers, few were in uniform. A small number had uniform caps, some wore green riding breeches, here and there one saw a green jacket with metal buttons but the majority were in civilian clothes embellished by odd bits of the paraphernalia of soldiers. Some carried rifles, some had revolvers, a few had both. But they marched proudly, the marchers and the spectators conscious that the occasion was a historic one.

We watched the whole parade pass. There was no sign of the Republican judge but in one of the leading ranks, wearing tan riding breeches and with a Sam Browne belt over his tweed jacket, we had seen the red-haired man in whose barn Spot had been kept safe from the Sinn Feiners.

It was immensely interesting to be a spectator at the birth of a new state, to watch the development of new institutions, to hear the endless talk about what the future might bring. Change was all around. The royal cyphers on buildings and on postmen's uniform were replaced by the insignia of the new regime; Government red paint ('England's cruel red') on letterboxes got a coat of green; the postage stamps still had the King's head on them with 'Saorstat Éireann' overprinted in black; the decision to make the native language a compulsory subject in all schools sent Protestant teachers to evening classes in Catholic schools and in the holidays to Irish colleges in the West, for none of them had a word of Irish. Everywhere people were thinking of patriotic new names for streets which had been called after landlords or events associated with Empire building; King's County and Queen's County became Offaly and Leix, Queenstown was now called Cobh and Kingstown, Dun Laoghaire. Military establishments which had got their names from royalty and generals and great battles now commemorated the heroes of Ireland.

Those who were disposed to laugh found subjects for derision. The behaviour of members of the apprentice army was informal indeed; turned out in such gear as they possessed, they looked more like rural duck-shooting men than soldiers; a private might salute his officer with 'How are you Mick?'. Army cars were sometimes driven by officers with 'other ranks' riding as passengers. There were comments about the appearance and the accents and the antecedents of the new leaders. In his wooden hut in the Diamond, blind Peter Reilly, on being asked by a small girl for a bottle of marking ink for Captain White's linen, was heard to mutter that Ireland must have had a notable victory indeed if the result had been to put a collar and tie on that little shit.

But time brought order and normality. In the public offices business was being conducted as before; the local court, with our neighbour on the bench, was, except for the opening preamble in Irish, very little different from what it had been under British rule. The soldiers got their new green uniforms and learned to salute correctly and move about smartly and generally comport themselves as do soldiers the world over. An influx of new officers who were strangers to the district simplified the enforcement of discipline and in a short time the traditional class distinction between officers and men began to appear.

Down in Dublin there were bitter wrangles between those who supported the settlement and those who called it betrayal.

It was astonishing to me that there should be any opposition to the acceptance of the Treaty. It had seemed that the spirit of the IRA was rapidly being crushed when the Treaty came and I had seen the rejoicing of the people and heard their expressions of relief when the shooting and the dangers and the suffering had come to an end. Then it seemed that some who had welcomed the settlement allowed themselves second thoughts, particularly when they learned that de Valera who, to some, had become the fount of all wisdom, was opposed to its acceptance. Nevertheless, one felt that the men who had signed the agreement in London had correctly interpreted the wishes of the majority of the people.

Following Dáil Éireann's majority decision to ratify the Treaty the former guerilla forces split; those who supported the Treaty being inducted into the National Army and those who rejected it taking up arms against their former comrades. Thus began the Civil War which developed into a more bitter and deadly squabble than the fight with the British Forces.

We saw nothing of the Civil War. There were a few anti-Treatyites in the Clones area but they did nothing to molest or hamper the institutions of the Free State. The civil and military bodies went about their duties in peace. Dublin and the trouble-torn counties were a long way off.

It was during this time that I found myself in deadly danger. I had been friendly with a youth who worked in the electricity station and who was very ingenious at making pellet guns out of pieces of metal piping and discarded springs and washers and bolts. He gave me a small revolver; it was the real thing. (It did not occur to me that he might have had some connection with the IRA.) The gun was probably useless as an offensive weapon but the trigger and the hammer worked and the magazine revolved and it felt impressively heavy in my pocket.

One morning I read in the newspaper that the Free State Government, its forces harassed and its institutions threatened by the attentions of the Irregulars, had decreed the possession of lethal weapons to be a capital offence. I spent a very uneasy day, conscious of the shadow of the gallows hanging over me. Late that night I stole out of the house and down to the bridge at the bottom of Whitehall Street where I dropped my gun into the canal. It hit the water with a splash which I was sure must have been heard all over the town. But the threat of the gallows had been removed.

Those who before the Treaty had been influential props of British rule – 'the Ascendancy' – naturally had misgivings about how they would fare in the new state. Some emigrated rather than live under a flag other than the Union Jack, some went because they were fearful of how their neighbours, on becoming the masters, would treat them. But the majority remained. No doubt there were instances of uncharitableness but it must be said that the new Government behaved with correctness towards their former political opponents. People who attain power through revolutionary methods tend to be intolerant of the supplanted governing class; in the Irish Free State the enmity died quickly.

I remember one notable example of the changes in attitudes.

In the midst of the pre-Treaty trouble the town was deprived of supplies of coal through a railway strike. When it was learned that our cellar was almost bare Father was overwhelmed with offers of help. They came from Loyalists and Republicans alike and we did not go short. Some time after the Treaty a similar situation arose; the town was without coal and we had none. Father, now a civilian, spent days calling on those who had previously been so ready to come to our aid but nowhere was there coal to spare; even the creamery manager, who in the previous shortage had sent his lorry in from the country with an offer of generous supplies, could not help. We had resigned ourselves to being without fires when our neighbour, the Republican judge now renamed District Justice, came to our door. He had heard that we were short of coal, he said, and he would be glad if we would accept the loan of a few bags from him. Those were the first words to pass between our neighbour and ourselves. And he was the man whose death I had planned! My conscience is still sensitive to the mention of his name. It was Owen Conlan.

The disbanded members of the Royal Irish Constabulary were not made to feel unwanted in the Irish Free State. I think we could have gone to live anywhere in the country without fear of molestation. Many former members of the force went back to their family farms in the South and West, some commuted their pensions to buy smallholdings; amongst the younger men some accepted invitations to serve in the British police force in Palestine.

My parents decided that we must leave Clones. We had no family ties there, it was a small town with very limited employment opportunities and there were five children to be educated on a very small pension. Father had heard of prospects of employment in the North, and the suggestion that we should settle amongst Mother's folk in Newry met with unanimous approval.

We left a friendly town. The Parish Priest called to say goodbye and to whisper to Father, wryly, that he had admired the stand he had taken over the education of his sons. The South was aflame with civil war and across the Border in the North there was a brooding calm amidst the embers of sectarian strife.

Ten

Newry in 1922 was a town with a hangover. The atmosphere was sour and full of hostility, the people divided demoninationally and politically, each side resentful of things past and suspicious of the other side's every move, apprehensive about the future. The 'A' Specials in ill-fitting uniforms, formidably armed, were there in large numbers; on duty in the streets, racing through the country-side in a variety of vehicles, standing guard over important instal-lations, watching and searching and sharply observing the towns-people.

Although this was one of the few areas which John Redmond's Nationalist Party had held against Sinn Fein in the 1918 elections, the Republican movement had since taken a strong hold in the district. With the coming of the Special Constabulary and the 1920 Act which placed the town in Northern Ireland, Sinn Fein and the IRA had grown in strength. Police had been ambushed and killed, on one occasion in the main street of the town; there had been savage reprisals by the Specials; some of the town's menfolk had sought refuge across the Border; some were, under orders made possible by special legislation, prohibited from returning to their homes in the North. There had been curfew which kept the resentful townspeople indoors after dark; we were told about the young man from the South, suspected of being connected with the IRA, who had been taken from his lodgings late at night and whose cries had been heard by the curfewed people as he was dragged through the deserted streets to a shed on the Armagh Road where, on the following morning, his monstrously mutilated body was found. We saw the line of Protestant houses at the foot of the Camlough Mountains which the IRA had burned out in a fierce night raid in which several of the occupants had been killed.

Nearby two brothers, one of them mentally defective, had been taken from their cottage home and shot dead at the roadside because they were believed to be IRA men. A short time before we moved house Father spent some days in Newry making preparations for our move and on Sunday morning as he left the Cathedral, in the main street, Wolff Flanagan, the Resident Magistrate, who had been to the same Mass, was shot dead virtually on the threshold of the church.

We arrived in the aftermath of these happenings. Except for the shooting of Wolff Flanagan, which was an act of delayed vengeance, the campaign of violence had, in fact, come to an end; peace had been restored by force of arms but the air was full of recrimination and mistrust.

Newry was very different from Clones or Rathfriland or Athlone. It was bigger than any of them, it had a ship canal along which small steam-driven vessels brought grain to the local mills, timber from Scandinavia and coal, for which Newry was a major distributing point, from the mines of Britain. Along the quay there were red-brick grain stores, coal yards, timber stacks, depots from which potatoes were exported to England and hardware and ironmongery warehouses owned by builders' suppliers and the importers of agricultural machinery and implements. The quay was a busy, noisy place, a place of fluttering pigeons and dark dust and many smells. The shops in the main street seemed always to be full and the Thursday market brought Belfast 'cheap-jacks' with their stalls and farmers with a variety of horse-drawn vehicles into the town.

Newry had a football team and an operatic society which staged a light opera every winter in the Town Hall. It was there that I had my first experience of the professional theatre. Dobell's touring company played a 'season' of Victorian memodrama for two weeks each year; the plays in their repertoire were *A Royal Divorce, Under Two Flags* and *East Lynne*. In the intervals between acts Dobell's actors and actresses revealed themselves as singers and musicians and the soubrette, all dimples and waving eyelashes, came amongst the audience selling autographed photographs of herself and other members of the company. We also had visits from Charles Doran's Shakespearean Company and in the Newry Town Hall I saw Anew McMaster, then a young actor who had just started his own touring company, in a performance of Hamlet which made a lasting impression on me.

93

The Newry people were born performers. On the smallest excuse it was possible to organise an evening's entertainment from amongst the ample supply of people with talents to display. Newry was a town in which there was always something to be seen or something to do.

The Abbey Christian Brothers' School was very different from the High School in Clones. It was an all male school. Our classmates in Clones had been male and female Little Englanders, the pupils in the Abbey were Republicans; almost every one of them and their teachers were believers in a political doctrine with which I had no sympathy. But my brothers and I were not unduly apprehensive about the conflicts which might develop. Jack and Tim and I were enrolled in the secondary school and Tom, who had not yet reached the age for secondary education, went to the primary school.

Looking back over the years I still feel a little pride at the logic with which we dealt with problems created by our minority attitude. One concerned Gaelic Football which was officially the school game. The Gaelic Athletic Association was, we believed, politically motivated, many of its leading players and administrators were prominent in the Republican movement, it had silly rules about who could or could not be allowed to participate in its activities and the Republican tricolour was flown at some of its matches. Jack, Tim and I – without any guidance from our parents who did not dictate a family attitude in such matters – decided that we could not refuse to take part in a school activity but that we would not have anything to do with Gaelic Football out of school hours. We played in school games but when the Abbey decided to enter a team in a local competition for boys' teams and all three of us were picked for the first match, we struck our names from the team list. Since we had made no secret of our feelings our action was accepted with little comment.

The fiercest outcome of our political differences was a bare-knuckle fight with a farmer's son. For half an hour he and I were allowed to belabour one another until a Christian Brother intervened and sent us home. We had reason to believe that he had observed the whole contest and appeared on the scene only when he felt that we had both had the hiding we deserved. When my opponent grew to manhood he joined the Royal Ulster Constabulary.

I was at the stage when the question of an occupation was

94

beginning to impinge on my thinking. I knew that I was being well taught albeit under fairly Spartan conditions. Corporal punishment was freely used but my apprenticeship in the Deerpark School in Athlone had taught me to bear such trials philosophically.

In those years secondary education in Ireland was based on a programme of examinations (originally conducted by the Inter-mediate Education Board for the whole of the country) which were taken in successive years; Junior Certificate at fourteen, Middle at fifteen and Senior at sixteen. I had taken the Junior Certificate before we left Clones but Irish had not figured in my education there. It was a compulsory subject for all pupils at the Abbey. As I was neither a diligent student nor an Irish language enthusiast, the extra burden of making up the leeway in Irish became a matter for agitation. I pleaded with the Headmaster to relieve me of a load which I assured him was prejudicing my whole future. I seemed to be on the point of creating a school record by being excused Irish when he found out that I was the son of a very fluent native speaker. My case was thereupon lost.

Much has been written and said about the Irish Christian Brothers. Some have sought to belittle their work but over the years since my first day at the Abbey my respect for them has grown. I know how high their reputation stands amongst present-day edu-cationists; in earlier years when opportunities were few their con-tribution to the education of Irish Catholics must have been immeasurable. My schooldays were before the arrival of free secondary education. In the Abbey School we knew that when the envelopes were handed out at the beginning of the term more than a few contained no bills. One could never know who was getting free tuition but it was known that in a Christian Brothers' school a promising boy was not refused education because his father could not pay the fees.

During our early years in Newry the Boundary Commission was an unending topic of conversation, for Newry was one of the places which the Nationalists confidently expected would be transferred to the Free State. That the area was predominantly 'nationally-minded' had been demonstrated in election after election; if the declared intention of adjusting the Border 'in accordance with the wishes of the inhabitants' meant anything, Newry's future in the Free State was assured, or so argued the Nationalists. And they were not alone in this opinion. One of the town's leading Unionists exchanged his Newry house for the Warrenpoint house of a Republican businessman and it was generally understood that they had swopped houses so that when the expected change came each would be a secure citizen of his preferred state.

When members of the Boundary Commission, in a fleet of large cars, paid a visit to the town, people stood and watched them pass slowly through. Stories were told about the cool reception they had given to Unionists who had appeared before them to argue their case for the retention of Newry in the United Kingdom.

When, out of the blue, the *Morning Post* published what it asserted were the findings of the Commission, the news was greeted by the Nationalists with derision, for the article said that the Border would remain virtually unchanged. When there was no official denial of the *Morning Post's* forecast, there were expressions of indignation. When it became clear that the Commission's recommendations had indeed been 'leaked' and that the high hopes which had been inspired by all the lengthy deliberations would be unfulfilled, there was dismay. After all the fine talk about majority opinion settling the destiny of Fermanagh and Tyrone and large areas of Armagh and Down and possibly leading to a united Ireland, the outcome was shattering. The Southern Government, which had made no secret of its expectation of a profitable settlement, cried out in protest but the protests sounded hollow for one of the members of the Commission was a representative of the Free State Government. They had been crushingly wrong-footed.

The outcry died quickly, the Boundary Commission was quietly forgotten, and in time the Government of the Free State accepted the Border as it had been drawn in 1920. Ireland, it was said, had been tricked again by perfidious Albion and for every Irishman with Nationalistic aspirations, Lloyd George's place in Republican Ireland's rogues' gallery was assured.

Newry had two cinemas, the Frontier and the Imperial, with admission prices of 4d, 6d and 9d. In each of them there was a Saturday matinee to which we were admitted for 2d. Those were the days of the great silent epics, of Tim Mix and Buck Jones, Eddie Polo, Charlie Chaplin, Clive Brook, Harold Lloyd, Buster Keaton and many other pioneers of universal popular entertainment. In the newsreels we watched the closing stages of the Civil War in the Free

State; the new Irish Army trundling its small cannons behind lorries, moving from town to town in armoured vehicles not unlike those in which the Black and Tans had travelled, spreading its hold on the country and ultimately forcing the Irregulars to give up the struggle.

During one lunch period I walked along North Street, a tumble-down part of old Newry, to the Butter Market and found myself in the midst of a Hiring Fair; a fair in which the merchandise was human beings. Those doing business were standing about in small groups, talking quietly; a sturdy man holding out for what he thought he was worth as a ploughman, a rosy-cheeked servant girl listening and nodding as the conditions of the offered engagement were explained to her by a farmer and his wife, a mother handing over her fourteen-year-old son on the understanding that in return for his apprentice labour on a farm he would be kept and given three meals a day and after six months she would be paid perhaps five or six pounds.

Hiring fairs were peculiar to the northern part of Ireland. Happily they are held no more.

The most exciting event during my years in Newry was the public meeting at which Eamonn de Valera was billed as the principal speaker. He was then in the political wilderness, having come out on the losing side in the argument about the settlement with Britain and not yet having propounded his formula for entering Dáil Éireann in the face of his stated objection to the compulsory oath of allegiance to the British Crown. The Republican group which had organised the Newry meeting had put posters all over the district announcing that de Valera would address the great gathering to be held in the Town Hall. But under an order made by the Northern Ireland Minister of Home Affairs, de Valera was a prohibited person; the law said that he would not be allowed into Newry. The sponsors of the meeting said that come hell or high water, their star guest would be in the Town Hall on the night and at the time appointed; the Unionists and the police said 'not bloody likely' and the townspeople awaited the outcome with light-hearted anticipation. Bets were laid about whether or not the great man would put in an appearance.

About ten days before the date fixed for the meeting the town was encircled with a ring of armed Special Constables who scrutinised every person and searched every vehicle coming into the town. Day after day we watched them peering into cars, climbing on to lorries, driving their bayonets deep into loads of hay and manure. One felt a certain sympathy for the distinguished fugitive as each day the ring got tighter, the search more diligent. It was impossible, it seemed, for any man, let alone one whose appearance was so well known, to penetrate these defences.

The Town Hall in Newry is built on top of the river which runs through the town; the roadway along the front of the Hall is, in fact, a bridge. On the evening of the great meeting I was there in good time, sitting on the stone parapet directly opposite the front door of the Town Hall, well above the heads of those standing on the footpath. As the time for the meeting approached my friends and I watched the faithful arriving; earnest men and women come to greet one who to them personified incorruptible Republicanism. There was still twenty minutes to go when it was announced that the Hall was full. The crowd outside got bigger and bigger, spreading out across Trevor Hill; from every direction they had come, people of every shade of political colour, many from country districts, some from neighbouring towns; they had come to cheer or to scoff or just to look on. By the time the town clock above our heads showed eight o'clock I was at the centre of a great multitude of people of all ages and conditions; a good-humoured, expectant gathering. Policemen and Special Constables were everywhere, watchfully moving amongst the crowd, standing in small groups, clearing a passage for the occasional car passing through.

We heard that the meeting inside the hall had started; it had been decided to begin without the guest of the evening. This announce-ment brought a derisive cheer from the 'antis' who interpreted it as acceptance of defeat by the organisers. Those who had been so sure that de Valera would fulfil his engagement grew silent. Jokes about the missing leader were made. The hands of the clock moved to eight fifteen, to half-past eight, and the crowd began to show signs of restlessness; there was talk of going home. At a quarter to nine one of the cars moving through the crowd stopped in the middle of the roadway, only a few yards from where I was sitting, and de Valera stepped out. There he was; unmistakably it was de Valera himself, the tall dark-clothed figure, familiar to anyone who had read a newspaper; the long-jawed white face, the solemn, enquiring eyes looking unblinkingly over the heads of those around him.

The clamour of voices around the front door and the flashes of cameramen's magnesium flares brought to the far limits of the crowd the news that the impossible had happened, that the event which had held the town in suspense for a fortnight was taking place before their very eyes. A great clamour spread out from the centre to the furthest limits of the crowd; cheers and angry shrieks and much laughter and, at the centre of it all, almost within reach of where I sat, stood the great man himself, a look of guileless solemnity on his pale face.

The cameras flashed again as District Inspector Fletcher put his hand on de Valera's shoulder and led him to the waiting police car which moved off with a banging of doors.

Eamonn de Valera was not one of my heroes but walking home in the dark I was not the only one who might have said, in the words of Percy French – 'I cheered, God forgive me, I cheered with the rest.'

Next morning de Valera was taken to Adavoyle railway station, then the last stopping place before the Border, given a single ticket, and put on the Dublin train.

(I have sometimes wondered would the history of the difficult years between 1916 and 1923 be as it is if in 1913 the Intermediate Education Board had appointed the shortlisted candidate, Edward de Valera B.A., to the post of Inspector of Schools. He lost on a split vote.)

My parents, like many Irish parents of their generation, were very ambitious for their children. Father had almost an obsession about security; for him the first test of a career was that it should be permanent and pensionable. He had known insecurity as a child, when his household was at the mercy of the climatic and economic hazards affecting life on a small farm at a time when there were no government subsidies, no state pensions for the old and no financial aid for the unemployed. The penalty for failure was the workhouse. Small wonder that the Royal Irish Constabulary was an attractive career for Irish farmers' sons.

The 1920s were lean years. We had seen the beginning of unemployment benefit and as we passed the labour exchange going to and from school the reality of unemployment was before us every day. The queues of idle men grew longer, business was bad, wages low and the opportunities for school-leavers very few indeed. Public scholarships were almost non-existent; in my last year at school two university scholarships, each of a maximum of £40 a year for three

99

years, were provided by the education committee for County Down. Most of the boys at the Abbey School came from homes in which there could be no thought of finding the money to send a son or daughter away for a university education. The highest hopes were teaching, the bank, the civil service, the police force, the priesthood or one of the religious orders; the possibility of going into business was not discussed because such industry as there was in the district was not, even in prosperous times, on a scale which could provide worth-while openings except perhaps for the sons and nephews of the owners. Not more than about one-third of those leaving school could hope to go straight into stable employment. This situation weighed heavily on parents like mine. As we grew up the question of what we would do for a living was increasingly discussed.

Throughout his schooldays Jack had let it be known that only a life at sea would satisfy him, but as he came nearer to working age and he realised that his wish would not be fulfilled, he declared that he would not work in an office of any sort. After much discussion and argument and advice tendered by friends, he submitted himself as a candidate for the Royal Ulster Constabulary, attended a series of interviews and tests first in Newry, then at the County Head-quarters in Downpatrick, and finally at the Police Depot in Newtownards, and was accepted.

We had lived all our lives in small towns in which good employment opportunities were few and we knew that if we were to fulfil our parents' wish that we should 'get on in the world' we would leave home as soon as our schooldays ended. To everyone in our home that was accepted as a fact of life. Nevertheless Jack's departure left a blank, for we four brothers had been close together and he had been our leader, a leader with no respect for authority and a versatile talent for breaking rules. He found ways of getting into football matches without paying; if the owner of a fruit garden felt that his fencing was secure against marauders Jack found a way in and we followed; he questioned the rulings of teachers and policemen and, all too often, our parents. He was fearless and there had been moments in our young lives when courage was needed. When he went away we all thought of him, a boy amongst men, feeling the restraints of discipline to which he would not take kindly. Until then we had not been conscious of the orchestration of ideas which had existed between us. After he had gone our activities were less adventurous.

At this time I was wrestling with the problem of my own future. I was not a good student, my work at school had never been more than the minimum needed to keep me free of trouble with the teachers. But there had been moments of praise of which I took full advantage by granting myself periods of rest; the company of kindred spirits could always lure me away from academic pursuits. In any case it was not manly to be thought to be a 'swot' and I moved in circles in which it was more praiseworthy to be manly than to be 'clever'.

Everyone seemed to want to become a teacher. In those bleak, competitive days teaching looked an attractive occupation. Teachers, I was told, had good pay, excellent prospects, long holidays, short hours and respect. But I found the prospect of spending my days in the company of schoolboys unattractive. 'The Bank' was a possibility. The banks held examinations for which large numbers entered but it was generally believed that the jobs went to those whose sponsors had good accounts; that ruled me out. A local solicitor with a large practice suggested to my father that I should become apprenticed to him and qualify as a member of his profession. This pleased me because I had a secret ambition one day to study law but just then the prospect of five or six years during which I would be paid only a nominal wage and work for a series of examinations, was not in line with my thinking. Father, to whom the law was almost a religion, would have liked me to accept but I knew, as he must have known, that my continued dependence on him would have created problems for the two brothers and the sister who were following me. I suggested that I should sit for the Clerical Officers' examination in the Northern Ireland Civil Service. If I drew a blank the legal apprenticeship offer would still be open.

My candidature for the Northern Ireland Civil Service posed a special problem. Two boys from the Abbey had just sat the examination and, as they were amongst the brightest in the school, no-one was surprised when they were called for interview. Both were rejected. They had also entered for the Free State Civil Service and come high in the list of successes. There was a furious outcry about the treatment our candidates had got in Belfast. In the Abbey it was entirely understandable that we should see religious discrimination as the reason for the rejection of boys who throughout their school careers had shown exceptional ability. The Headmaster made no secret of his opinion. He announced that he would not enter any more boys for posts at the disposal of the Government of Northern Ireland. Nevertheless, I decided to enter in the following year although the Headmaster's decision meant that in preparing for the examination I would be on my own.

The candidates for the Civil Service Clerical Examination in 1926 filled the Great Hall in Queen's University and we all knew that of the hundreds there about two dozen would be called for interview and perhaps half of that number offered appointments.

I thought I did a good essay and I enjoyed my week in the city where the new Classic Cinema had an organ and there were orchestras in the Imperial and the Royal Avenue Cinemas. Our two picture houses in Newry had upright pianos.

After about a month I got a letter from the Civil Service Commissioners in Belfast inviting me to come for interview. This was good news; I had got into the final. But the interview carried twice as many marks as any subject in the written exam and this was the test which the school's candidates had failed in the previous year. I felt like someone about to take part in a duel.

The Civil Service Commissioners held their interview board in the Ministry of Finance offices in Donegall Square West. I was brought into a large waiting room where I found about ten candidates already assembled and waiting to be called before the board. I was in a grey hand-me-down suit, but they were in sober navy blues and browns and, in one or two cases, formal black jackets and striped trousers. They looked and sounded cheerful and confident, they seemed to know one another and they talked amicably about rugby football and dropped names which meant nothing to me. I felt a stranger in a strange place. I sat alone and read the morning paper because interviewers, I had heard, were very clever at testing one's knowledge of current affairs.

Every fifteen minutes or so a uniformed messenger would come to the door, call out a name and take one of the candidates away. I must have waited for more than an hour as candidates went and others arrived. I found myself getting angry. I felt gauche and inadequate and envious of the urbanity of the others and I thought about the Newry boys who had come here a year before and been sent home empty-handed.

At last my name was called and I was brought into a conference room with five very important-looking men sitting along one side of a polished mahogany table. (I didn't know that in those leisurely days the interview board for mere clerks was made up of four very senior civil servants and a Parliamentary Secretary.) The man in the middle seat invited me to sit in the chair opposite him. Their attitude was, somewhat to my surprise, genial and informal. Quite early I realised that I was not nervous; I was talking freely and actually enjoying myself. After about ten minutes of questions about my hobbies and world affairs and local news it was all over. Going back to Newry in the bus I felt light-hearted, not because I thought I had made a lasting impression on my questioners, but I was fairly sure that I hadn't lost ground. In any case the last trial was over, it had not been too severe and my future was now firmly in other hands.

There must have been a late delivery of mail in those days for I was coming from the tennis court in the afternoon sunshine when I met my father who had come to meet me and give me an official letter with my name on it. It told me very formally that I had qualified for appointment as a Clerical Officer in the Northern Ireland Civil Service.

Posts in the lower ranks of the Civil Service may be very small beer nowadays but in the barren 1920s success at the first attempt in an open competition was more than a minor triumph. In our small school I would be amongst the year's successes. I was elated, not because I was going to be a civil servant, for I had not the remotest idea what that meant in terms of work or responsibility or prospects, but because my future was settled. I was independent. I was now free to direct my own life.

Father suggested that I should go at once and tell the Headmaster rather than that he should hear the news elsewhere. I called at the Brothers' house and the Headmaster brought me into the 'parlour', a rare treat for a pupil. I confessed that, contrary to his wishes, I had sat for the Northern Ireland examination and I handed him my letter. He was delighted and generous in his praise of my achievement. He made me stay and have tea and cakes with him and I felt very privileged as he talked about the dizzy heights to which I might rise if I worked hard and led a virtuous life. And that was the end of my schooldays.

Eleven

On 28 June 1926 I went through the doorway of Arnott's Buildings in Bridge Street, Belfast, to begin my career as a civil servant. I went up a dark staircase to the first floor and showed the messenger in the small cubicle the letter instructing me to report on that day to the Headquarters of the Ministry of Labour. He brought me along a dingy corridor to a room where a tall, well-dressed man who might have been in his late twenties, indicated, somewhat to my surprise, that I was expected and told me to come with him. We went to the end of the corridor, then through double doors into a long room full of girls, more girls than I had ever before seen in one place. They sat amongst rows of bookshelves containing large volumes in which, I later learned, they noted the number of insurance contributions paid by every person in Northern Ireland with an insurance card. But my first impression of that room was an assembly of lolling female forms, of bobbed hair and curls, a multitude of shining legs and the smell of cosmetics. They all seemed at once to turn their eyes on me and I blushed wildly.

My destination was at the far end of the room where half a dozen men and two girls sat around a cluster of tables. These were to be my immediate colleagues. I was introduced and found a chair. The man in charge sat beside me and explained what was expected of me. The work was elementary and straightforward and within an hour or so of my arrival I knew enough to make a start.

I knew no-one in the Northern Ireland Civil Service, I knew no-one in Belfast, I had no name of a friend or a friend's friend or an old boy of the school on whom I might call. As the hours passed on that first day I began to feel alone and unsure of myself and the awesome sight of the array of girls between me and the door added

104

to my feeling of isolation. I felt alien to everyone around me.

During that first week in Belfast my spirits got lower every day. My male colleagues were men in their late twenties or early thirties, men who had served in the forces in the 1914–18 War and, except for the man who was in charge of us, they were all temporary clerks. Their casual conversation was about barrack-rooms and square-bashing, about happenings in the various theatres of war and about experiences in French brothels. When the girls were out of earshot their vocabulary was competitively lewd. I was not particularly puritanical but the impact of army language and erotic anecdotes appalled and depressed me. I thought of the years ahead of me in the company of men who talked and thought as they did and I wanted to get away from it all. Worst of all, before the week was half over I was dreadfully homesick and homesickness was something for which I had made no allowance. I had always been reasonably self-reliant and in my later years at school my relationship with my parents had become decreasingly dependent. From childhood I had known that leaving home would be part of growing to manhood and I had looked forward to the diversions of the city after the social limitations of a small town. But by the middle of that first week my desire to go home, to be with my mother and father and Tim and Tom and my sister Dorothy, was overpowering. I was angry with myself for falling victim to what a week earlier I would have regarded as childish sentimentality. But I counted the hours until Saturday afternoon when I would be free to take the bus to Newry and sit down for a meal at home and meet my friends in Hill Street at night and talk about the week's happenings in the town. And if Sunday should be fine we would take our bicycles out and go to Warrenpoint for a swim in the baths. If I were doomed to work in Belfast for the rest of my life I would go home to Newry every week-end. Those week-ends in the summer of 1926 were joyful interludes in a depressing and disappointing existence.

One disappointment concerned my financial prospects. The literature supplied to me about the Clerical Officer rank had said that the salary scale was £80 a year rising to £250 plus cost-of-living bonus; the bonus on £80 was then £60 so that my starting pay was £140 a year. This compared well with the pay of an assistant teacher and was quite a bit better than that of a young banker. But I soon learned that the cost-of-living bonus was adjusted half-yearly and the index figure which governed bonus was then in a steady decline.

My annual increments for the first four years would be £5 (plus bonus) and at the rate at which bonus was falling my increments would no more than compensate for the bonus cuts. My salary, I calculated, would remain virtually stationary until my fifth year of service after which my yearly increments would rise to £10 (plus bonus). I felt that I had been cheated.

I began to learn something about the staff in the office. The girls were young, almost all of them temporary clerks. The majority of the men in senior posts had been in the British Civil Service in Dublin; they were either natives of Northern Ireland or Southern Protestants who were glad to serve in the North rather than be absorbed into the service of a Sinn Fein government. Most of the men clerks were veterans of the Great War who had been appointed with temporary rank; a few had been appointed to the permanent staff and the remainder were waiting hopefully for permanent status. I belonged to the small group who had entered straight from school; some who had come in during the early years had been selected after 'nomination', but from 1925 entrance had been by competitive examination. We were called the 'schoolboy entrants'; those who had come in after war service were the 'ex-servicemen' and the third class, the superior ones who had come from Dublin, had, it was said, been referred to by the wife of one of them as 'the real civil servants'. If indeed the men who had come from Dublin felt that they were special people, it was not without justification: they brought to the public service in Northern Ireland the practices and traditions of the British Civil Service and government has been the better for their influence.

My new associates were kind to me but they professed to being surprised at 'an intelligent young fellow' being so foolish as to enlist in employment which was so uninteresting, poorly paid and devoid of prospects of advancement. This surprised me because, in fact, I felt that my prospects were better than theirs and I wondered why, if they thought so little of their jobs, they had apparently done nothing about moving elsewhere. It took me a little time to understand what was behind their unencouraging comments.

The 'temporaries' were ex-servicemen hoping to be made permanent and possibly to progress to higher rank. In the very early years there had been little competition from younger men but the recent institution of yearly examinations for new entrants threatened not just their promotion prospects but their continued employment. It was a time of retrenchment and each Friday the man from the Cashier's office bringing the weekly wages (being permanent I was paid monthly) carried a small bundle of official envelopes each of which contained a week's notice for someone. Most of my ex-service colleagues were married men and I soon became aware of the shadow which hung over them every Friday; if the Cashier's man came and went without leaving an envelope, everyone relaxed. The recruitment of people like me, straight from school and with permanent status, was an added threat to the prospects of the 'temporaries'.

The work in the office was elementary and there was not enough of it to keep all of us busy. I learned quickly that it was not playing the game to ask for more work, to have an empty desk or to fail to look busy at all times. This pretence made the days dreary, but idle hours brought staff reductions and that would have meant the dole for some of my companions.

During that first summer the thought of leaving the Civil Service was rarely out of my mind. I scrutinised the employment columns of the newspapers, wrote off for the prospectuses of correspondence colleges, explored the possibility of studying law in my spare time. But it was no good and I began to accept the possibility that it would be years rather than months before I could hope to escape.

My first months in Belfast were amongst the dreariest and loneliest in my life. My 'digs' were in a small terrace house in Eblana Street, in a red-brick neighbourhood which lies betwen Botanic Avenue and the Ormeau Road and includes a group of streets with Biblical names, known collectively to Belfast people as 'The Holy Land'. My fellow-boarders were a middle-aged bachelor who worked in an insurance office and a seedy widower, a small, fat man of whom I saw little because of his irregular hours. The landlady was a demure little woman whose personality was utterly overwhelmed by her husband, the most unbearable bore I have ever met. He was unemployed, as were so many at that time, and was there at all hours, torturing us with wearying accounts of the experiences of his dull life.

A frequent visitor to our house was the landlady's nephew, Ernie, a friendly youth of about my own age who lived nearby with two unmarried aunts. He and I occasionally went to the pictures or to a football match. One day I asked our landlord about Ernie's parents.

Instantly, as the first spark of self-righteousness began to light up his eyes, I knew that I had dropped a clanger. He spoke his line soberly: 'Ernie's father is *non est*. His Auntie Maud is his mother.'

Even to one with little knowledge of man's better achievements in bricks and mortar, Belfast looks an undistinguished city. Compared with Dublin, the only other city in which I had set foot, it was, and still is, noticeably lacking in ornamentation. It has few graceful public buildings and the providers of its commercial property seem to have been little concerned with visual harmony. They built sturdily and inelegantly with mathematical concern for space and cost. I think my first impression of Belfast was that its inhabitants had little interest in heroes. Dublin decorates its public places with statues and busts and sculptured heads and ornamental plaques commemorating political leaders and distinguished soldiers and dead revolutionaries and men and women who wrote or preached or sought to lead men along paths to virtue or glory but, with the possible exception of Queen Victoria, the people of Belfast seem to have thought very few worthy of posthumous veneration.

When I came to live there in 1926 I knew almost nothing of the geography of the city. I had heard of the Catholic Falls Road and the Protestant Shankill Road but I was surprised to discover that these two crowded segments of the city, inhabited by the militia of militant sectarianism, ran side by side almost from the city centre out to the foothills which rise above its western suburbs. The Catholics of the Falls and the Protestants of the Shankill literally look into one another's back yards. And seeing them from close range one wondered how the enmity which for so many generations has marked them as great nurseries of religious intolerance could have endured, for the occupants of those closely-packed, neighbouring streets have had so much in common. They have been equally touched by economic depression, by bad housing, by the dictates of autocratic employers, by participation in foreign wars, by emigrating sons and daughters, by social change, by the emergence of organised labour. There have been occasions when, under the stress of material deprivation, they looked like making common cause and turning their combined anger on the people or the institutions whom they saw as their oppressors, but any such moves were brief and unproductive. A prudently-dropped hint from a more affluent area, a suggestion that 'the others' at the end of the street were plotting to take over, a whisper of 'Popery', invariably put the shutters up against collaboration. Inherited religious prejudices and fostered fears were too strong for the bonds created by immediate and very real grievances.

In that summer of 1926, with very little cash in my pocket, I spent many inexpensive evenings walking, finding out the sort of city to which I had come; the tightly packed streets, the surrounding hills, the riverside, the Victorian opulence of the Malone Road which the industrialists had reserved for themselves. On flat expanses of waste ground reclaimed from the marshes, men gathered to play 'House' (now called 'Bingo') or 'Pitch and Toss' and all over the city, in entries and small parks and muddy side streets, shabby, down-at-heel men played marbles until the evening light had gone. On Saturday afternoons the footpaths were busy with the footsteps of men hurrying to football matches. Those were the activities of people who were idle and poor in an undernourished city.

Belfast's saving grace is its setting. In its meanest street one is within sight of green, rising hills; the fields are never far away. It is an unbeautiful city set in a green river valley.

I must have been a couple of months in Belfast when I discovered that a seat in the gallery in the Grand Opera House cost only one shilling, a discovery which was the beginning of many years of theatre-going. Companies from London came for a week or, on special occasions, for two weeks and Monday night became my night at the theatre. In the gallery we sat closely packed together on hard wooden shelves and amongst the galleryites there were usually a few bright spirits to provide us with entertainment during the intervals. The front stalls cost 5s 9d and one wondered what sort of people could afford so much for an evening's entertainment.

It was in the Opera House that I first saw the Abbey Theatre productions of O'Casey, Esmee Percy in Shaw's plays, Gilbert and Sullivan, the Carla Rosa operas, and many, many great actors and great plays. Those first experiences of theatre have illuminated and enriched my life.

One morning in the office a benign young man who had come all the way from Cork to work for the Northern Ireland Government invited me to become a member of the Civil Service Rugby Club. I knew nothing about rugby but I had been reasonably good at both

Gaelic and Soccer football. I joined the club mainly for the opportunity it would give me of meeting people of my own age and from my first appearance at a practice game I found myself amongst kindred spirits. In the crowded changing hut the air was full of words spoken in the accents of the southern counties.

I took up rugby with enthusiasm. I had always been a robust player of field games and I was stimulated by the continuous physical effort required of a front row forward, which was the role assigned to me. Not less important were the social diversions which the game brought into my life.

In my second year playing rugby I succeeded in getting a place in the first team. I played rugby for fifteen years and although I was no more than an average club player, I got enormous pleasure from the game, from matches won and lost, from carefree experiences and from the enduring friendships it brought me.

In my early years playing rugby I was one of a small group who lived in the University district. The President of our Club was Sam Sloan, a very senior civil servant, two of whose sons were members. His house at Rosetta was open at all times to us and his hospitality towards impoverished clerks was generous. There I learned to play a coarse game of bridge in between talk about rugby. We took up dancing and with the Sloan sons and daughters we went in organised parties to the Carlton and the Plaza and to Caproni's in Bangor.

Forte's fish-and-chip shop in Shaftesbury Square was one of our regular meeting places. We crowded into one of the snugs, with, perhaps, one or two girls squeezed in amongst us, and bought chips at threepence a time or, if we were flush, fish and chips for sixpence. We were there to talk rather than to eat and, as the order for food was renewed only when Mr Forte showed signs of impatience, a long night's diversion could be had for a small outlay. Later, when we had outlived our pledges of temperance, six of us met every Saturday evening in the Grand Central Hotel where, in the Londonderry Room, with a five-piece orchestra playing for the pleasure of the gathered townspeople and their ladies, we each bought a round of six bottles of Guinness for three shillings. If it was in the prosperous early days of the month we went across Royal Avenue to finish off the night with magnificent mixed grills in the Cosmo Restaurant in Garfield Street at half-a-crown a head.

My most interesting and in a sense most successful Rugby Club effort had nothing to do with the game. We were to play Garryowen in Limerick on St Patrick's Day. This trip was the highlight of our season for apart from their reputation for robust rugby, Garryowen were celebrated throughout Ireland for the hospitality and the entertainment they provided at the dinners which followed matches with visiting clubs. I had been in the team in the preceding year and during the evening, when we had been wined and dined, the most unlikely-looking Limerick players revealed themselves as singers and reciters and entertainers of every sort. Our only response to their talented performances was provided by Tony Butler who, as well as being an accomplished centre-threequarter, had a pleasant tenor voice and a reasonable repertoire of inoffensive songs. The rest of us were silent and I came home feeling that whatever might be said about our prowess on the field we had, despite Tony's valiant contribution, been outplayed during the evening. In the weeks before the second Garryowen fixture, weeks in which we were all concerned about the possibility of getting a knock which might have affected our chances of playing in Limerick, I wrote a monologue made up of bits and pieces of popular songs, ballads, recitations and Palgrave's *Golden Treasury*. I mentioned it to no-one and I left to later the question whether I would have the nerve to make it known that I had a party piece. How it would be received if I were to recite it didn't bear thinking about. I put it away.

The first stage of our journey was to Dublin. We stayed at the Four Courts Hotel where, not for the first time, I was mistaken for Dixie Dean, the Everton and England Soccer centre-forward. Next morning we caught the early train and arrived in Limerick before noon. As I remember it, we won the match and when we were back in the hotel bar, waiting for the evening's entertainment to begin, I decided to reveal to some of my friends that I had composed a recitation. I read it to them and they insisted that I must render it at the dinner. To say that I was not displeased at their reaction does not mean that I was not apprehensive.

I hope Garryowen dinners are as good now as they were then; good food, drink in more than generous measures, cheerful company, entertaining speeches and singing forwards and three-quarters and half-backs. My confidence waned as the talents of our hosts were displayed. Our Tony Butler responded splendidly. Then my name was called. It was a well-fed, amply wined audience, and almost from my first words I knew that they were listening to me. As I went on their interest grew, they were laughing and cheering and responding to every line as I had hoped they would. My effort was a hilarious triumph and for me a new, marvellous experience. My doggerel had been just right for the occasion.

For several years following that Garryowen trip I was in demand to speak my piece at dinners and parties and concerts, sometimes in the company of minor professionals, until I had to take a decision to stop before someone threw something at me for the rubbish I was peddling. But it had been written for a type of audience which unashamedly revels in unsubtle coarseness and over several winters my rendering of it brought enjoyment to a good many people in smoke-filled rooms in Belfast and Dublin and London and in various premises in between. I was flattered, not so very long ago, to overhear my monologue spoken at a cheerful gathering and so well received that I was almost tempted to claim authorship.

Northern Ireland came into being in 1921 in an atmosphere of political turmoil which, particularly in Belfast, took the form of a religious war between Catholics and Protestants. By the time I came to Belfast the violence had come to an end but the signs of it – burned buildings and bullet-scarred gable walls – were there to be seen and feeling was still high in the most densely populated parts of the city. The Catholics, large numbers of them crowded into the streets along the Falls Road, were cowed and dispirited; they had seen riots and death, the burning of homes and business premises, the violent expulsion of their men from the shipyards and factories and building sites. They had stories of murder and cruelty, of the wild exploits of the Special Constabulary, the bigoted outbursts of political leaders. The Protestants had something to say about the involvement of the IRA in the city's troubles but the Catholics discounted any allegations that blame lay on their side. They feared their Protestant neighbours with the anger of people who had been subdued by force and left without any means of retaliating against their persecutors.

Catholics in the Northern Ireland Civil Service in those days were very few. Because of the hard times through which many had lived and from which they had emerged as losers the Northern Catholics were not disposed to claim anything from what they regarded as a hostile government; in any case, they believed that worthwhile employment under the Unionist administration was available only to Unionists and friends of Unionists. It was my experience that some Catholics, and especially those in Belfast where, I had been told, the Bishop had advised them against seeking Government employment, looked with suspicion on Catholic civil servants. We had joined the enemy; we were lost souls. When we were seen to practice our religion it might be hinted that we were secretly Freemasons. It was not easy to establish kinship with one's co-religionists in Belfast.

Within the Civil Service I saw the other side of the coin. To many of my colleagues Catholics were strange animals of which they had astonishingly little knowledge. When we talked about religion, which was not very often, I learned of their beliefs about the power of the Pope and his clergy and no words could persuade them that I was not subject to malevolent direction by black-robed priests to whom Rome had entrusted its master plan for world domination. I was astonished to meet youths of my own age who had never met a Catholic until I appeared in the office, who believed, as one of them told me, that in the event of their coming under a Nationalist government the Pope would require his obedient Irish flock to banish the Protestants from the land.

Although I had many experiences of the prejudices and the lack of understanding between the two communities – to each of which I was a cuckoo in the nest – the native kindness of the people compensated for moments of embarrassment. I had grown up in a family which was free of strong political loyalties and had joined the Civil Service without any feeling of having done something unconventional or unworthy. Many people were, as I was, anxious to live normal lives after troubled years. The competition for jobs was fierce and my attitude was simply pragmatic. I was, for better or worse, a citizen of the new state of Northern Ireland and I was claiming my piece of it.

My first reaction to the Civil Service had been that it was something to get out of as quickly as possible but my attempts to escape came to nothing. As time went on work became more interesting and as my non-official pursuits began increasingly to brighten my leisure hours the desire to change my occupation lost its urgency.

I had taken up rugby with enthusiasm and through it had made many friends. I had become a regular theatre-goer. In the Ministry we had a debating society and in evening debates we got some pleasure taking the mickey out of our elders and betters. My brother Tim had enrolled at Queen's University in 1927 and during his years there we shared digs. We went to debates in the Students' Union and occasionally, if the University Soccer team in which he played was a man short, I filled the vacancy. We went to house-parties and dances, played bridge and pontoon and poker, frequented fish-and-chip shops and pubs, tried our hands at billiards and snooker, visited our friends in their digs to talk about sport and religion and politics and Sir Crawford McCullough who it seemed would be Lord Mayor of Belfast for evermore. We took girls to the pictures or to dances or, if we were out of funds, walking along the Malone Road.

In the office I had got to know more about my colleagues. Many of the ex-servicemen had been in the Ulster Volunteer Force and on the declaration of war in 1914 had joined the Ulster Division (which they referred to as the YCVs, the Young Citizen Volunteers). Some of them had been wounded and when one heard of their experiences in the trenches their shortcomings as officials, for some of them were very poor material, were overlooked. A later generation would have shown less forbearance than they towards a government which had done so little to fulfil the extravagant promises which had been made to those who volunteered for war service. But they were the lucky ones; they had come through alive, albeit many with serious disabilities, and they had jobs. Towards me they were friendly and helpful. Bob Stewart, a big, easy-going man who took a fatherly interest in my welfare, told me about the Battle of the Somme. In his quiet Ulster voice he described his experiences on 1 July 1916 when the Ulster Division advanced into the German lines, a day in which many of the friends of his youth died. His account of what he experienced made a lasting impression on me and since then I have stopped at many a village war memorial and looked down the list of names which still bear witness to that day.

In 1931 all Government departments except the Ministry of Commerce were gathered into the new Parliament Buildings at Stormont and the change brought the migration to the eastern suburbs of Government officials of every rank and class. I moved with three kindred spirits into a trim, detached house at Belmont where we were attended to by a kind and patient landlady.

The change to Stormont widened still further my circle of acquaintances in the Civil Service and my knowledge of what was

114

happening in other departments.

We were a young service, not overworked and carefree. Young women were coming into the service in numbers and their presence brightened the scene. During the lunch hour on a summer's day the spacious grounds of Stormont had something of the atmosphere of a leisurely university campus. We talked about sport and the cinema, criticised our betters, explored the estate and watched, without enthusiasm, the coming and going of members of the Houses of Parliament.

We got to know by sight the members of the Civil Service hierarchy. Sir Wilfrid Spender, the head of the Service, was a very tall, gangling man with eager, uncomprehending blue eyes. George Chester Duggan, Spender's deputy, a handsome thoughtful man, had an immense reputation as an administrator. He was a distinguished graduate of Trinity College, Dublin and he had served in the Chief Secretary's Office in Dublin Castle. It was said that in filling senior posts he had strong bias towards Trinity men and indeed TCD ties were very much in evidence amongst the ambitious men in the junior administrative grades. The brightest star in Agriculture was George Scott Robertson, a small, bespectacled, ungracious Scot whose rapid advancement was all the more resented because he had successfully crossed the barrier between the technical and administrative classes. The Permanent Secretary in Home Affairs was Major George Harris, a convivial man who caused some raising of eyebrows by having a glass of stout with his lunch each day. Education's Permanent Secretary was A.N. Bonaparte Wyse, a remote, quiet man whose *pince-nez* gave him an appearance of profundity; the fact that he was a Roman Catholic was a matter of some wonder. The permanent head of my own Ministry was Major Hamilton Conacher, white-haired and benevolent in appearance, rather like an aged front-row forward who hadn't quite made the first fifteen. We saw these men and many lesser dignitaries from a distance and if we were as remote from them as flies on a window-pane, we were not inhibited about having opinions about them and allowing our prejudices to be fed by the gossip which was part of life in the corridors of Stormont.

We got occasional glimpses of Cabinet Ministers. Lord Craigavon, the Prime Minister, was then the dominating figure in Northern Ireland politics; a very big, bucolic, tight-lipped man whose reputation for wisdom and understanding has grown, perhaps overmuch, since he passed from the scene in 1940. Dawson Bates, hated by his political opponents, was Minister of Home Affairs; he was small, white-haired, slightly stooped, always looking preoccupied. Those who worked on his corridor said that he spent much of his time colloguing with shabby little men in bowler hats. Sir Edward Archdale, Minister of Agriculture, looked what he was, a landlord. John M. Andrews, a hardworking teetotaller, was as interested in the prosperity of his linen mill as in his political responsibilities. Lord Charlemont, the Minister of Education, we never saw. In a small city-centre office J. Milne Barbour of the Linen Thread Company presided over the Ministry of Commerce, for which he took no salary. Some civil servants, with traditional cynicism, wondered if, making allowance for the tax liability related to his considerable income, the sacrifice was as great as it might seem. Looking down the list of Cabinet Ministers one could be forgiven for thinking that Northern Ireland was about the only place on earth where people still voted for their landlords.

Of the Opposition politicians the best-known was 'Wee Joe' Devlin, a rubicund, cheerful-looking man, always nattily dressed in a dark suit, shining black shoes and white spats. I met him once. We were playing a rugby match in Dublin and after the game we assembled in the lounge of Jury's Hotel where 'Wee Joe' was having a drink with some friends. On learning that we were Northern Ireland civil servants he bought a round of drinks for the whole company; an act of generosity such as I had never before seen.

In those days of economic depression, unemployment and poverty a minor civil servant on a small salary could console himself that he was secure and a reasonably well-off member of the community, particularly if he worked, as I did, in an office in which there was daily evidence of widespread distress.

To the comfortably off the payment of state money to the idle was still regarded as socialistic extravagance, the subsidisation of indolence. The 'Dole' or the 'Boroo' as it is called in Northern Ireland (because the early local offices of the Ministry of Labour were called 'Unemployment Bureaux') was still a not very respectable form of public charity.

The plague of the unemployed was NGSW; disallowance of benefit because the claimant was Not Genuinely Seeking Work. The onus of proof was on the applicant. Every six weeks he was required to produce proof that he was genuinely seeking work. This condition, which was very rigorously applied, sent the unemployed walking the streets to call at offices, shops, factories, warehouses and building sites asking for notes certifying that they had applied for employment but that there were no vacancies. Some firms, in order more efficiently to deal with the stream of callers, had printed certificates which were handed out during appointed hours. At factory gates one saw queues of weary people waiting for the precious slips of paper which would help them demonstrate that they had been active in the hopeless search for jobs.

I spent some time in the Branch which dealt with the scrutiny of claims for benefit. It was depressing, difficult work.

One afternoon, in the absence of a colleague, it fell to me to interview a woman who had come to enquire about the rejection of her claim for benefit. She was a generously proportioned widow with the ready tongue of one who is not accustomed to being thwarted. Her employment record was such that her case was quite hopeless and very early in our conversation I realised that I must phrase with care my commentary on the inevitability of the Ministry's decision. She mentioned that during the war her late husband had worked in a munitions factory and despite my patient explanation of the irrelevance of this information, she kept repeating it and with each repetition presenting me with the problem of finding new words to say, without giving offence, that her case was a hopeless one.

I became conscious of the fact that everyone in the room, which was a big one, was listening to our conversation, wondering, I had no doubt, if the dialogue would end without some ill-chosen word or unfortunate inflection on my part bringing on my head a torrent of abuse. But the interview ended on a low note and when the lady got up to go, apparently resigned but by no means cheered at its outcome, I felt that I had handled a difficult situation rather well. She walked silently to the door, opened it and turning to the rows of silent men, now poring over their papers, she addressed the whole company. She spoke calmly and purposefully.

'During the war my husband made bombs. He spent four years making bombs. I wish to Jaysus I had one of them now.'

Much of my time during my three-day Christmas holiday in 1934 was spent reflecting on the associations which, over the years since I had come to Belfast, had provided interest and diversion and occupied more and more of my spare time. Just before going on leave I had been told that on 15 January I would be transferred to Enniskillen, which was just about as far from Belfast as any Northern Ireland civil servant could be sent. That holiday at home in Newry was a time for being sorry for myself, a time for brooding on the social deprivation which the change would bring.

There would be no more theatre-going. And no more participation in dramatic activities; I was one of the founder members of a dramatic society which had been formed in the Ministry and which by 1934 was well established as one of the leading dramatic groups in the province. Only a year earlier, at the finals of the Northern Drama League Festival in the Empire Theatre, I had received a first prize from the hands of Desmond McCarthy, the distinguished dramatic critic. Amateur acting was entertaining and interesting and time-consuming and I knew I would miss it.

The three previous summers had been spent living out of Belfast. Half a dozen of us, all rugby players, had decided that the summer months would be better spent at the seaside rather than idling in Belfast. One of our number was in the department responsible for the letting of coastguard cottages which were surplus to the needs of the service. There was, it seemed, very little demand for these spare houses and from 1 June to 30 September each year we became tenants, at an inclusive rent of nine shillings a week, of a coastguard house in Donaghadee, a town whose existence was recognised, *in absentia*, by Thomas Hardy when he wrote, 'I have never been to Donaghadee/That vague, far townlet by the sea.'

For the summer months we travelled daily to and from the office, took turns at cooking, explored the Copeland Islands, drank beer and generally enjoyed ourselves. With two of our party I joined the Golf Club where the subscription was two guineas a year. It was not a notably sociable club, with most of its members business and professional men from Belfast amongst whom, it was said, the local residents were not very welcome. We were a small group who played together without seeing too much of the other members; in any case we could not afford to mix with the free-spenders who frequented the bar and the card-room.

The move to Enniskillen would take me from the company of the Donaghadee commuters; it would be a parting from friends who had brought interest and entertainment, if not any serious purpose, into my life. Although this was not a time of deep political thinking in Northern Ireland, some of us had developed a mild interest in political issues. Despite the carping of its critics, the Unionist Party was firmly in control and the signs were that it would be there for all time. I was not attracted to the arid thinking of either the Unionists or the Nationalists because it seemed to me that, if change was to come at some remote future time, it should be brought about through socialist thinking rather than the sterile, interdenominational squabbling which passed for debate between the two principal parties. My man was Harry Midgeley. To me he represented incorruptible Socialism. I went to his meetings and listened to his stirring words. An elderly colleague, a life-long Socialist, hearing me speak in praise of Midgeley, took me aside.

'Midgeley,' said he, 'is not the Socialist he seems to be. He's a Unionist and a bigot at heart'.

It was a good many years before I could believe that my old friend's remark was not outrageous slander.

In remote County Fermanagh I would be far from political argument. But there would be rugby football and I would have a complete change of work for I was to be on the outdoor inspection staff. And I was going to what the tourist brochures called 'Ulster's Lake District'.

Twelve

County Fermanagh, in 1935, was Somerville and Ross country. After a slow train journey from Belfast, I arrived in Enniskillen on a wet winter's day. As I walked for the first time along the long, meandering main street I saw in the window of a public house a yellow poster advertising the Fermanagh Harriers Hunt Ball. In bold letters in the middle of the poster, I read: MUSIC BY BILLY SCOTT'S BAND AND LORD LOFTUS.

When I think of Fermanagh, that simple message, which I was to see many times, epitomises much that was novel and entertaining about Enniskillen. During my time there Lord Loftus became the Marquis of Ely and his senior title looked no less striking on the billboards and in the shop windows. He played at all of the dances and not alone did he 'guest' as a saxophone player but during intervals in the music His Lordship would display his skill as a magician, producing billiard balls and playing cards and other articles from all sorts of unlikely places.

On my second day in Enniskillen I bought a two-year-old Austin Seven car for fifty-five pounds, settled the hire purchase arrangements, insurance and driving licence in the morning and before the sun went down had my one and only driving lesson along a quiet stretch of the Irvinestown Road. I was a motorist. In little more than twenty-four hours since coming to my new station I had achieved a status which had been far beyond my reach in Belfast. On official journeying I would get an allowance of 3¼d a mile and with petrol at 1s 3d a gallon, my travelling in that expansive area would earn more than sufficient to sustain me as a member of the motoring public. The acquisition of that small car brought a sense of property such as nothing else in my whole life has. I was equipped and eager to take to the road.

The responsibilities of the outdoor staff of the Ministry of Labour were the investigation of claims for old-age pensions and the inspection of places of employment to ensure that the law requiring employers to put stamps on the insurance cards of their employees was observed. Three of us, myself, an older colleague and an Inspector, were responsible for the whole of County Fermanagh together with a large slice of Tyrone. My particular area was to be the eastern part of Fermanagh plus the Clogher Valley in County Tyrone as far as the village of Caledon.

My first call was with a man who had claimed an old-age pension. I found him in his small farmhouse on the slope of the northern shore of Upper Lough Erne. I laid out on his table the forms to record his means from all sources so that I could calculate whether his income was such that the state would be willing to supplement it. Before leaving Belfast I had had a week's thorough tuition in dealing with claims and the forms which I carried in my new OHMS bag gave all the necessary questions and spaces in which to enter the applicant's replies. But the circumstances of my very first client had not been visualised by my tutors. I started off all right by writing opposite the first question that he was 'employed'. To my second question – what wages did he get? he said, 'None'. As I had been warned that, the grant of pension being subject to proof of poverty, applicants might tend to understate rather than exaggerate their means, the poor man had some difficulty in persuading me that he was telling the truth. My doubts disappeared when he produced a sealed parchment agreement which spelled out in copperplate writing his responsibilities and the rewards which they attracted. He was employed as a herd; his job was to look after an 'out' farm, to mind his employer's cattle, maintain the hedges and ditches, help with the harvest, clear the weeds and keep the property secure. For those duties he got no money. He lived rent free, was allowed the milk of one of his employer's cows, he took one calf each year which he was allowed to graze free of charge for eighteen months, he had about half a rood of garden in which to grow vegetables, he could keep not more than two pigs for fattening and not more than forty hens.

My nice new forms had been designed on the assumption that people worked for money. Some thinking would be needed to demonstrate to Stormont that I considered this seventy-year-old relic of feudalism to be so poor as to be worthy of state aid at a rate not exceeding ten shillings a week. I was later to discover that there were, in Fermanagh, some hundreds of herds more or less similarly engaged.

In the centrally-heated offices in Stormont the outdoor officers were sometimes referred to as the 'Foreign Legion'. It was a job to be avoided for it meant being buried in the country, exposed to the weather and far from the bright lights of the city. But I enjoyed it. I enjoyed the informal, carefree atmosphere of our small office, the fact that each day I arranged my own working hours and decided where I would go. I enjoyed the sunshine and the rain and the rich spring blossoms. I liked driving my small car along bushy lanes into remote places where the sound of an internal combustion engine had not before been heard. And in a county in which there was great poverty there was some satisfaction in being the man who brought the pension to the old.

In spite of the wettings and the dog-bites – of which I must have had a couple of dozen in three years – the arguments and alter-cations with defaulting employers and the long hours, I found interest and entertainment in my work.

Ever present in our minds was the possibility that the law relating to employees' insurance was being disregarded or pensions being obtained by dishonest means. Occasionally a pension claimant tried to anticipate his attainment of the qualifying age of seventy by forwarding a crudely altered birth certificate or the birth certificate of an older cousin or brother who had died in infancy. Some such fraudulent claims must have been successful for it was said that a well-known Catholic periodical once published the acknowledge-ment – 'Thanks to St Anthony for old age pension received at 68.'

Information about misdeeds often came to us in anonymous letters. Occasionally an informant signed his name, as did F. McCool of Lisnaskea who wrote to tell me that a businessman in the town was evading his legal obligations. I visited the accused man and found that the accusation was false. For an hour I searched the town for the writer of the letter which had sent me on a foolish errand. Angrily I stomped into the police station, handed the letter to the Head Constable and asked, 'Do you know that fellow?'

The Head Constable read the letter, scratched his head and said, 'Aye, he used to be around here but he hasn't been in these parts for a good while. His Christian name was Finn.'

I had been searching Lisnaskea for Finn McCool, the mythical Ulster giant who according to legend had, in one mighty mudslinging act, created both Lough Neagh and the Isle of Man.

Each month a batch of pensioners needed new pension books; they applied for them by filling in forms set into the back of their spent books. Four or five questions had to be answered, the form had to be countersigned by 'a justice of the peace, a schoolteacher, a police officer of at least the rank of sergeant' or some equally worthy person. Little thought had been given to the drafting of the questions on the form. One of them began something like: 'If you are single or a widower/widow how much have you or if you are married how much has your wife/husband...' and so on for three or four lines of very small print. The reply should have referred to income but at the first attempt about one-third of the pensioners wrote 'yes' or 'no' or left the space blank. In those cases I sent out a new form with a circular letter explaining how the question should be answered. But there were always a few failures who had to be written to twice or even three times. A pensioner who lived on a barren hillside above Roslea ignored the difficult question at the first try, at the second he wrote 'No' and at the third 'Yes'. When I sent him a fourth form with a letter in which my impatience was unconcealed it came back promptly, blank except for the single word 'SHIT' written boldly across it. Each filling of the form had been a laborious exercise, each time he had had to walk a mile to have it countersigned by an important person. He had had enough. When I called at his two-roomed tumble-down cottage where the signs of poverty were all too plain, I could not but admire his spirit. For all he knew, his angry word could have cost him his pension but there was a limit to what he would stand from bureaucrats.

I put the offending form on the table.

'Did you write that?' I asked.

'Yes,' he growled.

'That form was opened in my office by a young girl.'

My lying statement so distressed him that I felt very guilty. We sat down together and filled in a new form.

When I got back to my office I sent the four useless forms to Headquarters and suggested a more simple wording of the difficult question. The change was made, thanks to an old man whose pen was mightier than he knew.

123

Very quickly I found plenty of diversions in Enniskillen. I played rugby for the town team and during my time there we won the Provincial Towns' Cup. I joined the Golf Club where I won a few prizes and the Yacht Club which had a large membership of agreeable people, about half a dozen of whom had yachts on Lough Erne. The law then required the pubs in towns with fewer than five thousand inhabitants to close their doors at nine o'clock, an hour earlier than closing time in larger towns. Enniskillen was one of the early closing towns although some said that its true population had been undervalued by the deliberate act of a teetotal faction who on the day of the census had moved temporarily across the Border so as to ensure that those who took a drink would, for at least an hour each day, be saved from themselves. Clubs enjoyed much longer opening hours than public houses and the Yacht Club in Enniskillen was a popular and convivial place.

Young bank clerks and civil servants were well thought-of about the town and I found that when I bought a pair of shoes or a shirt I was not expected to pay across the counter; a monthly account would do. I found myself in parties going on long journeys to Hunt Balls north and south of the Border. And if one wanted to ride with the harriers a horse could be hired for the day for five shillings from the man who owned the ice-cream shop. I did not hunt, nor did I shoot or fish although, had I so wished, that could have readily been arranged.

At week-ends, particularly in the summer months, those who had cars went to Bundoran, to bathe or play golf, to drink as 'bona-fide travellers' in the lush new bar in the Great Northern Hotel or at the 'Hamilton' or the 'Palace' or the more demure 'Central', the clientele of which was once described as 'bank clerks trying to look drunk and parish priests trying to look sober'. But that was more than thirty-five years ago.

Golf on the Bundoran course could be a hazardous enough pastime. Over the eighteen holes one was repeatedly playing back from the perimeter to the precincts of the hotel and after each visit to a green at the centre some players felt the need to refresh themselves in the hotel bar before resuming their round. In showery weather the population in the bar ebbed and flowed and it was not unknown for a player to finish his round in a different fourball than the one in which he had started out.

In my small car I travelled north to Londonderry and Strabane,

into south Donegal to bathe in the Atlantic breakers, to the Yeats country in County Sligo and into Monaghan, Cavan and Leitrim. Occasionally I spent a week-end amongst my friends in Belfast or at home in Newry.

Our office in Enniskillen was a remnant of the old county gaol, a two-storey stone building facing on to an open space known, understandably, as Gaol Square. The rooms to the right-hand side of the wide, stone-flagged, central hallway were occupied by the Customs and Excise staff and those on the left by the Labour Exchange. We of the Inspection Staff occupied two upstairs rooms and my table was at a front window from which, I was told, public hangings once took place.

Relations between the Northern Ireland officials and the Customs and Excise people were less than cordial. The C&E men were disposed to look on Northern Ireland civil servants as inferior people. For our part, we regarded them as a bunch of rather conceited idlers who had a livelier interest in their status than in their work. But that must have been a prejudiced view.

I believe it was in connection with the Jubilee of King George V that the Manager got a special instruction to fly the flag on three successive days. On the morning of the first appointed day he sent for Tommy the Cleaner. Taking the Union Jack from the cupboard in his office, he handed it to Tommy, saying, 'Tommy, put that —ing flag up.' (The Manager was rarely capable of enthusiasm early in the day.)

Tommy came up to my room, moved my table back from the window and, reaching perilously outwards, fixed the flag to its cord and raised it to the top of the flagpole.

The Customs Surveyor, arriving at the office half an hour later (I should mention that the unpunctuality of the Customs staff was a cause of some irritation to us), saw the Union Jack at the masthead and shouted for the cleaner. Tommy, whistling quietly, made his way to the Surveyor's office.

'Tommy, who told you to fly that —ing flag?'

(A dour man at the best of times, he, like the Manager, was inclined to be particularly cheerless before noon.)

'The Manager, Sir.'

The Surveyor went to his cupboard and produced a Blue Ensign which must have been newly supplied to him from London so that the Royal occasion could be fittingly celebrated by a display of HM Customs and Excise's very own flag.

'Take down that —ing flag and put this one up.'

Tommy came to my room again, moved my table, opened the window, hauled down the Union Jack and replaced it with the new Blue Ensign. He folded the Union Jack, went off, still whistling, ambled innocently into the Manager's office and was quietly returning the discarded flag to the cupboard when the Manager looked up from his desk.

'What are you doing with that —ing flag?'

'Putting it back in the press, Sir.'

'Why?'

'There's another flag up, Sir.'

'What other flag?'

The Manager walked to the window, leaned out and looked up.

'Where did you get that —ing flag?'

'From the Surveyor.'

The Manager said no more. He went to the cupboard, brought out his flag and placed it back in Tommy's hands.

'You go and take that —ing flag down and put this one up!'

Again I was disturbed as Tommy, grumbling about the problem of trying to serve two masters, once more went through the tedious operation of changing the flags. He folded the Blue Ensign and muttering, 'Jaysus the Surveyor'll kill me', went downstairs again.

He was back almost immediately. This time his hands were trembling as he tore at the cord, disconnected the Manager's flag and hoisted the Surveyor's.

From his ground floor window the Manager had been watching. He was waiting for Tommy.

'Tommy, what did I tell you?'

'Sir, the Surveyor said–'

'I don't give a damn what the Surveyor said.'

'But, Sir, he said–'

'He said what?'

'Sir, he said... he said... I must take my instructions from him because... because...'

'Because what?'

'Because he said, Sir... Sir, he said they are the senior service.'

Although the Manager was really angry he did not raise his voice. But he spoke firmly.

126

'Tommy, you go and tell him that we are the —ing landlords.' (A punch line which, as spoken by Tommy, we on the Northern Ireland side thought worthy of a round of applause.)

After further negotiations with Tommy, acting as intermediary, crossing and recrossing the main hallway several times, the Blue Ensign was removed from the flagpole. The Surveyor telephoned his superiors in the Customs House in Belfast, the Manager got into touch with Parliament Buildings, Stormont. Consultations, it seemed, took place between the Headquarters of the Ministry of Labour and the Office of the Chief Collector of Customs and Excise for Northern Ireland. The outcome of the consultations came down the wires to Enniskillen in mid-afternoon and the Union Jack was raised to the top of the flagpole. Quiet, if not exactly peace, came back to Gaol Square.

Life in Enniskillen and the ways of its inhabitants were influenced by two considerations. It bore the dignity of a county town and the countryside around it was generously decorated with the habitations of 'gentry'. As one old woman put it, 'You wouldn't travel far in Fermanagh without seeing a gentleman's seat.'

Amongst the 'County' folk we had the full range from Earls to minor squires, many of them people with status but little wealth who farmed their land, shot and fished and did their messages in the town.

The best-known of the local landowners was the Earl of Belmore, an elderly, very large, slow-moving man. When he was driven in his horse-drawn cab from his beautiful house at Castlecoole into the town his first stop, as often as not, was at Mrs Brady's confectionery shop where he would stand at the counter sipping a glass of lemonade as his order was being attended to whilst outside his manservant sat patiently on his high perch on the ancient conveyance.

The most coveted honour available to the wives and daughters of the town was membership of Lord Belmore's Badminton Club which met in the Orange Hall every Thursday afternoon, the day and time being fixed so that it was beyond the ambition of those who worked for a living or whose domestic arrangements precluded afternoon recreation. Invitations to membership were the prerogative solely of His Lordship who attended each Thursday's session in a non-playing capacity, as befitted the Club's only male member, to watch the play and take tea and cakes with the ladies.

127

Although His Lordship's terpsichorian gifts were not of star quality he rarely missed a formal dance in the Town Hall.

In those days white tie and tails was the dress of men on such occasions and when the Lord of Castlecoole came to the Town Hall to attend a 'ball' those around the doorway stood back as he strode into the room and surveyed the scene, his large head moving lazily above a great area of white shirt-front protruding from the surrounding black of his suit as though by pneumatic pressure. He would then move across the floor and take his seat beside the young lady whom, without warning or formality, he had chosen to be his partner for the evening. The duty of one so honoured was to sit with His Lordship and engage him in conversation until, at a time chosen by him, she was led by the hand to the centre of the room, there to stand, the great man and his (usually diminutive) partner until, with the help of a few rousing bars from the orchestra, the assembled guests responded to the signal that the time for Lord Belmore's Lancers had come. Leading the Grand March on the arm of the septuagenarian Earl was the young lady's moment of public triumph. Next day she would be invited to take afternoon tea with him and he would enter in his diary her name, address and date of birth thereupon enrolling her in the distinguished company of ladies each of whom, on every birthday, received from the Earl of Belmore of Castlecoole a present of a pair of silk stockings and a large box of chocolates. A good many years after I had left Enniskillen I met a faded beauty who proudly told me that her birthday had been so marked for more than twenty years.

In keeping with the townspeople's consciousness of being citizens of no mean town, social events were organised with style. Orchestras from far afield played at the dances, at the amateur dramatic society's productions in the Town Hall the front half of the audience came in evening dress, tennis tournaments were conducted with efficient formality. Before joining a private party for an evening of Bridge one ascertained whether black ties were to be worn.

The mirror was held up to life in three weekly newspapers; the *Fermanagh Herald* which was the organ of Nationalist opinion, the *Fermanagh Times* which reflected official Unionist thinking and the *Impartial Reporter* which carried the motto 'The Truth, the Whole Truth and Nothing but the Truth', to the pages of which I devoted an absorbing hour every Thursday evening. In it I followed the progress of the Spanish Civil War, the Italian war in Abyssinia and the British abdication crisis on which it had many reproving words to say. But even for readers who were concerned with foreign misdeeds and monarchical problems Millicent Trimble's recording of the local scene was absorbing reading. In her own weekly column she wrote eloquently about deaths and marriages, about notable arrivals and departures, about the achievements of Fermanagh men and women at home and abroad, about concerts and dances and soirees and sporting events. Her column reflected her pride in the community in which she lived. In the autumn it was her practice to review the arrangements for the forthcoming 'season' and come the spring she presented a nostalgic account of the worldly pleasures experienced in the months past. An interim report on social happenings presented a memorable picture of a pleasure-loving people:

Were it not for the stir of the social world, life and business would be very dull in Enniskillen in January and February.

We have had a succession of dances. Each had its own special character. The glory of the Fermanagh County Hospital Ball, the rollicking gaiety of the Fancy Dress Dance, the hunting Pink and 'horsey' atmosphere of the Hunt Ball, the Legion Ball with its many ribbons and medals on the breast – and now, the Constabulary.

Comments on a local sports meeting did not neglect its social diversions–

The tea tent was well patronised and many parties sat around enjoying their tea and talk. The Earl of Belmore seemed to approve of the fare provided, which was a good advertisement as the ladies in the working party also fed the military party and the competitors from the same menu.

Some might have seen, hopefully, in the use of one teapot to serve so mixed a company, the beginning of an egalitarian society in Enniskillen.

The *Impartial Reporter* was generously uncritical in giving space to local versifiers. I recall the final stanza of a tribute to a girl whose record of school attendance had been exceptional:

To Lily Rooney let's wish success.
Love and luck and no distress.
As husband may she find a jewel,
The girl who never missed a day at school.

In the early years of the Northern Ireland Civil Service the possibility of promotion was so remote as rarely to be a subject for serious thought. It seemed that when the government departments were being formed there was something of a rush to fill the more senior posts by accepting as many as possible of those officers of the British administration throughout Ireland as offered their services, by recruiting local men of ability who wished to serve the new government and by giving employment to people who, in various ways, had taken part in the political movement whose activities had persuaded the British Government that the Six Counties of Northern Ireland should be given a subordinate government within the United Kingdom. All of those elements quickly coalesced to establish a sound administrative organisation. But by the middle Twenties financial stringency prompted a scrutiny of expenditure and the staffing of government departments was closely examined. This was under way in my early years in the Ministry of Labour; senior posts were being suppressed or downgraded and staff was being reduced. As a result, the numbers admitted by examination were small and promotions were rare happenings. To people with short service, advancement in rank was something for the distant future.

In the basic grades, we were resentful of the arrangement under which each year a small number of university graduates was recruited by way of the British First Division Examination. They belonged to an elite class destined for the top posts and their introduction half way up the ladder reduced still further the opportunities of the more lowly placed.

Because promotions were uncommon they aroused considerable interest; one tended to listen readily to allegations of preferment on grounds other than merit. One would hear that the promoted man had been in the same regiment as the Establishment Officer (a Principal Officer with great power in staff matters), that he was a member of the Masonic Order or the Orange Order, that he was related to a Member of Parliament or even a Cabinet Minister or that the power of the old school tie had been invoked. In a very highly competitive situation the unsuccessful were reluctant to believe that decisions were taken on merit alone.

Graduates of Trinity College, Dublin, seemed to comprise a magic circle which encompassed all ministries. Many of them had come from Dublin departments, some had been recruited as

130

Assistant Principals without examination and the fact that ex-Trinity men tend to wear their university ties on all occasions was for us visual evidence of a powerful fellowship within our ranks.

The Plymouth Brethren, for reasons which I have never been able to find out, seemed to have disproportionately high representation in the middle ranks and were seen as a sinister and very influential group. When one of their most exalted members was transferred to still higher rank in another ministry, it was said that he left his Bible to his deputy – also one of the Brethren – with a page turned down at the text, 'I go to make a place for you'. Sure enough, in the fullness of time, the deputy was transferred on promotion to become again second-in-command to his old boss.

It was not uncommon to see men who worked in government offices preaching the Gospel at street corners, particularly in Belfast's Great Victoria Street on Saturday nights. When the preacher belonged to an office where members of the Brethren were in places of power, it was easy to be persuaded that ambition rather than the love of God was the motive. However unworthy those thoughts might have been, there was certainly one well-known colleague who, on attaining a rank which did more than justice to his capabilities, ceased to proclaim his religion in public and took up with enthusiasm the pursuit of more worldly enterprises. I have served with a number of members of this sect and I can only say that I found them no less worthy or just than anyone else.

I had been less than two years in the Ministry when I was called before a promotion board, much to the surprise of everyone, including me, for in seniority I was virtually at the bottom of a very long list. I couldn't possibly have the smallest chance of succeeding; my friends were, I felt sure, wondering what powerful influence was at my disposal. The interview consisted of ten minutes answering questions put to me by four very senior officials who were known to me only as remote, important people to be seen occasionally in the corridor. The single vacancy went to a man much older than me who, after some years of temporary service, had been made permanent at about the time of my appointment. My colleagues very quickly had the explanation of my surprise appearance before the board; the promotion had been a disgraceful piece of nepotism and I had been included amongst the candidates so that it could be said that the promoted man was not the only junior person considered. They were probably right. But I felt that somewhere on the long ladder between me and the top someone must have spoken well of me.

Most young civil servants were ambitious for promotion but without immediate thoughts of advancement; one thought hopefully that one day a rise to the next rank would come; possibly with a bit of luck there might be two steps up before retirement. But that was all in the distant future; we made the most of what we had, enjoyed ourselves and hoped for the day when we would be noticed.

In 1937 it was decided to create a new grade called 'Senior Clerk' which would be an intermediate grade between Clerk and Junior Staff Officer (for which the maximum salary was £515 a year). The new grade would have a salary scale rising to £400 a year and it was known that there would be a good many appointments to it. I and my contemporaries looked forward to the changes it would bring.

When the first list came to our office in Enniskillen and I saw that it included a good many of my friends, but not me, I was disappointed. When a second and a third and a fourth list followed without my name, although it seemed that everybody except the completely incompetent had been chosen, I felt angry and abandoned. One or two Protestant friends suggested that my religion was the reason for my failure but I could not believe that anyone could be so petty; I had never seen signs of prejudice of this sort amongst those with whom I worked. I wrote a strongly-worded memorandum complaining about my treatment. A week later the door of my dingy office in the Old Gaol building opened and the Establishment Officer of the Ministry walked in. Once or twice I had been in a room with a Principal Officer; here I was alone with the most exalted of all Principal Officers who had come all the way from Belfast. He asked me to take him to Maguiresbridge. He was a fisherman and he said he wanted to have a look at the river. On the way he told me that I was to be promoted. When we got to the village and stood on the bridge, looking down at the running stream, he told me, between comments about fishing and life in rural Ireland, that he had been very impressed with my memorandum. Whilst he did not say that he thought I had been treated unjustly, the fact that he had made the journey to Enniskillen on no errand but to talk to me, was clear acknowledgement that my complaint had been justified. A few days later I got a letter telling me formally of my promotion and calling me back to Belfast.

There had been many highlights during the three years I spent in

Enniskillen but there were dark days too. During that time my youngest brother Tommy died. We had been close friends and when he left school he had taken up the solicitor's apprenticeship which had been offered to me. He had shown considerable promise in his studies and had played games as no-one else did. But an attack of rheumatic fever left him with a heart which no longer matched his glowing spirit. I was with him when he died at the age of twenty-one. For months afterwards there were days when I drove out into the country to sit alone in my car and cry. Even now, more than forty years later, it pains me to open the secret place where his memory lies.

I came back to Belfast intellectually enriched by my three years in the country. It may be that the experience of sorrow enhanced my evaluation of friendship. My work had brought me amongst people of all sorts and I had found time to read two books in every week of my three years. I had enjoyed to the full many late nights and early mornings, had met scholars and sportsmen, poachers, idlers and hard-working souls in talkative gatherings in the towns and villages. And I had spent three years of days and nights amongst kind people who had shown me generous hospitality.

Thirteen

I took up duty in January 1938 in the branch supervised by Robert W. Steele in the Headquarters of the Ministry of Labour at Stormont. I did so without enthusiasm, for I was one of about a dozen of various junior ranks temporarily posted there to get a new voluntary insurance scheme launched and without any idea that the move would lead to a dramatic change in my circumstances.

During my earlier years at Stormont I had worked close to Steele and had known him as an efficient, extremely hard-working, rather dour man from County Londonderry who had gone to Trinity College, Dublin, where he had graduated with high honours. Whilst his contemporaries with comparable academic labels had come into the service in the elite Assistant Principal grade, he had been content to accept a junior executive rank and apply his talents to the management of one of the Ministry's many branches, remote from the centre of power where the more fortunate graduates spent their days dealing with loftier policy issues. Robert Steele, one concluded, had not displayed the external graces which were being sought by those concerned with appointments to the cadet grade.

The branch which he presided over in 1938 was concerned with the interpretation of social insurance law and with the drafting of statutory regulations. It was regarded as one of the most important branches of the Ministry and was reputedly staffed by people of proven excellence. But I was just one of a fairly nondescript lot brought in for a special job which would last perhaps six months, following which places would be found for us elsewhere. I hoped that my future would be back with the inspection staff. I was a carefree bachelor, I had got used to the freedom and the opportunities for social diversion which the outdoor life provided and I knew that without the expense allowances payable in respect of official travelling, I would not be able to continue to afford my own car. Having just been promoted, I could not expect further advancement soon; the question of where my future would be most likely to prosper was not of immediate concern.

In spite of my eagerness to get back to the nomadic life, I began, almost against my will, to find myself getting growing satisfaction from working under Bob Steele. His ability and his capacity for hard work were impressive and well-known but I found that this rather remote man had sides to his character which I had not suspected. He had a delightful sense of humour and a special talent for generating enthusiasm and interest in those around him. He was a warm-hearted, fair-minded man totally committed to objective administration and fiercely antagonistic to injustice or intolerance in any form. He gave his opinions, whether or not they were popular, with uncompromising directness which suggested a Covenanting background. Working under his guidance became more and more a stimulating experience.

I cannot recall Steele ever saying a word of praise for anything I ever did, for it was not in his nature to be patronising, but as I gained confidence in my new environment and entered freely into the daily discussions about our work, I began to see that he thought well of me. When, in the middle of one discussion, the name of my previous boss was mentioned, the momentary glance which he gave me as he muttered 'that bloody bigot' told me for certain that Bob Steele believed that I had had a raw deal in the recent scramble for promotion. After about six months, when those who had been brought to the branch as temporary reinforcements were being dispersed, he told me that I would not be moving on. He had arranged that I would stay as a permanent member of his staff. To be found acceptable to a man I had grown so much to respect was a very heartening experience, and I sold my small car without too many regrets.

One morning in April 1939 I was told to make myself ready to appear before a promotion board that afternoon. Normally candidates for such engagements were given several days' notice; days which they usually spent reading reference books, studying Acts of Parliament and Regulations, consulting the newspapers and questioning colleagues about all sorts of obscure topics so as to stock their minds with facts which would enable them to display a wide range of knowledge in response to the questions which they were likely to be asked. (Most of this research was totally wasted effort.) This summons gave me no time for research and it was different in other ways. I learned that everyone in the clerical and executive grades under the age of thirty-one, including some with higher rank than mine, was being called and that the interviewing board would be the Ministry's Permanent Secretary and his three Assistant Secretaries. Despite the shortness of the notice this was to be no ordinary board. Corridor gossip said that in all Ministries the same thing was happening. It had been decided, I was told, to search throughout the Service amongst the younger men who had entered in the clerical grade for one or two who might be worthy of advancement to the select Assistant Principal rank traditionally reserved for graduate entrants. Each Ministry was to look for candidates suitable to go on a short list from which, if promising people were found, a final selection would be made.

The more I learned about what was happening the more angry I got. I remembered my first promotion board when I had been used to give respectability to the advancement of somebody's favourite. I had gone unnoticed for years. Bob Steele had rescued me from obscurity and I knew that I had by then become his front runner for promotion to Lower Executive rank, but my experience of past happenings told me that the parade to which so many were being invited and from which one or two would be chosen, could have no meaning for me. I would be competing with people who had already been preferred to me.

When I sat down before the Permanent Secretary and his Assistant Secretaries my blood was really up and I didn't care if it showed. I dealt with their questions and their conundrums without caring whether I was being indiscreet or offensive or simply wrong. I talked more freely than I had ever before talked to senior officers; I was resolved that these men who had previously probably never heard of me, would remember our first meeting. I laid before them my stock of knowledge, some of it very scant, on every subject they raised and I didn't hesitate to question or contradict careless comments from the other side of the table. I broke all the rules recommended by wise men for the guidance of candidates at interviews but I was enjoying myself and I didn't give a damn. And I was being listened to. The four very important men across the table were, I began to see, interested in what I was saying. The interview,

136

for which twenty minutes had been allotted, lasted an hour. I went back to my room wildly excited. If the purpose of the exercise had been to find a place for some well-connected favourite, I had not made the job any simpler for its promoters.

I was one of eight who, a week later, went before a board made up of Sir Wilfrid Spender, the head of the Civil Service, and six Permanent Secretaries. I could not expect to repeat my earlier performance but I was not too unhappy at how it went. At least I had made the final. The very exclusive rank for which we were competing would not be for me but I had surely earned my promotion to the executive grade.

After a couple of weeks it was announced that two of my competitors on the short list had been made Assistant Principals and a few days later my promotion to Lower Executive came through. Not having regarded myself as a likely appointee to one of the plum jobs, I was satisfied. Having been, I felt, a forgotten man, I had climbed back into the light.

On a Saturday morning, about ten days later, the Establishment Officer called me to his room and after a brief preamble about the rewards of virtuous living, for he was a God-fearing man, calmly told me that Sir Wilfrid Spender was waiting to see me and offer me an Assistant Principalship in the Ministry of Finance. In his expansive, carpeted room on the second floor of Parliament Buildings, Sir Wilfrid was indeed waiting for me. He greeted me warmly and almost apologetically explained that the recommendation in my case had been delayed because the Minister of Finance – then John M. Andrews – had been abroad. He had just returned to the office and had given his consent to my promotion in his Ministry. Could I start there on Monday?

A bright sun was shining as I went into the city centre to Mooney's pub. Bob Steele was amongst those who helped me to celebrate. I was now on a new mountain; the top was away out of my reach but with luck my stopping place would be far above what a 'schoolboy entrant' could have expected. Before going back to my digs that evening I bought a two-year-old Morris 8 car with ten thousand miles up for £72.

Bob Steele was to rise to high rank in the public service; although we had no further official contacts, there were many occasions when we met and talked. He never once suggested that such success as I have had owed anything to his sponsorship but I know that his generous support of my case at that time was the most important influence in my whole career.

Almost thirty years after those happenings Bob Steele died in retirement. His funeral brought together an impressive gathering of young and old, of all ranks, who had reason to remember him with respect and affection. When we had laid him to rest we retired to a local inn where we sat late into the evening, hearing accounts of many ways in which this able, generous-hearted man had brightened the lives of others. Throughout my career I did not know his equal.

Sir Wilfrid Spender was an Englishman who at the time of the 'Ulster Crisis' in 1912 had resigned his commission in the Army and offered his services to Carson and the Ulster Unionists. He had taken a leading part in the establishment, organisation and training of the Ulster Volunteers, the semi-military body which was to have resisted Home Rule by force, and by 1920 was in the inner councils of the Unionist movement. When the Government of Northern Ireland came into being in 1921 he was made Secretary to the Cabinet and after a few years succeeded Sir Ernest Clarke as Permanent Secretary of the Ministry of Finance and Head of the Civil Service.

His appearance and demeanour suggested guileless innocence. He was not a man of great ability but, despite his years amongst the political activists, he carried out his duties with integrity and a great desire to be seen to be fair. To the civil servants, then a much smaller community than now, he was a father figure and it was known that he was accessible to anyone, however lowly his or her rank, who felt aggrieved. But 'The Colonel' as he was called, was not without prejudices. His dislike of the IRA was probably only marginally stronger than his dislike of the Special Constabulary, whose organisation, authority and appearance offended his military mind. He made no attempt to hide his lack of respect for some politicians, including some senior ones; I knew him to refuse to attend a meeting when he learnt that Sir Dawson Bates, the Minister of Home Affairs, would be there.

George Chester Duggan was second-in-command in Finance, with the rank of Senior Assistant Secretary. He was probably the ablest civil servant Northern Ireland has had; a handsome, humorous, slow-speaking, rather shy man dedicated to objective administration and quietly cynical about the machinations of politicians. Although originally, I believe, a northerner, he retained the rich Dublin accent he had acquired during his years at university in Dublin and his service in Dublin Castle. There were many stories touching on his unenthusiastic attitude to the non-administrative areas of government to which Spender was devoted.

King George V had died. Duggan was immersed in some complex financial problem when a colleague came into the room.

'I was looking for Spender,' said the visitor.

'He's down in the Cabinet Offices. A very serious matter has come up.'

'Oh! What's on?'

Duggan sat back and explained.

'You see, when Parliament is sitting the flag flies at the top of the flagpole. When the King is dead the flag flies half way down the pole. Today, Parliament is sitting, and the King is dead.'

His eyes were twinkling and he shook his head slowly as he turned back to the papers on his desk.

'Flags are very tricky things.'

In the Treasury Division of the Ministry of Finance my duties brought me into regular association with senior men in all ministries, men who lived in a very different world from that of the junior ranks of the Ministry of Labour. Because all expenditure and proposals for new legislation had to have Treasury approval, I found myself dealing with initiatives and schemes affecting a great variety of government services and attending meetings at which questions of high policy were discussed. Although my role was no more than that of 'devil' for my more senior colleagues, the change brought about by my new status was dramatic. Amongst my new duties was occasional attendance in the officials' gallery in the House of Commons or the Senate.

Sitting through a debate in Stormont was never an inspiring and rarely even a moderately interesting experience. The standard of debate was – as it probably is in most elected assemblies – low. Most of our public representatives were dull people with little capacity for eloquence or originality or humour. Proceedings which political correspondents decorated with the cliché 'the cut and thrust of debate' were, for the silent occupants of the gallery, usually a dreary and uninteresting spectacle. In a House in which the Government side always won 'by a distance' the suspense which comes with uncertainty about the outcome of a contest was manifest only on those rare occasions when it became known that a number of Government back-benchers were unhappy about some aspect of their front bench's proposals. But the civil servants knew from long experience that the 'crisis' was no more than a small passing cloud which would dissipate after a few hurried conversations in the corridor or, perhaps, a quickly convened party meeting. There were, of course, moments of diversion.

Hughie Downey, a barman who was for some years the Socialist Member for Dock Constituency had a nice talent for wry observation. Commenting on a speech by Edmund Warnock, a distinguished, silvery-haired, self-assured lawyer whose eloquent pronouncements did not always meet with the approval of the man from Dock, Hughie said that the Member for St Anne's had 'become dazzled by the glare of his own headlights'. And at a time when Harry Midgeley, although still sitting with the Opposition, was struggling in the difficult no-man's-land between Socialism and Official Unionism, speaking on all possible occasions and trying neither to betray his past or prejudice his future, Hughie observed that he was 'like a corncrake. He never shuts up from morning to night but you're never right sure what field he's in.'

Tommy Henderson, the Independent Unionist Member for Shankill, assailed the Government with resounding clichés, always with a twinkle in his eye. In one debate he dealt at length with the deprivation suffered by some of his constituents as a result of inadequate plumbing arrangements in their houses. As he related, with unadorned frankness, how some of the people of the Shankill had contrived to deal with certain personal problems arising from inconveniently-sited toilet facilities, John F. Gordon, the Minister of Labour, a dapper little man whose trim appearance belied his trade union background, began to make distressful, protesting noises. Tommy addressed himself to the outraged John F.

'I see the Minister of Labour is shocked. He should be. I'll bet he performs the functions of nature in the lap of luxury.'

He is probably best remembered for his vivid expression of his hope for a future which would see 'the British lion marching down the Shankill Road hand in hand with the floodgates of democracy.'

Tommy Henderson was an uncompromising Unionist. He was very popular on the Shankill Road and he had no enemies anywhere.

The subject of religious prejudice is one which no reasonable man approaches without misgivings; observations about another man's bigotry tend to be unprofitable. In Northern Ireland they can lead to controversy and acrimony and they are usually biased. But any story which touches on life in Northern Ireland over the past fifty years would be incomplete if it were to omit reference, however prejudiced, to what has been, all too often, a divisive influence both in public and private life. My working life has been in an environment about which many accusing observations have been made, particularly in recent times. An account of my career would be less that complete if I were not to deal frankly with the occasions on which, to my personal knowledge, such matters impinged on my life.

Some of my fellow Catholics would say that it was more than a little naïve of me to expect to succeed in a career in the Northern Ireland Civil Service, whose membership when I joined was almost entirely Protestant, under a Unionist Government that appeared to be there for all time, whose leader, Sir James Craig, had said that they had created 'a Protestant Parliament for a Protestant people'. Perhaps I was naïve, but although I was aware of the prejudices and fears which ran through our community, I had grown up in comparatively small towns where both denominations had lived together in reasonable harmony, in a household in which religious intolerance was regarded as unChristian; there was no time when there had not been Protestants amongst my friends. I really did not expect anti-Catholic prejudice to be a barrier to any rewards which I might earn. I am a gregarious person and when I came to Belfast I quickly made friends with kindred spirits in the various Government offices. I associated wth them in non-official pursuits, played rugby with them, got drunk with them, lived in the same digs with no feeling of being in any way at a disadvantage in their company. Indeed, I sometimes felt that the care of their souls benefited from my being in their midst, for my regular attendance at Sunday Mass tended to prompt some of my fellow-lodgers to a more diligent observation of their religious conventions.

The promotion which took me to the Ministry of Finance brought about a spectacular improvement in my position and my prospects but I did not think of it as a Catholic victory in a Protestant world. And in my new surroundings I was treated with understanding and kindness. There was no thought in my mind that my religious beliefs were of the slightest interest to any of my new colleagues.

One morning, it must have been about a year after my transfer, Sir Wilfrid Spender, followed by Henry Sherrard, my Principal Officer, came into my room (I had already achieved the exquisite distinction of having a room to myself). Sir Wilfrid looked somewhat agitated and without even sitting down he came straight to the point.

Major Maynard Sinclair, who had been elected a Member of Parliament at about the beginning of the war, had been brought out of the Army to take up the office of Financial Secretary to the Ministry of Finance. Sir Wilfrid explained that it had been necessary for him to propose a member of staff for appointment as private secretary to the new Financial Secretary. With the agreement of the Assistant Secretaries, he had recommended me for the job. He had felt obliged, although to him it was not of any significance, to mention to Major Sinclair that I was a Roman Catholic. Sinclair had asked for a few days to think about the proposal and had that day come back with the information that his political advisers had told him that it would be injudicious of him to have a Roman Catholic private secretary. Spender made the words 'political advisers' sound unclean.

'I thought it only right that I should tell you about this,' he said. 'I can only say that I am surprised and disappointed and very sorry.'

I felt that some comment was due from me but what could I say? I was still rather new-fangled with my enhanced status and I felt more than a little flattered that this supreme civil servant, who was under no obligation to mention this matter to me, should, without imposing any pledge of confidentiality, be so open and frank on so delicate a subject. As I had no ambition to be anyone's bag-carrier, even in a job which would have brought me to the notice of all sorts of powerful and influential people, I did not feel particularly deprived. I said something about understanding that the selection of a private secretary was a personal matter for Major Sinclair and I assured Sir Wilfrid that I was not put about by what he had told me. Not so Henry Sherrard. He was a Dubliner, a Trinity College graduate, an ex-serviceman of the First World War, a British 'establishment' type (to whom Dun Laoghaire was still Kingstown). He thumped the table, called me a fool for taking the thing so lightly and said that if he were the victim of such a scandalous decision he would 'pull the damned place down'.

A few days later Spender sent for me to tell me that, on Sherrard's recommendation, he had decided to grant me a special increment of pay in recognition of the good work I was doing. (The private secretaryship would have brought a similar benefit.)

It was about this time that I learned more about how I came to be transferred to the Ministry of Finance. The final board before which I had appeared had recommended me for promotion in my own Ministry, but the Minister of Labour, John F. Gordon, had refused to approve the appointment of a Roman Catholic to an administrative post in his Ministry. Spender and G.C. Dugan and W.A.B. Iliff (an Assistant Secretary in the Ministry of Labour who was to leave us for a distinguished career with the World Bank) had got together and decided that I must not be deprived of the advancement which I had earned because of the Minister's narrowmindedness. John M. Andrews, the Minister of Finance, had approved their plan to rescue me.

Those events took place about forty years ago and I am now the only survivor of the participants. Sir Wilfrid Spender's diary, to which the happenings of each day were faithfully committed, will, I hope, eventually become available for public scrutiny. I would expect that some reference to these conversations will be found therein.

Fourteen

Since coming back to Belfast I had lived in lodgings in Elmwood Avenue in the University district, in a large comfortable house inhabited by cheerful, lively people. Late in 1938 we got a new boarder, Dr Jupp Hoven, a German who told me that he had come to Ireland to do research into certain aspects of social change attributable to the effects of the Plantations. He and I became friendly.

Jupp was very small, not much over five feet, stocky, greyhaired, about forty years of age, a solemn-looking man who, as many small men do, carried himself rigidly. But he was not without a sense of humour and he liked company. He introduced me to the wines of the Rhineland and I spent many late nights sitting in his room, drinking hock and talking. The talk was mostly about Ireland, about which he was very knowledgeable, and he allowed me to borrow freely from his large collection of books of Irish interest. He rarely spoke about Germany, which was not surprising at that period of the Hitler regime. One night, however, under the influence of many glasses of wine, he confided in me that he had had a spell in prison for 'political activities'.

Hoven travelled over much of Ireland, visiting libraries and universities, meeting people, compiling voluminous notes. He was a prodigious worker and quickly acquired amazingly detailed knowledge of the country, its people and traditions. He sought out and introduced himself to historians, social workers, politicians, clerics, industrialists and writers. On getting the name of someone who might be able to help in his investigations he would send off a letter asking for a meeting which, it seemed, he invariably got. He was extremely correct and courteous and on his visits he invariably brought a large bunch of flowers for the lady of the house.

From time to time I heard suggestions that Hoven was a spy, for war with Germany was then becoming more than a possibility. But it was not easy to think of this rather innocent-looking little man as a secret agent. Nevertheless there were a few circumstances which prompted the thought that he was more than a travelling academic. One man of whom he spoke with affection was Frank Ryan, an Irishman who had risen to high rank in the Communist forces in the Spanish Civil War. Hoven had visited Ryan in a Spanish prison where he was serving a life sentence. He had had meetings in Dublin with Father Michael O'Flanagan, the revolutionary priest whose oratory had provided so many headlines in the newspapers after 1916. He told me of other leaders of the Irish revolutionary movement whom he had met.

In May 1939 I saw Jupp Hoven off on the Dublin train on his way back to Germany. I had accepted his invitation to spend my holiday with him in August, first at his home in Aachen and then in Berlin.

Some weeks later, I had a visitor, a large untidy man with no gift for small talk.

'I believe you know Jupp Hoven?'

'Yes.'

'You intend to visit him in Germany?'

'Yes.'

'His photograph is in every police station in Ireland. We think he is a spy.'

I said that I had heard others express similar views, but I was sure he was all right. In the tense atmosphere of those days any German travelling outside his own country, showing curiosity about all sorts of things, would find it hard to avoid arousing suspicion.

My visitor had a proposition. If, during my visit to Germany I would observe and on my return report on Hoven's associations, his activities and his friends, the reimbursement of the cost of my holiday might be arranged. I refused the offer. I said that if during my holiday I should see or hear anything detrimental to the security of this country, I would feel obliged to pass on the information. But I would not be paid to spy on a friend whilst enjoying his hospitality.

As August approached the signs of the approaching storm were too ominous and my holiday plans came to nothing.

Some years ago I picked up a book *Spies in Ireland* by Enno Stephan. In it I saw a photograph of Jupp Hoven in the uniform of a

145

German Army officer. According to Mr Stephan, my old friend, having been 'studying sociology in Ireland' was recruited into the German Intelligence service early in the War and was instrumental in having Frank Ryan brought from his Spanish gaol to Berlin. But the plan to involve Ryan in stirring up disaffection in Ireland came to nothing; the poor man died a few weeks after reaching Berlin. Hoven was then attached to a group given the job of organising an Irish Brigade from amongst the Irish servicemen in prisoner-of-war camps, but the operation was a failure. Hoven was, according to Stephan, regarded by his superiors as 'politically unreliable' because of a youthful association with a left-wing group; he was transferred to the Army in 1942.

If Jupp Hoven is still alive perhaps I will one day find out whether the acceptance of the offer of a free holiday might have led me to a new career in the shadowy corridors of international espionage. But I must say that Mr Stephan has not convinced me that Jupp has a place in a book about spies.

I was just three months in my new post when the Hitler War started. Several senior people, including G.C. Duggan, were seconded for service with new or expanding British Departments. C.H. Petherick, who succeeded Duggan as Senior Assistant Secretary, let it be known that he would not release any further members of his staff, other than young people with junior rank, for war service.

I had spent the month of July preparing for war. I had been given the task of drafting a series of instructions which, on the outbreak of war, would tell senior members of the staff how and where they would operate in the conditions which were expected, and give guidance on the role and the responsibilities assigned to each and every one of them in a great variety of preconceived situations. This was highly secret work which brought me into consultations with all of the 'top brass' of the Ministry and called for daily meetings with the Permanent Secretary. My completed memoranda were bound in stiff covers and given the title 'The War Book'; copies were placed in the secret repositories of the Ministry and the Cabinet Offices. But my 'War Book', over which I had spent many hours in confidential discussion and secret composition, was never opened. The beginning of the War was nothing like what I and those who knew much more about war than I did, had expected.

Memories of six years of civilian life in wartime do not come in

146

any order. On Sunday morning, 3 September 1939, we had listened with glum resignation to Prime Minister Chamberlain's broadcast statement that Britain was at war with Germany and in the succeeding days we got horrifying stories of the German attack on Poland. The newspapers carried photographs of children in British cities and towns being put on buses and trains to be 'evacuated' to the safety of rural billets. We tried on our gas masks and hoped we would never have to use them.

After the Germans had subjugated Poland there was a pause in the fighting (the term 'phoney war' was used) and there were many rumours about peace negotiations. Then, in the summer of 1940, the German Army moved into Holland and Belgium and France with, it seemed, invincible power. They had produced armaments and aircraft which had rendered traditional defences useless, the Maginot Line which we had been told would hold out against any army on earth was an anachronism; whole regiments of heavily armed men had been dropped from the air. The Germans seemed to be unstoppable and suddenly the menace was very near.

Those months after June 1940 were the most depressing of the whole war; it seemed that the forces of evil were going to walk over Europe. I remember, on a cloudless summer day, sitting in my office in Stormont, looking out over well-cut lawns and wondering if German soldiers would be there within weeks. There had been many who had been comforted by the feeling that we were comparatively remote from the probable arena of war. Some, including one or two in high places, had thought that the building of air raid shelters and the organisation of a civil defence service in Northern Ireland was a waste of money for, they argued, no aeroplane could carry a load of bombs all of the 500 or 600 miles from the nearest point in Germany to Belfast. They were to learn otherwise.

When the air bombardment of British cities began we hoped that our patch on the outer edge of Europe would have a pretty low rating in the Germans' plans. In the spring of 1941 we had one or two minor visitations from enemy aircraft; perhaps they had strayed from their appointed routes, some of us thought hopefully. Then, on Easter Tuesday night, as week-end holiday-makers were returning to the city, the German planes came roaring in and for three hours rained death and destruction on an ill-prepared city. More than a thousand people, including several of my friends, died that night. When the raid started I was in my fiancée's home in the southern suburbs. No bombs fell near us, but from an upstairs window I watched fountains of debris from exploding bombs rising through the beams of the searchlights in the Crumlin/Oldpark/Antrim Road area where I knew that my brother would be out on duty. Next day I spent dismal hours walking through wrecked streets until I found him.

The second big raid came on Whit Sunday night. The death toll was somewhat less than on Easter Tuesday but much of the city centre was destroyed. This time I was in my lodgings in Elmwood Avenue, much nearer the target area.

The occupants of 50 Elmwood Avenue applied themselves methodically to the steps recommended for self-protection in air raids. The household consisted of the landlady, an intelligent, calm, cheerful person, her daughter and usually five or six boarders of different ages and occupations.

When the alert sounded the more active ones saw to it that the shutters were securely bolted, the bath, handbasins and sinks filled with water in case of fire, candles brought out lest the electricity supply should fail, fires extinguished. The assembly point for the whole household was the large ground-floor living room. Miss Mack, an elderly, socially superior person who normally kept herself to herself in her first floor bedsitter, would make one of her rare appearances amongst us. She would come downstairs, draped in her fur coat and carrying her jewel case. Tenderly she would be manoeuvred into a recumbent position on a mattress under the large dining-room table; for the period of the alert she would lie there, her furs wrapped around her, her jewels clasped to her bosom. The Dublin couple, from whose mealtime conversation one deduced a background of tweedy opulence, would appear carrying two large suitcases colourfully decorated with the stick-on labels of famous shipping lines and faraway hotels. Having chosen their resting-place, they would inflate their two airbeds, settle down on them and with apparent indifference to the sound and fury outside, while away the time scrutinising the pages of out-of-date copies of the *Illustrated London News* and the *Field*.

Coffee would be made. Those who were not lying down or on a fire-watching tour of inspection of the top floor, sat or stood around the empty fireplace. In the tense atmosphere, with so diverse a company, conversation tended to be intermittent and trivial. The

Dublin husband and wife shared occasional moments of pleasure when one of them spotted in the glossy magazine pages the photograph of a distinguished personage who had been amongst the *dramatis personae* of their prosperous days. From the darkness beneath the large mahogany table an observation about the brutality of the Germans or the splendid behaviour of the British Royal Family would remind us that Miss Mack was still there.

That was how our household was disposed on Whit Sunday night as we listened to the frightening drone of the raiding aircraft, the sounds of the city centre being torn apart, the detonations of the exploding bombs and the return fire of the anti-aircraft guns. On that night fear was in every heart in Belfast.

The bombardment was under way for some time when the sound of a descending footstep on the stairs brought us all to silence. We had forgotten about our air raid warden whom I shall call Mr Smith. He had come to us when his firm had transferred him from Dublin to Belfast and his family had, wisely, decided not to move house in the conditions then prevailing. Their loss was certainly not our gain. To call Smith a bore would be an understatement. Even the most tolerant, forgiving and patient amongst us (and in every large household there are such people) found him unendurable. But, to his credit, he had volunteered for service as a part-time air raid warden and now he was going out to do his duty. As we heard the front door close behind him there was a general murmur of sympathy not, I regret to say, untinged with relief.

Five minutes later we heard the front door being opened. Expectantly we listened. It closed with a dull thud. There was silence; total silence in the room and no sound from the hall. All eyes were on the door. As we watched, the handle began to turn, the door slowly opened, a head appeared. Under a black steel helmet, peering from the thick embracing folds of a navy-blue Balaclava helmet, was a very white, oval piece of face, the solemn face of Smith, his nose looking uncommonly long, his dark postage-stamp moustache touching the waves of the dark knitting in which his inadequate chin was buried deep. We remained still and silent as his small brown eyes looked around the room, as if counting the house. Then he spoke, addressing the whole company:

'I forgot my teeth.'

Something had to be said and I, standing with my back to the fireplace, said it.

149

'Well, what's the problem? They're not dropping sandwiches.'

On no other occasion in my life have I been the cause of ten full minutes of uncontrollable laughter. As it went on a feeling of guilt troubled me. Smith, it must be said, took it all very well.

Because I had been assigned to special duties connected with emergency situations, I had been prohibited from joining any of the civil defence services. When the all-clear sounded I made my way to the city centre, past burning buildings, through streets criss-crossed with fire hoses, around areas in which unexploded bombs had been found, to the Law Courts which had been designated as the meeting place for the emergency group. From the roof of the building, as the dawn broke, I watched the city centre being consumed in flames and down below where I stood open vehicles were bringing dead bodies into St George's Market.

I was married in September 1941 in a quiet country church in County Down and set up house in Bangor, which is both a popular seaside resort and a commuters' settlement. In those bleak wartime years holidaymakers were few, the hotels were unoccupied, the boarding-houses empty and the wide streets unnaturally quiet because of petrol restrictions. The town had a half-empty appearance except during the morning and evening stampedes to and from the railway station; almost all of the working population of Bangor earn their living in Belfast.

Although we were to remain in Bangor until 1948, when we went back to Belfast, my memories of it are mostly of the wartime years, of the things we lacked rather than what we had.

For the benefit of the war effort the annual leave allowances of people in the Government services were drastically cut; in my case from six weeks to two. In the winter months I travelled to and from the office in darkness, seeing my house in daylight only at week-ends. Food rationing, inadequate public transport, high prices which put scarce luxury goods out of the reach of people on fixed salaries, the non-availability of many simple household needs of newly-married people setting up house; these were daily trials in what I remember as a rather dull time. The 'small ads' in the newspapers contained offers to exchange all sorts of goods for others which had disappeared from the shops and it seemed that there was no limit to what people were prepared to barter for golfballs. I remember a poignant one-line advertisement which said, 'Titled lady wishes to buy second-hand mackintosh'.

Bangor Bay was an assembly place for convoys. Great gatherings of ships came and went without any contact with us on shore, and from their shapes and sizes one could only guess at their cargoes and their destinations. There were nights when we wakened in terror to the sounds of mighty explosions which shook the house, but in the morning the ships would be peacefully at anchor in the bay. We assumed that the nocturnal reverberations came from depth charges launched in pursuit of marauding submarines. One afternoon we walked along the sea-front to see the Bay crowded with large ships, many of which were obviously passenger liners. Next day, 26 January 1942, the first units of the United States Army to land in Europe in the Second World War, came ashore and marched through the streets of Belfast.

My wife and I joined the Drama Club and the Golf Club. At a time when the opportunities for professional entertainment were few, amateur dramatics flourished as never before and our involvement brought us many enjoyable nights. On a summer day in 1943 I won the Captain's Prize in a field of more than a hundred golfers. It pleases me to know that in commemoration of that victory my name, in letters of gold, is still to be seen on a large notice-board in the clubhouse.

After about two years in the Ministry of Finance I was given responsibilities which expanded my official horizon. I was made Secretary of the Civil Service Committee for Northern Ireland, a Whitehall-Stormont body concerned with ensuring that certain rights acquired by pre-1920 local government officers and civil servants would be honoured under the new administration. I was also appointed Secretary to the Joint Exchequer Board whose responsibilities related to the financial relationships between the British and Northern Irish Governments. For some years I had, therefore, the distinction of being the executive officer of the two statutory committees set up by the Government of Ireland Act of 1920. Those offices brought me periodical visits to London and contacts with British Treasury officials.

It was part of the job of the Secretary to the Joint Exchequer Board to secure that august body's agreement to certain financial transactions between the British and Northern Irish Exchequers under various statutes, regulations and agreements. To that end, when reference to the Board fell due, I would begin by assembling the figures on which the calculations would be made and, as an official of the Ministry of Finance, I would write to myself in my capacity as Secretary to the Joint Exchequer Board, forwarding the figures and requesting that the amount of the due financial transaction be ascertained and approved. I, the Joint Exchequer Board Secretary, would thereupon make the necessary calculations and send them to the Board members, three or four very important people in the corridors of power in London, inviting their agreement to my sums. On receiving their acquiescence, I would write, conveying formal approval to an expectant me, the Northern Ireland civil servant. In carrying out this sensitive operation some care was needed to ensure that I was not replying to myself in advance of the receipt of the initiating letter (from myself). It should not be necessary to add that this was very important work.

Quarterly I prepared the calculation of the financial adjustment between London and Belfast under what was called the Reinsurance Agreement, the purpose of which was to equalise, as between the British and Northern Irish taxpayers, the burden of the cost of unemployment benefits. The calculation was an extremely complicated one involving figures of expenditure under a number of headings and relating those figures to insured populations, actual populations, numbers unemployed etc. The whole exercise covered several pages of figures set out in a sequence determined by the terms of the agreement. Since the calculations were made only four times a year it was not worth while committing the details to memory; the sensible thing was to read and learn the formula each time it was needed and then forget it, or so I thought until the day the Minister, without a moment's warning, let it be known that he would like someone to explain to him how we calculated the amounts due under the Reinsurance Agreement. I picked up my files and went into his room.

The Minister of Finance was then Sir Milne Barbour, an elderly taciturn man and I decided that the simplest way of satisfying his curiosity would be to place before him a copy of the most recent calculation and take him through it stage by stage. I started with the easy confidence of a man on familiar ground but before I was half way through my exposition, I realised that I was lost. Somewhere along the way I had overlooked or misinterpreted a figure or a plus or a minus and I was adrift – talking nonsense and even running out of that, for half of my brain was frantically looking for a way out of my predicament. Should I admit that I had gone astray and start all over again? If I did, could I be sure that I would not repeat my mistake? My confidence was disappointingly low. The Minister's attention was still with me, he was showing no signs of loss of interest. I decided to go on and hope for the best. Line by line, talking all the time, desperately choosing words to adorn the figures, without making sense of them, with digressional references to past difficulties or future problems, my moving finger led my silent listener's eye down along the remaining pages until, somehow, I came to the end of my meaningless recitation. With the voice of a man making light of some mighty achievement, I signed off with the words:

'And that's how we calculate the payments due under the Reinsurance Agreement.'

I waited, breathlessly, for questions.

Sitting back in his large armchair, like a benign Buddha, Sir Milne Barbour spoke.

'I am very grateful to you, Mr Shea. Thanks to your very lucid explanation, the Reinsurance Agreement will never be a mystery to me again.'

I think he was telling a lie. He must have seen the great beads of sweat on my forehead.

Fifteen

At the outbreak of war, unemployment, a perennial problem in Northern Ireland, was depressingly high, possibly higher than it had ever been. However, as the factories became engaged in the manufacture of supplies for the war effort, the situation improved rapidly. Within a couple of years the economy of the province had been transformed. There were jobs for everyone. Money was plentiful.

Our new-found prosperity prompted some fresh thinking about the financial arrangements between us and Westminster. I found myself inclined to question some of the changes which were being sponsored, but decisions on such matters were taken at a level at which my small voice would have had little influence.

The Act of Parliament which established Northern Ireland gave the subordinate Government very limited tax-raising powers. All of the main taxes – income tax, customs and excise duties etc – were collected by the appropriate British departments. From the United Kingdom's yield of revenue the net amount attributable to Northern Ireland was passed over to our exchequer. That receipt, together with the comparatively minute income raised by the Northern Ireland Government through its tax-raising powers, made up the bulk of the Province's revenue. One special charge on our funds was the Imperial Contribution, required under the 1920 Act as our donation towards certain United Kingdom services, mainly the defence forces.

Initially Northern Ireland's essential public services were organised and their levels of cost settled by its own Government with the approval of its own Parliament in the light of its financial resources and without any obligation to take note of British standards. One exception was the social services, for which at an early stage it became necessary to negotiate special arrangements so that we could maintain those benefit schemes in parity with the corresponding schemes in Great Britain. Over a wide range of public services rates of spending were settled locally and the organisation and development of them depended on local initiative, the overriding consideration being the amount of money at the disposal of the Government. Early in the game, however, civil servants began agitating for parity of conditions with British civil servants; by 1939 they had gone a long way towards achieving that objective.

The higher British taxes made necessary by wartime spending brought spectacular increases in revenue; Northern Ireland's income from British taxes collected in the province rose steeply, giving us, compared with pre-war years, enormous surpluses of income over expenditure so that each year many millions were re-transferred to the British Exchequer by way of the Imperial Contribution. Initially this change inspired Ministers to speak words of praise about our financial contribution to the war effort but very soon politicians, including some members of the Cabinet, began to ask if we could not hold on to some of the surplus funds. (The inflated Imperial Contribution was, of course, no more than our proportionate share of financing a world war.)

The call for 'parity of treatment' or 'step by step' began to be heard inside and outside Government. We were part of the United Kingdom, the preponderance of our taxes were exactly those applicable throughout the rest of the United Kingdom, all of our citizens were, therefore, entitled to precisely the same financial rewards as were available to similarly circumstanced people in Great Britain. The logic of the argument was undeniable.

Rapidly our negotiations with the British Treasury began to change. The principal of 'parity' was accepted and the test for approval of more and more proposals became, 'What are they doing across the water?'. The British Treasury conceded that, subject to consultation with them, we would be free to apply Great Britain standards to virtually all of our services; so long as those standards were not exceeded, financial support would be assured. (There were exceptional services, particularly those associated with law and order, for which, it was conceded, our obligations were proportionately higher than in the rest of the United Kingdom.)

There was a political element in this change. Unionist politicians must have seen that as our standards, particularly in the social services, rose above those in Southern Ireland the economic argument against union with the South would grow stronger. Nationalist politicians, apparently blind to this consideration, were no less emphatic than Unionists in the agitation for the application of the higher British standards. Presumably they regarded any device to get extra money out of the pocket of John Bull as a praiseworthy operation.

My concern was with the business of government. We were becoming agents where we had been principals. I felt that a community, having been given authority in the management of its affairs, however limited that authority might be, should maintain and use it to the limit. Decision-making was good for politicians and civil servants and the community. I was all for parity, that is, for the allocation of total funds sufficient to enable us to apply British standards should we so wish; but we should decide for ourselves how the funds should be allocated.

The Beveridge Report was published in 1943. Hailed as a blue-print for a post-war paradise, it proposed enormously increased rates over the whole range of social security and welfare benefits with corresponding increases in the rates of contributions by employees, employers and the State. I felt that this was the moment to stop and think where the pursuit of 'parity' was leading us.

The principal markets for what we have to sell are in Great Britain. Would the pursuit of parity in wages and State-provided benefits not make it increasingly difficult for our industrialists to compete with British manufacturers? As Northern Ireland industry depends substantially on imported raw materials, its manufacturing costs are loaded with transportion charges on both its material needs and its finished products. To counterbalance these and other expenses arising from our remoteness, had the time come for the Government to consider taking steps to hold our living standards somewhat below those in Great Britain? We might begin by looking at the possibility of applying 'a minus factor' to the very generous Beveridge proposals.

My contribution to the office debate on Beveridge was a memorandum in which I expressed those views. I sent it on its way, not expecting it to get an enthusiastic reception, but I felt obliged to make my point and that this was the moment for it.

Some days later Maynard Sinclair, the Financial Secretary (later

156

to become Minister) called me to his room. With my memorandum before him he questioned me about my views without offering many comments one way or another. Finally, as he closed the file, he said with a rather wry smile, 'You know, you are asking me to commit political suicide.'

He was probably right. He had been one of the strong advocates of 'parity' in the fragmented form which I found unappealing.

Parity continued to be the measuring scale for more and more of our services and without doubt a great many people benefited financially from its adoption. But the price was the surrender of authority and the transfer of responsibility from Parliament to Ministers and civil servants. With ready-made blueprints endorsed by the mandarins in Whitehall so often available to Parliament its business became increasingly trivial. If we were following great Britain the question 'Can we afford it?' did not arise and the question 'Is it right for Northern Ireland?' seemed like looking a gift horse in the mouth. Instead of managing our own house we were living in furnished lodgings under a benevolent landlord. It is not surprising that many men of ability saw little scope for the exercise of their talents in political life.

When in recent times I have read of manufacturers complaining about the burdens of freight charges and imported fuel costs, I have had the feeling that my somewhat unconventional proposal might have deserved a longer look than it got.

During the war I had got one further step of promotion to the rank of Deputy Principal. By 1945 my work had, at one time or another, covered the Ministry of Finance's oversight of all of the public services so that I was, by then, pretty well known in all departments of the Government. Within the Ministry I had also had executive responsibility in connection with services such as the Irish Land Acts, the law relating to charities and entertainments duty which were directly administered by the Ministry.

Much of the work, particularly that relating to new legislative proposals, could produce challenging conundrums. Although I was then at a level that could be called no more than 'middle management', I found myself involved in correspondence and arguments and sometimes acrimonious disputes on issues of pretty high policy. Decisions did not rest with me but I had quickly got rid of any inhibitions I might have had about making my opinions known.

157

The Ministry of Finance in Northern Ireland fills the place occupied by the Treasury in Great Britain and it has always been subject to the sort of criticism which is directed at that institution: that its role is largely a negative one, that the main aim of its officials is to find ways of rejecting other people's progressive ideas. Although much of this carping is unjustified I cannot say that during my years in the Ministry of Finance there were not instances of official parsimony. I remember one.

Above me in the Ministry there were, in rising order of importance, a Principal Officer, an Assistant Secretary, the Senior Assistant Secretary and the Permanent Secretary who was also Head of the Civil Service. Formal approval to the spending of money, however small the amount, rested with them. I was expected to have clear, logical, justifiable opinions about a proposal; I would, as often as not, draft the document saying 'yes' or 'no' to the application before us, where necessary giving reasons for the decision; but the final word, was, by a rule of the house, communicated by one of my seniors. When my opinion was in harmony with that of the man who would sign the letter the outcome brought satisfaction to both of us but one of my rank would not be entrusted with the formal act of announcing a decision.

On the morning after the second big air-raid on Belfast the city was in chaos. The bombers had put virtually the whole of the public transport service out of commission. I walked all of the way across the city to the office – seven or eight miles – and not having been in bed during the previous night, I was not at my brightest when I got to my room in Stormont at about eleven o'clock. The telephone was ringing; the caller was Ronald Green, then an Assistant Secretary in the Ministry of Public Security, the Department concerned with Air Raid Precautions, the Fire Services and the Police. Green, a very practical and on that particular morning a busy man, wasted no time in giving me his message. Communications in the Fire Service and the Police were almost non-existent because the whole of the public telephone service had been put out of action. (We were speaking on an internal line.) His Department, after much searching, had found nine second-hand motor bikes which could be bought and he wanted to buy them for issue to the Police. His vote did not contain provision for such expenditure and he wanted instant Treasury approval for the purchase, the total cost of which would be something under £500. He had phoned the offices of the Permanent

Secretary, the Senior Assistant Secretary, the Assistant Secretary and the Principal Officer, none of whom was available. Mine was the first Ministry of Finance voice he had heard. Green was a kind man and he knew me well but he had no time for questioning or quibbling: 'I now want you to approve this expenditure.'

I accepted the mantle which he had placed on my shoulders. I said, 'Right. You can assume Ministry of Finance approval.'

As I put the phone down my Assistant Secretary put his head around the door to let me know that he had arrived. I felt bound to tell him about the conversation I had just had. He dashed off to his room. Twenty minutes later he came back, smiling triumphantly, and announced: 'I beat him down to six bikes.'

The war was then costing the country something more than twenty million pounds a day.

Reginald S. Brownell became Permanent Secretary of the Ministry of Education in 1939 in succession to A.N. Bonaparte Wyse, the first, and for forty-eight years the only, Catholic to attain that rank in the Northern Ireland Civil Service. Wyse had a scholarly appearance and those who had worked with him spoke highly of his administrative ability and his quiet, good-humoured personality. When he transferred to the Northern Ireland service in 1921 his family did not come north and during the eighteen years of his service in Belfast he travelled each week-end to his home in Dublin. He was recognised as the architect of the education service established in the major act of 1923, much of which still survives.

Brownell was ambitious, energetic and intense; a moody man whose sternness was relieved by a rich vein of dour humour. His impatience with those whose acquiescence was withheld from him, could bring forth, decoratively rather than with malice, the hackneyed profanities of his native Dublin. Those who knew him were not put out by his growling remonstrances or upset by his questioning cynicism for they knew that at heart he was a generous person who respected men who were fit and ready to stand up to him. He was an able, tolerant man, too individualistic to be a good manager; he used sound and fury as a flag of authority rather than a lash.

In December 1947, I reported to Brownell on my appointment as Principal Officer in his Ministry. I had met him for the first time a week earlier when, with half a dozen other candidates, I had appeared before him and his Assistant Secretaries. I had found a man who was not afraid to engage adult civil servants in argument about what many would have considered sensitive issues and therefore taboo in the neutral atmosphere of a government office. He and I had had a right set-to about a particular aspect of the Catholic Church's policy on education. (Although not wholly in agreement with the Hierarchy's pronouncements, I felt that this was not the time or place to question them.) I believe we both enjoyed the argument and I was pleased when I was told that I had been chosen to fill the vacancy. He welcomed me warmly.

The contribution which R.S. Brownell made to education has not, in my opinion, been adequately acknowledged. In Government circles he was known as an aggressive and persuasive head of a difficult department but he never became a 'public figure'. He was not a frequenter of the sort of social gatherings in which public reputations grow and blossom.

In 1947 the Minister of Education was Colonel Hall-Thompson, no intellectual heavyweight but a fair-minded man. During the long and bitter controversy preceding the passing of the Act of 1947, which modernised and expanded the whole structure of education, he showed notable courage in his handling of the noisy protesters who objected to the proposed increases in the grants to the voluntary schools, most of which were under Catholic management. For that comprehensive Act alone, the names of Brownell and Hall-Thompson are worthy of an honourable place in the history of education in Northern Ireland.

My first post in the Ministry of Education was Establishment Officer and Accountant; this meant I was responsible to the Secretary for the organisation, staffing and housing of the Ministry and for the management of its finances. The 1947 Act which was to come into effect on 1 April 1948 would introduce new and expanded services and would lead to more staff, greatly increased expenditure and considerable reorganisation. I had not done work of this kind before and I liked the idea of being directly involved with people and their problems.

From its beginning until the expansion which came with the 1947 Act, Education had been a small, inbred, rather remote Ministry; leisurely, conservative and unchanging. Its working arrangements in 1947 were those which had been introduced by the small group which had come from Dublin in 1921 and opened its first offices in

hired rooms in the Presbyterian Assembly's College. There were parts of the Ministry where one would not have been surprised to see quill pens still in use; not every member of the staff took kindly to the changes which were necessary to enable the office to fulfil with reasonable efficiency its larger responsibilities under the new Act. I remained on this work for two very satisfying years following which I was moved into the world of schools and schoolmasters and scholarships and the training of teachers.

It has been said, and it is probably true, that until comparatively recently I was the only Catholic to fill the office of Establishment Officer in the Northern Ireland Civil Service. Since that post is concerned with appointments and promotions and there have been many allegations of discriminatory practices in the Government service, I feel bound to speak frankly of my experience in those matters. All of the records of appointments and promotions were under my care; I was in the Secretary's confidence in all such matters. I read no record, heard no conversation, witnessed no decision which would justify any allegations of discrimination on grounds of religion or otherwise against officials of the Ministry. Brownell was not capable of such practices and it must also be said that Hall-Thompson avoided interference in questions affecting personnel.

Hall-Thompson ceased to be Minister of Education in 1949 and the circumstances of his going reflected credit on no-one but him. He had introduced in the House of Commons a small Bill, the purpose of which was to enable the Ministry to pay grant on the full amount of the new national insurance contributions for the teachers in those voluntary schools for which it was already bearing the full salary costs. The Second Reading in June 1949 was taken almost without comment, but when the subsequent stages came before the House some months later it was evident that some influential members of the Unionist Party had had second thoughts. Amongst the leaders of the revolt was Harry Midgeley, recently converted to Unionism, who made it clear that he was against making life easier for schools managed by people whose attitude to the Crown and the State of Northern Ireland was less than enthusiastic. In the wheeling and dealing which followed this internal revolt Hall-Thompson (who was not an Orangemen) found it necessary to have a discussion with representatives of the Orange Order, following which he resigned from the Cabinet and accepted the lesser office of

Chairman of Ways and Means. His friends thought he had been treated very shabbily.

For the rest of his life Hall-Thompson remained silent about the circumstances of his departure. I believe that if the inside story were known it would be seen to be no more creditable than the much-publicised account of the fall of Dr Noel Browne. He, at about the same time, left the Government in Dublin after, it was said, some behind-the-scenes communications between the Catholic Hierarchy and the Government. It could be that some of the Stormont people who cried 'shame' at the goings-on in Dublin had themselves acquiesced in a not dissimilar exercise which led to the sacrifice of a decent man within their own ranks.

Rumours that Harry Midgeley would be the new Minister of Education were greeted at first with derision, then, as they persisted, with annoyance; someone with a warped sense of humour was at work! The man had only just been made Minister of Labour.

The announcement that Harry had indeed been appointed to Education brought dismay and shocked surprise in the Ministry's offices in Massey Avenue.

Midgeley had been an outspoken opponent of increased state assistance to the voluntary schools, an attitude which was in accordance with his former Socialist affiliations. He had been particularly hostile to the recent Bill and had made it clear that he was prepared to dismantle the structure created by the 1947 Act which had so recently emerged out of prolonged and difficult negotiations. He had, indeed, seemed an unlikely candidate for Education. People asked if Brookeborough was mad. Others, remembering that every previous Minister of Education had had to leave because of a disagreement with his Cabinet colleagues or a clash with some of the powerful influences concerned with education, wondered if the Prime Minister was hoping that Education would rid him of his turbulent convert.

I had watched, with diminishing respect, Harry Midgeley's political journeyings. In my early years in Belfast, in times of much unemployment and great poverty, he was the vociferous radical, the most compelling and uncompromising home-grown advocate of Socialism; a small black-haired, swarthy man, a restless, impatient man whose days and nights were spent preaching and reading and arguing, disputing actions of employers or decisions of the Ministry of Labour. To me, in those early days, he was the one Socialist in our community who could be said to have fire in his belly.

Harry Midgeley had come into the House of Commons as the Socialist Member for the Dock constituency of Belfast, a working-class district where unemployment was high and the majority of the voters were Catholics. Harry was their champion until the Spanish Civil War brought a conflict of loyalties amongst them. His political beliefs placed his sympathy on the side of the Spanish Republicans; within his own constituency he was provided with the means of demonstrating, his critics would have said parading, his attitude to that conflict.

At the outbreak of the Civil War there were several Spanish cargo ships berthed in Belfast Harbour and there they remained until it ended. The ships' crews, at a loose end in a strange country, were befriended by, amongst others, the Member for Dock. He was frequently seen in their company in the constituency, he took them to meetings, sometimes bringing them on to the platform to bear witness to the sufferings of their fellow-countrymen at the hands of a Fascist military clique waging war against democracy. But Harry's reading of the Spanish situation was not acceptable to all of the Catholic electors of Dock and amongst those who took particular umbrage at his posturings was the local Parish Priest, a well-loved, down-to-earth man. During one confrontation, with the Spanish sailors looking on, the PP, his Glens of Antrim blood up, threatened to take off his coat to the MP.

Within the small Labour Party, Harry was also having difficulties. Jack Beattie was the Labour MP for Pottinger and neither he nor Harry was prepared to fill the role of number two to the other. On one occasion they had a bitter quarrel on the floor of the House of Commons.

At the General Election in 1938 Midgeley lost his seat in Dock; it was all too evident that a substantial number of Catholics, disenchanted because of his stance on the Spanish question, had voted for the Unionist candidate. Harry alleged, probably with justification, that the Parish Priest had encouraged his parishioners to give their votes to the Unionist. For the remainder of his life Harry Midgeley's antagonism to the Church of Rome became increasingly bitter.

In 1941 he returned to the House of Commons, still nominally representing Labour, but with many of his political utterances sounding uncommonly like echoes from Unionist platforms. When I had first listened to him his political thinking was pretty near James Connolly's concept of an Irish Workers' Republic. Now his appeal was for loyalty to the Crown and Commonwealth; he saw Rome as the enemy of freedom and democracy and he was the most bitter critic of the Southern Government's policy of neutrality in the War. The voters of the Protestant constituency of Willowfield took him to their hearts and he had a comfortable victory over the Unionist Party's candidate in a by-election.

His link with the Labour movement had for some time been a very frail one; in 1942 he broke it and established the Commonwealth Labour Party. Gone were the days when his political life depended on Catholic votes. His new party would be a pro-British, Protestant, working-class party.

In 1943 Brookeborough brought Midgeley into his Cabinet, first as Minister of Public Security, which was a wartime Ministry, and later as Minister of Labour, He resigned his Cabinet post to lead his new party in the General Election of 1945 but when Parliament reassembled he was Commonwealth's Labour only MP. In that solitary role he was still the fighting Harry Midgeley. But his fiery words, which for so many years had berated the capitalist system and Toryism in all its forms, were now more often than not turned on his former comrades sitting on the Opposition benches. Those who listened wondered when he would take the final step into the ranks of the Government party. This he did in 1947.

It was as a Unionist back-bencher that Midgeley had taken a leading part in the attack on Hall-Thompson's Bill in August 1949. In November, when the party bosses were preparing for the next round which was to bring about the downfall of Hall-Thompson, Midgeley became Minister of Labour.

In his final comment on Hall-Thompson's fall, Lord Brookeborough, the Prime Minister had said that he would ask the new Minister to 'look into the whole system of education'. This seemed an odd comment from the head of the Government which had recently restructured it. The staff of the Ministry of Education were not the only people who awaited with misgivings the impact of Harry Midgeley on his new Ministry.

In 1950 the business of the Ministry of Education was conducted, as it had always been conducted, in an atmosphere of Victorian formality which was entirely in harmony with the personality and the character of R.S. Brownell. In the Ministry of Education respect from one's juniors was the first fruit of seniority; the practice of this custom allowed of no liberties. The newly-promoted man would expect that the colleagues who had hitherto addressed him by his surname would, from the moment of his elevation, insert the prefix 'Mr'. Only where close friendships had been formed, and then with due discretion, were Christian names heard. In conversation there was much 'Sir-ing'; memoranda were phrased with excessive respect for the rank of the recipients.

The essence of Harry Midgeley's personality was informality; ebullient, back-slapping informality. According to Brownell, the new Minister looked down the list of senior staff which had been set before him at their first meeting and asked:

'What are the Christian names of these fellows?'

The Secretary replied, 'I don't know anyone's Christian name. We don't go in for that sort of thing here.'

The Minister accepted the local rule but his observance of it was without prejudice to his normal conversational ways when the company included people from outside the Ministry. At a meeting with a deputation (and there were many, many deputations received by him) the officers of the Ministry would address the chair as 'Mr Minister' and he would courteously 'Mr' each and every one of them, whilst to the visitors he was 'Harry' and he knew and used all of their first names. After one rather prolonged meeting of this sort, the Chief Inspector, a gentle-spoken, scholarly man, was heard to comment wearily:

'The trouble with the new Minister is that he's Harry to every Tom and Dick.'

From outside the Ministry came the story about the Minister leaving for home late in the evening. Coming out of his room he met the Secretary.

'Good-night Mr Brownell.'

'Good-night Minister.'

As he went down the stairs an Assistant Secretary was coming up.

'Good-night Mr Smyth.'

'Good-night Minister.'

At the bottom of the stairs he met a Principal Officer.

'Good-night Mr Mortimer.'

'Good-night Minister.'

Out in the hallway the cleaner was using a mop on the tiled floor.
'Good-night Billy.'
'Good-night Harry.'

Harry Midgeley had announced that he intended to carry out a comprehensive examination of the whole of the education service and put forward proposals for its restructuring. So far as I know he did not particularise his views on what was wrong with the system except that he felt in a general way that the voluntary schools were too well treated. No substantial proposals for change emerged during his seven years in the Ministry (except for one which, in fact, benefitted some of the voluntary grammar schools). At the beginning of that time the story most widely heard was that the new Minister would run the Ministry without dictation from its officials, that he would bring to an end the dominating position of Brownell who, it was said, had dictated the policies of previous Ministers. The allegation was not wholly without substance; Brownell was a man of strong personality and considerable ability, virtually all of whose working life had been spent in education. He knew its problems and difficulties; for many years he had been at the centre of educational development in Northern Ireland and the passing of the Act of 1947 was the crowning achievement of his career. If previous Ministers had been content to accept Brownell's views many would say that the education service was the better for it. But there was no denying that he knew of and enjoyed his reputation as the mastermind in education and he could be wildly indiscreet. It was not surprising that Harry Midgeley should see his Permanent Secretary standing in the way of change.

From the beginning Midgeley and Brownell were at cross-purposes; the Minister questioning and suspicious, the Secretary impatient and dourly defensive. Civil servants are trained to give loyal service to their political masters, whoever they may be, and Harry Midgeley was served faithfully and conscientiously by all of his staff. But he never ceased to suspect that in order to protect a bureaucratically designed system, his officers were less than frank in their dealings with him. As a result, simple proposals could become the subject of prolonged and sometimes acrimonious argument. Between the Minister and the Secretary there were frequent quarrels; there were days when there was no communication between them.

I don't suppose any Minister got so many letters, listened to so

166

many deputations or received so many complaining visitors as the Right Hon. Harry Midgeley. And not all of the complaints and requests were concerned with education. People who wanted houses, who had been sacked, who wanted to join the police or the army or the civil service, who wanted someone out of gaol, people with ideas about how Linfield Football Club (of which Harry was Chairman) would win matches, who wanted a reference or a word spoken here there or anywhere, people who just wanted a shoulder to cry on, wrote to or called on the Minister of Education. And since he was incapable of saying 'No' to a suppliant in need of help or sympathy, he promised favours which he was powerless to grant and gave undertakings which were incapable of fulfillment. As a result, his relations with his officials suffered. In local government where he had spent many years, concessions could be won and favours negotiated, but where the rules were made by Parliament and administered by cold-blooded officials under the scrutiny of parliamentary institutions, the letter of the law was the order of the day. He found it hard to accept that there was virtually no patronage at his disposal.

Midgeley never lost his mistrust of his civil servants and it must be said that Brownell's handling of his occasional brainwaves was not such as to improve relationships. Not surprisingly, the Minister sought help and advice outside the Ministry; he was ready to listen to anyone who had something to say about education. One morning, resuming a conference at which, on the previous evening, his officials had spent hours vainly trying to persuade him to a course of action, he announced that he had new proposals to put before them. These proposals had been gleaned the previous night, as he himself said, 'from a waiter in a high-class restaurant'. The anonymous waiter's contribution to educational thinking was listened to in silence.

One of the oddest of many contretemps between Harry and his officials concerned a girl who decided to become a nun so that she could devote her life to nursing the sick. She entered an order of nuns whose activities included teaching as well as nursing; when her superiors saw her brilliant examination results, they decided that her role would be to teach and an application for her admission to a teacher training college was duly made. The young lady's father called with the Minister, told of his daughter's deep disappointment at being denied the opportunity to follow her true vocation,

167

explained how difficult it would be for a young novice to question the judgement of her superiors and asked if the Minister could arrange for his daughter to fail in her application for admission to training. The Minister assured him that there would be no problem; the Ministry would have a representative on the interviewing board and he would be told to fail the unwilling candidate. Theoretically, since admission entailed the award of a scholarship by the Ministry, there was an implied right of veto. In practice, however, the role of the Ministry's representative at the interviews was, in collaboration with the college's representatives and on a basis of mutual trust, to join in selecting the best candidates. When the senior inspector concerned pointed out that he simply could not give the 'thumbs down' to a candidate whose academic record suggested that she would be amongst the best appearing before the board, the Minister was very angry. That was not his idea of the exercise of power.

One day Brownell came into my room.

'Do you know the motto of the Jesuits?' he asked, a broad smile on his face.

I said I didn't but if it was important I could find out. He told me the reason for his enquiry.

That morning he and the Minister had had a meeting with a group of distinguished clerics representing the Protestant churches. During a break for coffee, the Minister showed him a drawing, the outcome of the work of a committee of which Midgeley had been chairman, charged with the task of designing a pocket badge to be worn on the blazers of the Linfield football team. Beneath the chosen device Brownell read the motto which the committee had selected, *'In hoc signo vinces'*.

He handed the square of paper to the Moderator of the Presbyterian Church, asking innocently.

'Moderator, what sign does that refer to?'

'The Sign of the Cross.'

Harry went off to do some urgent telephoning.

Sixteen

My father died on Christmas morning 1952, a crisp, frosty morning with a covering of snow on the ground. A year earlier he had had a stroke which slowed him down but did not incapacitate him. Death came instantly and without pain which was just as well for he was too impatient to endure prolonged suffering.

Since coming to Newry he had made a new career, ultimately becoming Clerk of Petty Sessions for the area, a job in which his interest in legal processes served him well.

I think my Father influenced me more than anyone else has. It was impossible not to be impressed by his independence, his keen, alert mind and his great understanding of others. I once asked him why, when I was leaving home, he had given me no fatherly advice.

He said, 'Well, I said to myself, "If the fellow has any character he doesn't need advice; if he hasn't I'd only be wasting my breath," so I kept my mouth shut.'

His example was the surest guidance I ever had.

In 1945 I wrote a one-act play. For as long as I could remember I had wanted to try my hand at writing. Living in wartime Bangor with few social distractions and married to a wife whose artistic perception had become a joyful revelation to me, this was the moment to try.

I sent my script to Radio Éireann where it was accepted and broadcast and I was paid a fee of £3. No money I have earned has given me more satisfaction than that cheque. Some time later my little play was put on the stage by Bangor Drama Club.

Writing something, however small or trivial, which others are prepared to offer to an audience, is a uniquely satisfying experience.

And yet it is a relief to me to know that not a single copy of that first, small effort has survived. It was terrible. But because it aroused the kind attention of a few people, it opened for me a new interest and new experiences which brought me great satisfaction and some lasting pleasure.

My next attempt was a short story, prompted by a trivial incident. During a lunch-hour walk with a few friends in the Stormont grounds we met a little middle-aged lady hurrying back to her desk in the Ministry of Labour. Under her arm she carried a package wrapped in brown paper. It was wartime, food was scarce and roughly-wrapped parcels suggested black market dealings. One of my friends called out to this most unlikely pedlar of illicit goods:

'What's in the parcel, Miss Law – a roast of beef?'

'No, Mr MacDonald, a gun.'

The quick reply was all the better coming from so timid a person and it led to some banter about what might be in Miss Law's parcel. What if she was telling the truth? Who would she want to shoot? Possibly someone very important! And how would we look if, on coming back from our walk, we should see an assassinated mandarin being carried out on a stretcher? We had been told by this lady that she was carrying a gun – and we had done nothing about it! What would an inquisitive policeman or a good lawyer make of her story?

That evening I wrote a short story based on this incident and sent it to Radio Éireann where it was accepted with a complimentary comment from Francis McManus and a fee of £4. I made a one-act play of it which I called 'A Lady in a Cage', the title being from Chesterton's poem 'The Grocer':

> He keeps a lady in a cage
> Most cruelly all day
> And makes her count and calls her 'Miss'
> Until she fades away.

I entered 'A Lady in a Cage' for a manuscript play competition and it got first prize. I then submitted it to Samuel French, the London publishers, so that, if it was any good, I might reap the benefits of having it published and distributed through the world-wide Samuel French organisation. When no word came after a month I sent a reminder and got an immediate reply which said, 'We will write to you in the course of a day or two when we may have a proposition to put to you.'

This message, written on notepaper which bore the London, New York, Hollywood, Toronto and Nairobi addresses of Samuel French, could only mean that they were going to publish my play; it would become known to amateur societies throughout the English-speaking world and the rewards by way of performing royalties would be substantial. (I had just read of an author who claimed that a single one-act play had brought him an income of £500 a year for ten years.)

I needed money. We had just moved house to Belfast and I had had to borrow every penny of the purchase money. We had a daughter and another baby was almost due. A new source of funds would be welcome.

French's proposition came in a few weeks.

'We are prepared to publish "A Lady in a Cage" if you are willing to accept twenty guineas for the sale of the copyright to us.'

I was shattered. I had expected so much; I had been told that reputable publishers did not try to buy copyright outright. For amateur productions the royalty would be at least £1 and there could be fees from broadcasting at a guinea a minute or more.

I read the letter again. It had been signed by the Managing Director and there could be no mistaking what the offer was. I turned it down.

Over nine or ten years 'A Lady in a Cage' was broadcast on the BBC half-a-dozen times (including one broadcast in Arabic), it was published by Harraps in *The Best One-Act Plays of 1950-51* and it has been performed by amateur dramatic societies in the five continents. Had Messrs French bought it for twenty guineas they would have recovered the purchase price many times over.

The wish to write something, however inconsequential, which might be worthy of notice somewhere, had lurked in my mind as long as I could remember. My bachelor years had been busy, carefree ones and my gregarious nature had involved me in all sorts of agreeable distractions which left no time for sedentary pursuits. After my marriage, two influences stirred my ambition to write. One was my wife's interest in the arts and her uninhibited enthusiasm for original work of any sort. The other was my growing disenchantment with certain aspects of my work in the offices of the Ministry of Education.

Before 1948 Education had been a very small department, so

small that senior members of staff could find time to become involved in quite minor matters. As numbers grew with the Ministry's expanded responsibilities, the level of decision-making which, to my impatient mind, should have speedily moved to lower levels, remained at the top where the dominating figure of R.S. Brownell sat. With hindsight, I can now see that it was unreasonable to expect dramatic change. Brownell had been put in charge in 1939 when one energetic man could encompass all of the Ministry's activities and he had spent years working on the reforms which he saw to be necessary and which were achieved in the Act of 1947. He knew more than anyone else about the education service and had been deeply involved in every facet of it. It was only natural that he should want to keep the reins in his hands and that those who had spent years under his tutelage should be content to leave it so. But in two Ministries I had been used to responsibility and was impatient of the restraints I had now to bear. Midgeley's performance as Minister of Education was an additional cause of my discontent.

It had been an accepted tradition that the Minister of Education, being concerned with a service in which particularly sensitive interests were involved, eschewed political controversy, save when educational issues arose. Harry had no respect for forbearance of that sort. Hostility towards the Roman Catholic Church had become an obsession from which he took no rest. He read widely about the Church, about Papal infallibility, about the doctrine of transubstantiation, about the misbehaviour of Popes, the errors of bishops, misconduct of minor clerics, the evil consequences of what he called 'authoritarian dogmatism'. His public statements, which were frequent and widely reported, were salted with high-sounding expositions of his most recent discoveries of the discreditable actions of Church bodies, ancient and modern, or foolish statements by enthusiastic laymen or long-dead prelates. It was unlikely that a follower of Rome would have a bright future in his Ministry.

The Minister's anti-Roman Catholic utterances became more and more of an embarrassment and at one time I asked Brownell to allow me to transfer to another Ministry. He said that he would not let me go. He agreed that I had good reason to feel aggrieved and suggested that the Catholic members of the staff should get together and prepare a 'dignified protest' at the Minister's sectarian utterances. This was a ridiculous idea. I had to point out that an organised protest, however dignified, would give support to those bigots who saw us as agents of a foreign Church seeking always to undermine democratic government.

Coming home in the evenings, frustrated or angry or just bored, I looked forward to occupying my mind with something which gave me pleasure, writing what I wanted to write in my own way, answerable to no-one but myself, using whatever skill and imagination I might have. Not that I valued my work very highly; for me, writing was no more than an absorbing hobby, an engaging release from the preoccupations of work. If others sometimes liked what I did, the pleasure was all the greater.

I wrote a number of radio plays and short stories which were broadcast and I won another prize and a complimentary note from Lennox Robinson of the Abbey Threatre.

In the mid-1950's I began a partnership with John Kevin Maguire, a colleague in the Ministry, who had written notably good pieces for the local newspapers. Under the pseudonyms John Kevin and P.S. Laughlin we became quite well-known as writers for broadcasting and were very successful with radio plays and the dramatisation of celebrated local trials. I cannot remember how we made known our willingness to try variety scripts, but Radio Éireann commissioned us to do a series of eight half-hour variety programmes. We called the series 'Gallimauphry'. We wrote songs and monologues and sketches and littered the scripts with bad puns and topical jokes, good and bad. As we lived at opposite ends of Belfast much of the work of composition was done over the telephone. On Saturday afternoons we met in a downtown pub to bring our bits and pieces together, settle the shape of the week's offering, insert a few last-minute jokes and apportion the final typing so that the completed script would be in the post on Monday. It was incredibly hard work but great fun.

With John Gibson, then Drama Producer for the BBC in Northern Ireland, we went to an exhibition where, for the first time, we saw some of Sydney Nolan's paintings on the theme of Ned Kelly, the Australian bushranger. It was there and then agreed that Kevin and I would write a serial programme about his exploits. After many months of research we produced 'Ned Kelly – The Story of a Bushranger' in seven half-hour instalments. The broadcast of this programme aroused a good deal of notice and although it took place more than fifteen years ago, I still meet people who want to talk about it.

From the beginning of our collaboration Kevin Maguire and I agreed that each would be free to work independently of the other; this was only sensible since not all ideas lend themselves to collaborative development.

Having had reasonable success in radio and written a number of one-act plays which had done well with amateur dramatic societies, I decided to have a shot at writing a full-length play for the professional stage. Since it would be written in my spare time, in a household in which there were now three small children, I knew that whatever my capability as a playwright might be there would be no point in trying to write something 'significant'. It would be a straightforward story set in a local scene.

The germ of an idea came quickly. I started to write and as I wrote the characters shaped the plot (which I believe to be the best way to arrive at a dramatic composition). After about a dozen nights, working three or four hours each night, I had finished my three-act play. I sent it to the Ulster Group Theatre; two days later the theatre's director called on the phone to say that he liked it very much and wanted to produce it. I was delighted. I had only to wait until the theatre was ready to start rehearsals. But for many months after the excitement of that moment the silence was broken only occasionally when I enquired about the theatre's intentions and was assured that its interest in presenting my play had not waned in the slightest; the problems in the way of production were about to be solved. After almost a year and a half I came to the conclusion that in spite of the cheering responses which my enquiries had produced, such prolonged inactivity did not indicate any real desire to see my play on the stage; they were, I felt, just being polite in their assurances of abiding enthusiasm for my work. I sent the play to the Abbey Theatre, Dublin, where it was accepted. To this news the Group Theatre reacted with surprising ill-temper; I had to point out that they hadn't even given me a written acknowledgement of the receipt of my script.

My play, called 'Waiting Night' was produced in the Abbey Theatre where it was well-received but not successful. From such an experience an author has many thoughts about what might or might not have been. For one thing, I am sure that, since it was written in Ulster dialect, its chance of success would have been very much enhanced had it been produced at the Group Theatre which had then a very good company. But I had grown impatient with so many

174

months of waiting and, like every amateur, I was impatient to see my work performed. Perhaps I should have been more patient. But had I waited until the Group was ready I would have missed making a curtain speech in a famous theatre – one of the more memorable moments in my life.

Following the Abbey Theatre production I adapted 'Waiting Night' for radio, where it was very successful. It was also in steady demand from amateur societies in Leinster, Munster and Connaught (but never in Ulster). One very talented society from a village in County Limerick, having taken prizes at a number of festivals, went to the All-Ireland Drama Festival at Athlone and there won a first prize with it. Another notable achievement during its years on the amateur circuit was a performance which won for a County Kerry society the accolade of 'Best Play of the Festival' in a competition which included a play by one William Shakespeare.

'Waiting Night' brought me interest and disappointment and enjoyment and a little pride.

The postscript to my brief interest in the professional theatre was a play in which I sought to recreate the Orange and Green conflict which had for generations periodically disfigured our community. My story was set in Belfast, in a district where, after years of peaceful co-existence, sectarian prejudices, inflamed by political agitators, had once more resulted in violence. My play had Catholic gunmen, Protestant assassins, a fanatical Republican orator, a spell-binding hot-gospeller, riots, intimidation and death. I finished a first draft and was well-satisfied with its shape and its dramatic value. But it was 1958. Sectarian violence was a thing of the past; we had learned sense. A Belfast audience would not come to the theatre to be reminded of the sins of their forefathers, sins of which, thank God, our community was no longer capable. There was no point in wasting further time on what was clearly a non-starter.

I must have put my unfinished script in the waste-paper basket; over the past eight or nine years I have more than once searched eagerly for it but in vain.

Seventeen

When Harry Midgeley died in 1957 there was before the Stormont House of Commons a report which was the sequel to his most memorable quarrel with R.S. Brownell. He had overruled Brownell and granted teacher training scholarships to a number of students whose applications had been turned down on consideration of medical evidence. I had dealt with the cases and been present at a tempestuous brawl between the Minister and his Permanent Secretary which ended with the latter storming out of the room muttering angrily as the Minister wrote an instruction to him to grant the scholarships.

The Public Accounts Committee, a committee of the House of Commons, was obliged to inquire into the circumstances in which the Minister and the Permanent Secretary had disagreed. In a special report it ruled that Brownell was right and that the Minister had acted illegally in all but one of the cases.

Had Harry Midgeley lived a few weeks longer he would have been obliged to explain himself in a debate in the House of Commons. No-one who had seen him in action would have wagered a penny that the House would have endorsed the Committee's reprimand; Harry Midgeley in the full flight of his oratorical gifts was the most persuasive speaker I have ever heard. I once listened to him, fascinated and at the same time angry, as he addressed a gathering of teachers who had dined together following a schoolboys' international football match in which England had beaten Northern Ireland by seven goals to nil. The message of his oration was that Northern Ireland was an integral part of the United Kingdom, that we were proud of our British heritage and that it was an honour for our schoolboys to lose seven-nil to England. The whole performance was ludicrous but, declaimed with his seductive earnestness and his unerring instinct for the emotional nuances of words, he mesmerised his audience of intelligent people. They listened in breathless silence and when the ridiculous speech ended, cheered their heads off.

Harry Midgeley's years on his political plateau were, in my opinion, years of failure. Others, I know, would disagree. When he died one thought sadly of the young, fighting iconoclast and wondered what mountains he might have climbed had his character been shaped in a more mature environment and the circumstances which influenced his political life been less parochial.

The next Minister of Education was Maurice May, by profession an accountant, who had already established himself as one of the leaders in the commercial life of Northern Ireland. He was efficient, logical, unemotional; obviously a man to whom no reward in business or politics was unattainable. His death after only a few years as Minister of Education removed one of the ablest men in the Unionist Party.

When Brownell retired on pension in 1958 he sent for me. He wanted, he said, to talk to me as a friend; as evidence of which, for the first and only time, he used my first name. He knew, he said, that I felt aggrieved that my career was at a standstill (for I had then held the same rank for eleven years, abnormally long except for the unpromotable). He was good enough to say that I had deserved better, that I was well thought of throughout the service. He revealed to me much which I would not now wish to repeat about promotion opportunities in which my name had figured. His last words to me, as we shook hands, were:

'Because you are a Roman Catholic you may never get any further promotion. I'm sorry.'

There must be few people during whose careers there have not been moments of disappointment, for a man is an unreliable judge of his own merits. During one such time, early in my service, when I felt that I had got less than my due, I resolved that I would not torture myself with resentful brooding on what might have been. I would frankly and without equivocation or apology, let it be known that I believed that I had been wronged. And I would work like hell; it would be foolish to make life easier for any who might wish to undervalue me or to make injustice look respectable. I confess I got a sort of perverse satisfaction from this attitude.

177

Following my last meeting with Brownell I decided that I would adjust my life to his prognosis of my future. The rank which I had was a reasonable one; I would make it do and perhaps find compensation in greater involvement in those non-official interests which my wife and I shared and enjoyed. And with three lively children, home was a busy place. One part of my plan of re-adjustment would be to ask for a transfer to another Ministry.

A.C. Williams succeeded Brownell as Permanent Secretary of the Ministry of Education in 1958. I felt that it would be ungracious of me, until he had at least 'worked himself into the job' — he had been head of the Inspectorate – to tell him that I wanted to leave his Ministry. I had no reason to suppose that his assumption of the top post would in any way affect my prospects of further advancement. I had been no more than two years in the Ministry, back in 1949, when Brownell, in one of his indiscreet moments, had said to me, 'You're going to be an Assistant Secretary soon'. Almost ten years had passed since then. There must have been very few indeed, other than those found unfit for promotion, who had held my rank for so long. If there was a barrier against my further progress, and I believed that there was, it had been placed there by politicians, not by civil servants.

There were now very practical reasons for concern about my lack of progress. I had never been thrifty and the setting up of a home during the war years when prices had risen much faster than salaries, had left me in debt and it would be many years before I would be without an overdraft in the bank. By 1958 my children were coming to the age when, if they were to be given the opportunities we wished to give them, the demands on my income would rise steeply. The rank of Assistant Secretary would have brought a very comfortable rise in pay and that was the time in my life when it would have been of greatest benefit to my family. But as I saw others advancing ahead of me it began to look as though my career had come to a halt. I had known one Catholic who had become an Assistant Secretary during my service but I had also known Principal Officers, reputed to be men of ability, whose failure to progress beyond that rank was generally attributed to their religious beliefs.

My discontent was not lessened by the knowledge that I was well thought of. I was confident that I had done good work and from

178

what Brownell had told me it was clear that for some considerable time I had been on the list of those found suitable for promotion. But promotions in the senior administrative grades were, it seems, subject to the veto of Ministers, and for the most advanced posts to the acquiescence of the Cabinet. It was common knowledge that there were offices, the most notable being the Police Division in Home Affairs and the Cabinet Office, to which Catholics were not appointed. Although I made no secret of my resentment of such unwholesome conventions, I had no ambition to become involved in those services. The Ministry of Education had a reputation, a well-deserved reputation, for generosity towards the Catholic schools. If, within our own walls there was not to be fair dealing (and Brownell had led me to believe that that was so), where was it to be found? From time to time old friends with whom I had worked let me know that they felt that I had had less than justice but there were also depressing experiences.

One day at lunch a group of us got to talking about how a forthcoming vacancy would be filled. The conversation was no more serious than gossip about anticipated events of that sort ever is, until one of the company said, in the most matter-of-fact way:

'Of course, Paddy, you being an RC, I suppose we can leave your name out of the reckoning.'

I felt a pang of disappointment, not so much because of what had been said. The speaker was an old friend, a kind, liberal-minded man; his comment, simply and perhaps rather innocently, gave expression to what he regarded as an accepted fact of life. But I was disappointed and I was angry that his remark aroused no response from the others; the conversation went on as though it had not been made. These were friends and colleagues; as I felt my anger rise I wondered, had I been one of the majority around the table, if I would have felt obliged to speak even a few words of disapproval. I thought I would. I wondered if, throughout the hierarchy of the civil service, when this subject had been mentioned, as it must have been, anyone had ever thumped a table and called for some sort of stand or protest against such shabby intolerance. At that moment, for the only time in my long career, I felt isolated from those with whom so much of my life had been spent.

Early in 1959 an Assistant Secretary came into my room. He had just been to a tea party given by the Permanent Secretary to a group of London journalists on a tour of Northern Ireland as guests of the

Government. One of the journalists, of whom my visitor spoke resentfully, had, in the middle of what was a friendly gathering, shocked the company with the question:

'Does a Roman Catholic ever get a top job in Northern Ireland?'

The Permanent Secretary had, I was told, silenced the discourteous questioner by pointing out that his predecessor's predecessor had been a Roman Catholic. The man standing before me was clearly very pleased at how the ill-mannered Londoner had been squashed. I did not try to restrain my tongue.

I asked, 'Did he not tell him that Bonaparte Wyse has been dead for twenty years?'

Five minutes later, when I was alone, I wrote a two-line note to the Secretary asking for a transfer to another Ministry.

It took a few days to arrange the interview with Sir Douglas Harkness, then head of the Civil Service. I had asked for this meeting so that the reason for my discontent would be known to those at the very top. I went into his room prepared to deal with any suggestion that my allegations were not justified. I began by saying that I had reason to believe that I had, for a good many years, been classified as suitable for promotion, that in the whole civil service there was no-one of my rank who had been kept waiting so long for the rank for which I felt I had demonstrated my fitness. I said that after much thought I had come to the conclusion that my religious affiliation was the reason for my failure to make progress, that I was now resigned to the fact that because of my religion I would go no further. I had asked for a transfer so that the remainder of my service could be spent in an environment which I would find more congenial and possibly less demanding than the Ministry of Education.

At that point I stopped talking. My strategy was to hold my supporting facts and figures, a pretty formidable array of evidence, for use in rebutting his denial of my allegations. On the other hand, he might say that I was not amongst those regarded as suitable for promotion; that would effectively demolish my whole case.

Sir Douglas, a friendly, shy man, simply said, 'Where would you like to go?'

I replied that my preference would be the Public Building and Works Department of the Ministry of Finance. He said that he would see what could be done about it and the interview ended. My planned, well-prepared tirade against unworthy discriminatory

180

practices was left unspoken.

A week later I moved to the Works Department.

My preference for a move to the Works Department might have been seen by many of my colleagues as a sign of mental decline. To those outside it, the Works Department was the graveyard of forgotten men where nothing of any moment happened. I had chosen this office because, as I was no longer a contender for further preferment and had turned fifty, it seemed sensible to spend the remainder of my active years where the volume and the intellectual content of the work would not be too burdensome. And the office was far away from Stormont, remote from the corridors in which ambitious men engaged in the competition for better places. But, to be honest, behind my unambitious reasoning was a feeling, no more than a whimsical hope, that I might even do good work there.

From my first day in my new office I knew that I had made a change which I would not regret. I found myself amongst agreeable people whose down-to-earth approach to the most practical of jobs was wholly refreshing. Everything about the office was different from anything I had previously experienced. The responsibilities of the Works Department were, briefly, the housing of the Government, its departments and public institutions, and the general oversight of the construction industry. Our daily work included the buying and selling of property, the provision and maintenance of buildings for many different kinds of services and, as an interesting sideline, the care of ancient monuments. There was much discussion and negotiation with people from other Ministries, with architects and engineers and contractors and manufacturers and representatives of trade unions.

Within a few weeks I was completely at home in these surroundings, refreshed by the change to work where there was a considerable element of personal responsibility and trust, engaged with cheerful, enthusiastic colleagues in practical work, of which the results would be seen in bricks and mortar. Going through the Province to-day I see, with some pride, buildings, including some notable ones, for which I signed the contract on behalf of the Government. In that Division, because the heads of the professional branches were sensible, friendly, co-operative men, we managed to establish a relationship between the various disciplines which is not all that common.

My judgement that this was my sort of world was flatteringly confirmed one day when after a lengthy conference with representatives of the construction industry, the elderly head of a large firm of building contractors took me by the arm and whispered, 'If I were starting in this business again, I wouldn't mind having you as a partner.'

Some years after I had left this work I was honoured (and enormously pleased) by being made an honorary member of the Royal Society of Ulster Architects.

I had never regarded my literary work as more than an interesting pastime which brought me relaxation from the frustrations of daily work and occasionally supplemented my income. In the years which followed my change of work, the urge to write waned mainly, I believe, because my new responsibilities brought increased personal commitment and the sort of fulfilment which I had previously sought in writing. And the untimely death of my good friend Kevin Maguire broke what had been a productive partnership. Besides, my children were coming to the age when association with them was an increasingly demanding interest. And my wife, in her own right, had stepped forward.

Eithne had always had a keen and well-informed interest in the visual arts. Since coming back to Belfast there had been more opportunities to go to exhibitions and particularly to see the work of Irish artists. We bought a few pictures. In 1958, when our three children were at their most demanding stage, Eithne, having less time for leisure pursuits than ever before, decided to start painting; not just doodling at programme designs or Christmas cards, as she had occasionally occupied a spare hour. She bought an easel and canvasses, an assortment of brushes and a whole battery of tubes of oil paint. She commandeered our spare room and took possession of the door key; when she could disengage herself from domestic occupations she locked herself away and the smell of oil paint on the landing told us that she was expressing herself on canvas.

When the Royal Ulster Academy of Arts announced that it was about to receive entries for its annual exhibition, three oil paintings were brought out from the spare room, put in frames and sent in. In that year the Academy had decided to do something about improving the standard of work at its annual display, which for some years had consisted of large numbers of exhibits in which work of merit was lost in a mass of mediocrity. The selection of exhibits was, therefore, entrusted to 'outside' experts who would be uninfluenced by local names or reputations. Of the hundreds of paintings submitted, fewer than fifty were chosen, amongst them two of the three painted in our spare room. For Eithne it was a tremendous triumph to have her first attempts included in this important and highly selective exhibition. It was also a great occasion for the whole family. It opened a new exciting interest in our home, an interest which has continued to give us great pleasure and many happy experiences.

The Assistant Secretary in charge of the Works Department was due to retire early in 1963. As the date approached, there was the usual speculation about who would succeed him. Although the new man might come from any part of the Civil Service, I was, on seniority, the fairly obvious candidate. And I thought I had justified my place in the organisation. But my name was hardly mentioned by those who were trying to pick the winner; perhaps they knew that I had gone to the Department without prospects or promise of reward.

Captain Terence O'Neill was the Minister of Finance; he would make the choice. He hardly knew me for, although I had then been in his Ministry for four years, I had not been in his company more than half-a-dozen times. I was fairly sure that he would be less likely than some Ministers to be influenced by my religious beliefs.

When I was told that the Minister had approved of my promotion to the top post in the Works Department, I don't think I was really surprised; there have not been many who have had to wait fifteen years for that particular step. But I was very pleased and the announcement was made all the more heartening for me by the many kind messages I got from colleagues who made no secret of their pleasure at a representative of the 'minority' being admitted to the inner circle of Government administration.

In my years in charge of the Public Building and Works Department I served under Terence O'Neill both as Minister of Finance and Prime Minister; I have the most pleasant memories of my association with him. He was succeeded in the Ministry of Finance, in fairly quick succession, by J.L.O. Andrews, Ivan Neill and Herbert Kirk, with all of whom I had the most agreeable relationships.

At nine o'clock on the morning of 23 December 1969, I got a telephone message at my home telling me that I had been made Permanent Secretary of the Ministry of Education, the appointment to take effect on that day. I had to abandon my intention of spending the day Christmas shopping. By eleven o'clock newspaper reporters and photographers were in my office in Churchill House; shortly after noon I was in Dundonald House, Stormont, drinking a glass of whiskey with the Minister of Education, the ebullient Captain Bill Long.

This last promotion came as a complete surprise. More than a month earlier it had been announced that Education's Permanent Secretary, John Benn, would become Northern Ireland's first Commissioner for Complaints (a local government ombudsman). As the time for the change approached, there were many rumours about who would succeed him. This time I knew that my name was amongst those being talked about, but for all sorts of reasons, sensible as well as unworthy, I did not think there was the smallest possibility of my being offered the post. As the weeks passed one assumed that the chosen man, whoever he might be, had already been told, in confidence, of his good fortune. Had I been given a few days to think about the proposal, I might well have refused, for I was very happy amongst my friends in the construction business. But I got no warning or hint that my name had found favour; the message I got was sudden and brief and more than a little bewildering.

The Permanent Secretaryship of a Ministry is a post to which no-one, wherever he may stand in seniority, however intelligent or industrious he may be, can lay claim. It would be vainglorious of me to suggest what qualities are expected of the holder of this, the top grade in the Civil Service, but it is a rank which some of the ablest men who have adorned our service did not reach. I approached my new duties humbly and hopefully.

More than ten years had passed since I had left Education. There would be many changes there; being the Minister's immediate adviser would be a new experience for me, for my previous work had rarely involved policy considerations. I had less than four years to serve until retirement and the education service did not seem to be preoccupied with any major problems. Perhaps my last official journey would be blessed with calm waters. With a little luck I might be able so to arrange my affairs that my remaining time in the Civil

184

Service would not be too burdensome. That was a vain hope.

When I moved to Education in December 1969 there seemed to be some hope (how ridiculous it all seems now) that the political unrest which had been disturbing our community might be coming to an end.

A formula for peace, a programme of reform, agreed with James Callaghan, then the British Home Secretary, was under way. Changes were made in the local government franchise, in the management of the Royal Ulster Constabulary, the Special Constabulary had been disbanded, housing authorities were required to adopt just arrangements for the letting of houses, a Parliamentary Commissioner for Administration had been some time in office and the new Commissioner for Complaints, who would examine allegations of unfair practices in local government, had just been appointed. Of particular relevance to me was that the filling of senior posts in the Civil Service had been placed in the hands of the heads of the Service; promotions to the top jobs would no longer be subject to Ministerial wishes or prejudices. I must have been one of the first to benefit from these new arrangements.

The Northern Ireland Government had appointed a Commission to examine the structure of local government and one of my first duties in the Ministry of Education was to appear before it and give the Ministry's views on how the education service might be reorganised. All too soon for me, the Commission reported; a major restructuring of the education service was amongst the sweeping changes which it recommended. I, who had thought of the possibility of freewheeling my way to retirement, found myself involved in the biggest and most complex administrative operation of my whole career. Education being a many-sided subject, we had months of negotiations with a great variety of interests, including the churches, as a preliminary to the drafting of a comprehensive new Education Bill. And it was urgent; it had to be completed and presented to the Northern Ireland Parliament in about half the time one would normally allow for such a large and important operation.

More than once I have heard it alleged by political commentators that amongst the sins of the Northern Ireland Government which led to its abolition was its lack of urgency in implementing the reform programme then in hand. This is wholly without justification. During its last two years Government Ministers and civil servants applied themselves to the legislative programme with urgency and diligence and made progress which I believe could not have been surpassed.

I don't think I have ever been one to avoid responsibility; being busy is a condition which has always stimulated me. I involved myself totally in the preparation of the new Parliamentary Bill. This meant chairing meetings with colleagues dealing with the many facets of a service bristling with sensitive, often controversial, sometimes highly complicated points. The law which governs education in Northern Ireland (and, I suspect, in most democratic countries) is full of provisions which were the outcome of campaigns and compromises and deals and pledges wrung from our predecessors over a century and a half of government intervention in education and are still cherished by teachers or churchmen or whatever other interests promoted them. It was necessary to give all of those interests an opportunity to state their views on the future of the service; that meant meetings with clergy of all the main denominations, with teachers' organisations, of which we had an astonishing number, with local authorities and their officers, with the library services, with representatives of the parents.

At the same time I was getting on with the day-to-day work of the Ministry. Happily I found the Minister, Bill Long, an industrious, cheerful man with whom it was not difficult to establish a friendly, business-like relationship.

Never had I been so busy. Perhaps I could have so arranged the affairs of the Ministry that my personal involvement would have been lighter but there was a special reason for applying myself as I did.

My appointment had aroused rather more attention than such events normally do. It was noticed and commented upon not only in the Northern Ireland press, but in the Dublin and some of the London papers, almost all of them making the point that in fifty years I was only the second Catholic to reach the rank of Permanent Secretary in Northern Ireland. I was inundated with messages of goodwill from all sorts of people some of them generously flattering, some saying, frankly, that the reward had been long overdue. But the promotion had come when the Stormont administration was in the midst of change; urgently getting rid of practices which had sullied its reputation, establishing new arrangements which would remove grounds for allegations of discrimination or oppression or unfair dealing. There was no doubt of the Government's genuine desire to put its house in order, nor was there any doubt that the process had begun as a result of pressure from Westminster.

Some people, I knew, regarded me as one of the beneficiaries of the change of heart in the Unionist Government. That was, of course, a tenable point provided it did not reflect on my fitness for the job. Amongst those who had no faith in the Government's declared intention of mending its ways, the increased, albeit unspectacular, involvement of Catholics in various roles in the public services brought occasional sour comments. The term 'Token Taig' was sometimes heard.

Although I had had no personal experience of hostility or disfavour (the opposite was overwhelmingly the case) I very quickly resolved that in the official and the public sides of my activities I would make myself available for scrutiny to the fullest extent so that, for better or worse, opinions about my competence would be based upon observation and not on gossip or innuendo. I would be wholly involved in everything of significance in the office and would avoid no opportunity of being seen and heard outside. At a time when I should have been thinking of slowing down, I was embarking on a very full life.

I have always enjoyed company and it was with no feeling of apprehension that I accepted invitations to all sorts of functions. During my years in Public Buildings and Works I had been out and about a good deal and had come to be well thought of as an after-dinner speaker and (although the mood and the phrases would be different) I was not worried about being asked to make speeches. I took on these new social duties cheerfully and Eithne was given more and more opportunities of sharing in my activities. In the universities, the colleges of education, and the schools, at cultural gatherings and sporting events, opening ceremonies and prize-givings, we were shown kindness and generous hospitality; we made many new friends and were the recipients of many expressions of great goodwill.

In this busy, stimulating time there was one small blemish which it took me a little time to be aware of. Throughout the Province we were well received and the invitations came from Protestants and Catholics alike (I remember with particular pleasure the many happy gatherings in the schools in my home town of Newry) but Belfast, I began to see, was different. Except for my good, kind friends the Dominican nuns, those in charge of the management of Catholic education in Belfast, whilst always correct and friendly on official occasions, showed almost no desire to have me in their company on their own ground. Perhaps I was being spoiled by the attention I was getting elsewhere, but I cannot remember being invited to visit a Catholic school in Belfast.

This may be seen as a somewhat sour comment but I am not the only Catholic who has had the feeling that some of our Belfast co-religionists tend to regard success in the ranks of 'the others' as unbecoming in one whose label is that of second-class citizenship.

Eighteen

On the evening of 24 March 1972 Eithne and I were with some friends at a function in a hotel near Belfast. It was a well-dressed, well-attended gathering of well-to-do citizens who had come together to raise funds for a deserving charity. At a few minutes to eleven o'clock I went out into the car park, got into my car and turned on the radio to hear the news that permanent heads of Ministries had that afternoon been told to expect; that the Government of Northern Ireland was to be discontinued forthwith by an Act of the British Parliament and Northern Ireland would come under direct rule from Westminster. Going back into the crowded ballroom I stood looking at the colourful, carefree gathering and I wondered how they would respond to the news which I had just heard. That excellent man, Lord Grey, Her Majesty's Governor of Northern Ireland, who must have known of the fateful decision which had been taken in London, showed no concern. My thoughts went back to the dark night so long ago, when my father had taken two small boys out on to a grassy hill to watch a boisterous crowd celebrating the news that the Irish Question had been settled. Almost sixty years later it seemed that the solution was no nearer.

Within days the business of closing down the fifty-year-old Government had been completed. We no longer had a House of Commons or a Senate, the Cabinet had resigned rather than be dismissed, Ministers had packed their personal belongings and gone from their well-furnished rooms. To Bill Long, our departing Minister, I wrote conveying the thanks and good wishes of the staff, with whom he had been very popular; I got an appreciative and generous reply.

On a Saturday morning the Permanent Secretaries of the various

189

Ministries had coffee with the newly-arrived Secretary of State, William Whitelaw, and were impressed with his friendly sincerity. A few days later we met his junior ministers, Lord Windlesham, Paul Channon and David Howell, amongst whom administrative responsibility for our eight Ministries would be distributed. My new Minister would be Paul Channon whom I immediately liked for his frankness, his astonishing energy and his good humour. (I had read his father's diary which, I believe, will be read when Harold Nicolson's fat volumes are forgotten.) When, after about six months, he went back to London to become Minister of Housing he was succeeded by William Van Straubenzee, a friendly, benign and able man. Even those who were inclined to be critical of the new arrangements acknowledged that Westminster had not palmed us off with second-best ministerial talent. Working with them was demanding and stimulating.

The introduction of direct rule, backed as it had been by a massive all-party vote in the British House of Commons, was clearly an expression of no confidence in the parliamentary structure established under the Act of 1920. The change, which came with cruel suddenness, caused a variety of emotional reactions. Public opinion was sharply divided. There were some expressions of approval, there was also amongst Unionists bitter disappointment, anger and much uncertainty about the implications of the new scheme of things. To those who felt a deep loyalty to the British connection as seen in the trappings of the Stormont Parliament, the fact that the door of that institution had been abruptly closed, and by a Conservative Government, was seen as a cruel betrayal.

Civil servants are no less responsive to public feeling than anyone else but in spite of the expressions of dismay, the threats and posturings of politicians and political groups and the continuing acts of violence aimed at disrupting our society, the administration of the public service never faltered. In my opinion, the performance of the Northern Ireland Civil Service in those difficult days was beyond praise.

It was inevitable that with London Ministers new to the Northern Ireland scene, heavily-burdened with departmental responsibilities, searching urgently for political initiatives, senior civil servants should find themselves more closely involved with political matters than is normal. We, on whose official being any political birthmarks had been hidden under a cloak of official objectivity, found ourselves stripped of our protective covering, our predilections and our prejudices becoming more clear at each new meeting. Observing one another in these unexpected conditions, I believe that we all had one or two surprises. But whatever differences were exposed during this unique and fascinating experience, one never doubted the integrity of one's colleagues or their commitment to impartial government.

Civil servants are, very properly, required to refrain from public involvement in politics; they are expected not to take part in controversy where the subject may be related to matters of government policy. This does not prevent them from being members of political parties although, in my experience, very few are. Because of these considerations and probably also because close association with the ways of politicians rarely stimulates the sort of euphoria in which party enthusiasms flourish, political discussion amongst civil servants is not common; when it does happen, pulses do not beat faster. But under direct rule we sometimes found it necessary to be more forthcoming in offering opinions on what had been for us rather irrelevant albeit sometimes highly sensitive topics. Occasionally I felt that in these deliberations bearing on political happenings and initiatives some of my colleagues (particularly when their judgement of events was not in harmony with mine) revealed a less than adequate understanding of past political developments from which some of our contemporary difficulties had, in my view, sprung. They knew almost no Irish history and it must be said that some who had come to us from across the Irish Sea showed that they had acquired more knowledge of Ireland's past than had many of the native-born officials. Perhaps most Irishmen who were educated in Catholic schools have tended to be over-exposed to unscholarly versions of the story of their country. Nevertheless some knowledge of what had happened in times past was essential if one was to get below the surface of the unrest which was clearly not going to go away for some time. But did my sparse, probably imperfect, store of knowledge entitle me to find fault with others?

In an attempt to analyse my own thinking I wrote a memorandum setting out some of the issues which seemed to me to be important to an understanding of the relationships between what have been called the two communities. (With a view to stimulating discussion I had intended to circulate it amongst my fellow secretaries but the right moment for doing so without being gratuitously offensive, did not arise.) I reproduce it here. If it does no more than reveal the prejudices of one Irishman, perhaps its composition has not been a waste of time.

Before 1920

For hundreds of years Irish Protestants were amongst the most privileged people on earth. A minority in the country, they enjoyed power and opportunities far beyond the reach of the majority.

Over a long period, beginning in the aftermath of the Reformation, philanthropic bodies, Royal patrons and benevolent landlords provided and endowed, in Ireland, educational institutions of a high standard, from primary to university education, which were open only to Protestants. Admission to these institutions was not the birthright of every Protestant but for many generations good education was within the reach of a substantial proportion of Protestant Irish boys whose parents were not wealthy. The Catholics had no comparable opportunities.

In the ownership of property the Protestants were specially privileged, mainly as a result of Government action over centuries.

These advantages (which, in the main, had not been provided as a result of any initiative on the part of those who benefitted from them), resulted in the development of a well-informed, secure, law-abiding Protestant Irish middle class.

There were great areas of patronage at the disposal of government institutions, grand juries, the magistrates etc. These included senior posts in the Government service and in local government, cadetships in the Constabulary (the majority of whose officers were Protestants, whilst the rank and file were predominantly RC), appointments in the courts' services. The numbers of these and similar influential posts which were filled by Protestants was, over the whole of Ireland, disproportionately high. But, having for generations been the better educated and the socially more secure class, no doubt they were the best candidates. They also had the advantages which accrue from having people of one's own ethnic group in positions of power and influence not only in the public services, but amongst the land-owning class and in the professional, commercial and industrial world.

Before 1920 the Protestant schoolboy who took advantage of these special opportunities had little worry about a career. Whether he went straight from school to employment, followed a university course or served a spell in the Army before looking for a civilian job, he could always be fitted in somewhere without too much attention to his academic attainments.

This industrious, responsible class of Irish Protestants, as well as making an immense contribution to the government and the commercial and industrial life of Ireland, produced men who achieved distinction outside Ireland, particularly in the Army, the British Civil Service and the Colonial Services.

The position of the Catholic Irish was very different. During the period of the Penal Laws, whilst the Protestant community was prospering, Catholics were, by law, denied opportunities for education, they were prohibited from entering certain professions and the laws relating to the ownership of property bore heavily on them. At the middle of the nineteenth century the Irish Catholics were largely a depressed, impoverished community.

Until the appearance of institutions such as the Irish Christian Brothers, education beyond the minimum school-leaving age was, even when its development was not actually impeded by government action, outside the reach of all but a tiny minority of Catholics. Because there were no wealthy patrons to provide and endow the schools, Catholic secondary education, when it did develop was, for the most part, inferior to that provided in the old-establshed Protestant schools. It remained so until comparatively recently.

Before 1920, the Catholic boy not of wealthy parents, felt, and indeed was, at a disadvantage compared with the Protestant. His educational opportunities were more restricted, his employment prospects were at a lower level, he belonged to a community in which a substantial middle class comparable with the Protestant middle class could not have developed. He believed that the social disparity between Protestants and Catholics was the result of deliberate government policy. If he wished to escape from the social conditions of his parents he joined in the competition for a place as a trainee teacher, became a candidate for a minor post in the Civil Service, studied for the priesthood, emigrated or, after years of hard grafting, became the owner of a pub. In the early years of this century the unevenness of opportunity, as between Protestants and Catholics, had begun to decline. The comment of a Northern Ireland politician that 'the trouble about Catholics is that they are only one generation educated' was, as a generalisation, not so far from the truth.

The Home Rule movement and ultimately the passing of the Home Rule Act of 1914, gave hope that the Catholics would have a bigger share of power and opportunity but many Protestants, with generations of power behind them, truly believed that the Catholic Irish were unfit for the responsibilities of government. On the outbreak of war in 1914 the operation of the Home Rule Act was deferred. Whether the North's opposition to it could have been overcome or whether some sort of compromise could have been negotiated is arguable but any prospect of keeping the island in one piece died with the Rising of 1916. The partition of Ireland which had become more than a possibility in 1914, was made certain by the organisers of the 1916 Rebellion. (Republican zealots would not accept this view. But Leon O'Broin's book *Dublin Castle and the 1916 Rising* casts an interesting light on the proposition that the Rising was justified because of Britain's intention of 'welshing' on the Home Rule proposals.)

1920 Onwards

The establishment of Northern Ireland in 1921 and the Irish Free State in 1922 was a settlement which sought to bring peace to the country by giving security within the United Kingdom to the majority of Irish Unionists and Dominion Home Rule to the majority of Irish Nationalists. But the Nationalists saw in the 1920 Act's reference to the possibility of unity and in the speech by King George V at the opening of the Northern Ireland Parliament, implied acceptance by Britain of the inevitability of the reunion of Ireland. The appointment of the Boundary Commission which was to make recommendations about adjustments of the border 'in accordance with the wishes of the people' confirmed them in their belief that a united Ireland was not far away because they felt that since election results had shown that Nationalists were in a majority in large areas of the six counties, the Boundary Commission's findings would surely result in a process of amputations which would leave only a small, unmanageable residue around Belfast to the Unionists.

The failure of the Boundary Commission to produce the results expected by the Ulster Nationalists, left many of them feeling disillusioned and abandoned. Thus, from the beginning, many non-Unionists have regarded Northern Ireland as an artificial creation devised and maintained by wily British politicians.

The first Northern Irish Government took office in civil war conditions. In the lawlessness then prevailing there must have been doubts about the state's survival. And amongst non-Unionists there were many who, although opposed to men of violence, were prepared to condone various forms of non-co-operation.

In these conditions it could be said that illiberal policies and repressive laws were necessary to enable the six northern counties to maintain the degree of self-government they had so recently been granted. Hence the expansion of the Special Constabulary (which had been founded by the British Government), special powers legislation, electoral gerrymandering etc, might be defended on the ground that the alternative was anarchy and extinction.

Even when the violence ended there was on the Catholic side no enthusiasm for the new government. Since politics in the North had for many years been a Catholic *versus* Protestant argument, what was seen as a victory for one side was accepted as defeat by the other. Some Catholic politicians and Church leaders advised their followers to have nothing to do with the Government of Northern Ireland.

In time, mistrust lessened somewhat and there were increasing signs that the Catholics were prepared to make the best of the situation by participating in politics and by taking employment under the new regime.

By the late 1930s the political atmosphere had cooled appreciably. Catholics were becoming less interested in the non-co-operative posture of earlier years; more and more were coming into Government employment. Although there were several attempts to begin a campaign of violence, their failure showed that the vast majority of the people had rejected violence. During the war years the desire for reconciliation seemed to take on a new impetus; there were even signs of marginal changes in traditional voting habits.

In the twenty years after the 1939–45 War the Northern Ireland Government and the Unionist Party, by failing to build on the growth of goodwill, missed an opportunity of winning the trust of a large section of the Catholic community. A little magnanimity (for example some concern about the more blatant discriminatory practices in local government; more just electoral arrangements in Derry) would have gone a long way.

The close association between the Orange Order and the Unionist Party made it virtually impossible for a Catholic to be a member of the Party. Some years ago when a leading Unionist was quoted as saying that Catholics could be members of the Party, the Orange Order immediately said 'No'. After lengthy cogitation the Party announced that Roman Catholics could be considered for membership 'provided they are found to be suitable people'. Needless to say, the Party's Headquarters in Glengall Street was not embarrassed by any rush of applicants anxious to be adjudged 'suitable people'.

Despite efforts by liberal-minded men (Terence O'Neill notably) to change its image, the Unionist Party was seen to be a party established by Protestants for Protestants and too few of its leaders showed any real concern for this being so.

The Catholics of Northern Ireland did, of course, benefit in many ways from the Government's progressive legislation; any fair-minded person would be bound to admit that in material things they would not have fared so well in a united Irish Republic. But when Unionists point to these benefits and ask why Catholics did not more actively support the Government, they talk as though the Protestant community has been sharing its wealth with the less well-deserving. (This attitude was outrageously typified by the comment of a schoolmaster in my presence: 'We should never have given them Maynooth'.)

It is probably inevitable that any group or class which has controlled government continuously for more than fifty years, which has had a specially privileged position in the country for centuries, should feel endowed with a divine right to govern and should resent any suggestion that the power and the privileges which have been at their exclusive disposal for so long should be shared with those who have been outside and often resentful of their special position.

It would however be wrong to leave the impression that over

the past sixty years one-third of the people of Northern Ireland have spent their time brooding on these matters. Many, many people on either side of the 'religious divide' have, without any inhibitions or reservations, established the most cordial (what in other places would be called 'normal') relationships with their neighbours. If divisive issues impinged on their thinking, they managed to shut their minds to allegations of past wrongs and to discard inheritated prejudices.

Unhappily recent events have revived mistrust and hostility. Now, when solutions are being sought, it is as well to understand that the roots of the evils that beset us lie deep in history.

Personal

When I joined the Civil Service in 1926, I did not do so out of any burning desire to serve the Union. (Who did?) Nor did it occur to me that by entering the service of the Government of Northern Ireland I was being in any way disloyal to my co-religionists. I wanted a job at a time when jobs were hard to get and I was appointed as a result of a competitive examination. And yet, particularly in those early years. I sometimes felt rather like a cuckoo in the nest. Protestants would ask me how I had 'got in'. And Catholics, particularly in Belfast, looked on me with suspicion. I must have 'influence'; I was probably a 'bad Catholic', perhaps secretly a Freemason or the son of a Freemason. Until quite recent times members of my own Church, including politicians and clerics, showed little interest in the welfare of Catholics in the Northern Ireland Civil Service. We had gone over to the 'other side' and if we thought we were not getting fair play, what did we expect? It should be emphasised that this attitude was particularly a Belfast one.

I believe that there have been serious discriminatory practices operating to the disadvantage of Catholics in parts of the public service and particularly in the local government services. At the same time I regret that, until rather late in the day, Catholics failed to make full use of the opportunities which were there; too often they accepted second-class citizenship as their lot and they got little help from their political representatives. Generations of Nationalist politicians were miserably resourceless in finding ways of drawing attention to the more scandalous allegations of unfair practices.

Throughout my service I never found in a civil servant or a Minister any curiosity about my political opinions and I have made a point of not telling anyone how I vote. But I cannot say that I did not encounter evidence of prejudice against Catholics. My colleagues in the Civil Service I acquit of any such charge but I believe that, until very late in the life of the Northern Ireland Parliament, Catholics were seriously at a disadvantage in those grades in which advancement was subject to the approval of Ministers. That is not to say that all Ministers would have approved such attitudes; there were honourable exceptions.

That paper was written in 1972, a year before I retired from the Civil Service. Although from the outside, things do not look quite as they then did, I don't think I would wish to change it except to suggest that the time has come for someone to tell us more than has yet been revealed about the extent to which the Orange Order influenced not just the organisation and the thinking of the Unionist Party but the policies and the actions of the Government. Evidence of the Order's considerable association with the Party can be seen in the fact that over the life of the Northern Ireland Parliament, Unionist Members who were not Orangemen were rare exceptions. Membership of the Order seemed to be a prerequisite for nomination.

The Cabinet Ministers with whom I came into contact were, almost without exception, kind to me, conscientious in their attitude to the public services, anxious to manage their departments efficiently. In private conversation many of them showed a liberality of mind pleasantly at variance with the accepted public image of Unionist politicians. One wondered how men for whom one could feel genuine respect could have acquiesced, even participated in, illiberal practices which, in the end, brought discredit on fifty years of government. I believe the answer lies in the relationship between the Orange Order and the Unionist Party; the influence of Orangeism was, I believe, considerable, often malevolent, and always an impediment to good government. But my impressions come from sounds emanating from behind doors which were closed to me. Someone who was in those locked rooms should tell us about what went on there.

Nineteen

During my last months in the Government service I participated with colleagues in examining aspects of devolved government on which administrators as well as politicians were expected to have something to say. The decision to work towards a 'power sharing' administration had been settled in the Cabinet in London. We were invited to examine and comment on various matters related to a settlement of that sort; how such a government might be shaped, how the public services could be affected, what difficulties or problems might arise in the reallocation of departmental functions, the effects of withholding certain services, such as law and order, from the new administration. Those deliberations took us into some quite new places. I believe that it was around that table that the term 'Irish Dimension', about which much has since been heard, was first used.

I had ceased to frequent the 'corridors of power' when, following the 'Sunningdale Agreement', a new form of multi-party government came into being. Moderate people (a head count of whom, in our community, even Solomon would not be capable) hoped that at last we had found a formula which would lead to the banishment of sectarianism from our political life. The failure of that experiment is now a matter of history. In a society in which democracy normally means rule by the elected majority, perhaps it was an artificial creation doomed to failure in any case but the event which brought it to an end, the so-called Ulster Workers' Council Strike, was the most bewildering and in some respects the most frightening experience of my life.

Our home was then in a suburb in south Belfast; our neighbours were, in the main, business and professional people with a sprinkling of academics and public service employees. We had the good fortune to be in an area which had remained virtually undisturbed by civil strife, amongst many kind people. When the Workers' Council strike began and the shops and business premises were closed under threats of violence we were, as all around us were, discommoded and not a little annoyed. Mr Merlyn Rees, the Secretary of State, with advice from his security chiefs, decided to adopt a 'low profile' which meant that the bully-boys who were on the move, closing shops and offices, halting traffic, ordering people off the streets, searching inoffensive citizens, went unchecked. No names were taken, no attempt made to send the gangs home or to remove the obstructions which had been placed across the Queen's highway.

I watched a group of club-carrying youths stopping and searching cars within sight of a large police station and a military check-point and I began to feel what life must have been like in Nazi Germany. During those days we were in the presence of raw Nazism.

It was a time of rumours and one which swept through our area and indeed, much of Belfast, was that the Catholics were in danger; people told us that lists of all the Catholic households, which were not very numerous where we lived, had been circulated so that, on an agreed signal, action could be taken to 'clear them out'. I don't think I believed that there was any real danger of a pogrom but with the atmosphere more tense every day, the forces of law and order apparently standing by, and all too many signs of lack of discipline amongst those who had been allowed to take charge, it was not easy for any household to remain calm. However unfounded the rumours might have been, many people were afraid; we knew families who went to bed with suitcases packed.

Merlyn Rees cannot look back on his handling of the UWC strike with any pride. In at least one household in Belfast he got no marks at all for judgement or courage or concern for the fears of law-abiding citizens.

Although the rumours and the inconveniences and the strutting cornerboys brought moments of concern, I went about my business more or less as usual, albeit on foot, and was never molested. For me the most bewildering aspect of the whole business was the extent to which the stoppage had the acquiescence, too often the active support, of what might be called the middle and upper middle classes; the people of means and property, professional people, industrialists, the directorial classes, some of the teachers of our youth, one or two highly-placed civil servants. Their sympathy and co-operation, in substantial numbers, ensured the effectiveness of the stoppage. Their response was, with undoubted exceptions, surprisingly and depressingly strong; it was astonishing that so many apparently intelligent, educated people could, in the presence of open anarchy, feel anything but revulsion and fearful concern for the future of their community.

Those events confirmed my opinion that centuries of privileged treatment created in Ireland a governing class of which, after the partitioning of the country, the Northern Ireland Unionists remain a residue; a possessive, unbending remnant of a powerful ruling class. The principal demands of the strikers were forgotten when the power-sharing Executive was forced to resign. Middle-class support evaporated overnight once power had been taken from the hands of the non-Unionists (which, sadly, means the Catholics).

The notes which have gone to the making of this book were begun some years ago when I realised that I have lived in a generation in which there have been a great many social changes, two World Wars and, in my own country, more attempts than ever before to settle a centuries-old problem. In the cradle I heard of Home Rule. Attempts at Irish Home Rule in various forms seem to stand as milestones over the years and the sound of political controversy has always been there. I have heard men preach revolution, seen men of peace condemned as traitors, witnessed the cruel manifestations of sectarian hatred; on occasions I have been close to scenes of violence and death; I have seen its ugliness and its cruelty and listened to the unbalanced fanaticism of some of its advocates. My present political views are different from those of my prejudiced youth, but I am totally convinced that whatever may be said about the righting of past wrongs or the maintenance of inherited power and privilege, there has been no moral justification for violence or the threat of violence for political ends in Ireland at any time in the present century.

Some time ago, watching a television programme, I heard a veteran of the 1916 Rising, then a respected academic, say that he believed that he and his friends had been wrong to follow Patrick Pearse's call to arms. In the same programme a retired Cabinet Minister in the Republic, whose political career owed much to his opposition to the establishment of the Irish Free State, confessed that he had come to the conclusion that the Civil War had been a mistake. Lord Brookeborough, for more than twenty years Prime Minister of Northern Ireland and for all of his long political life the outspoken champion of Protestantism, revealed, after he had retired, that he was an agnostic. In his old age Eamonn de Valera admitted to having had a change of mind about his approach to the partition issue. And amongst his last poems W.B. Yeats wrote:

> I lie awake night after night
> And never get the answers right.
> Did that play of mine send out
> Certain men the English shot?
> Did words of mine put too great strain
> On that woman's reeling brain?
> Could my spoken words have checked
> That whereby a house lay wrecked?

Old men have their second thoughts but the influences which guided their earlier years have not died. The deprivation and the waste are not yet at an end.

Postscript

When I have told of the moment when I came close to qualifying for a martyr's crown someone has invariably expressed disbelief. But since, on the few occasions on which I have mentioned the matter, my listeners were men who had come to the end of several hours of wining and dining, perhaps an element of disbelief should not surprise me; after-dinner audiences do not, in my experience, expect to be served undiluted history.

The date was 12 July 1939. Orangemen's Day in Belfast. The 249th Anniversary of the victory of William III over James II at the Battle of the Boyne.

About mid-morning there came to my bachelor accommodation in the University district a message informing me that a group of my friends had come together in an upstairs Select Lounge Bar on the Lisburn Road and inviting me to be of their company.

The bar in question was not far away but my progress was somewhat impeded by the crowds lining the footpaths on the Lisburn Road, watching the Orange procession go by. A hot sun shone, the spectators were noisy and good-humoured, enjoying the passing parade of drumming parties and banners and bands and solemn marching men in dark suits and Orange sashes. It was, for them, a yearly festival and it would be several hours before the end of the procession would pass.

The upstairs Select Lounge Bar was crowded. My friends, sitting in a tight circle in a corner of the room, hailed me with welcoming calls. The other customers were Orangemen, dozens of them in full regalia with their womenfolk and a sprinkling of small children. It surprised me that so many had dropped out of the parade, but the presence of wives and girl friends indicated that many of them had

203

arranged beforehand to meet at this well-stocked oasis about half way along the seven or eight mile route from Carlisle Circus to 'The Field' at Finaghy.

It was a noisy, relaxed, cheerful gathering with no hint of discord or hostility. Through the wide-open windows came the sounds of the bands and the drums and the marching thousands.

When it came to my turn to buy a round of drinks I made my way through the throng to the counter and as I stood there waiting to catch the barman's eye, I became conscious of a gathering of Orangemen behind me. It looked as though, in response to some secret signal, I had become trapped in a semi-circle of dark suits and Orange sashes. I didn't dare turn around, but in the mirror at the back of the bar I could see that I had been encircled, cut off from my friends in a co-ordinated operation. Each time I took a quick look at the mirror my pursuers seemed to have come closer; unsmiling and silent and menacing. I just stood there.

'Is your name Paddy?'

The speaker was standing at my elbow; a stocky, solemn-looking man whose Orange regalia bore the insignia of high office.

Since my companions had been using my Christian name freely there could be no equivocation about my answer. I spoke unemphatically.

'Yes.'

My mind was already preoccupied with how I would deal with the next, inevitable question. It came quickly.

'Are you a Roman Catholic?'

From what had gone before I knew that he knew the answer. And he knew that I knew that he knew... The landlord and I (unless he was off playing golf) were probably the only Roman Catholics on the premises at that moment.

The semicircle of Orange collarettes was now close in upon me, expectantly waiting for me to speak.

I knew what my answer must be but in the few seconds respite which I claimed I had no feeling of nobility, no thought about how brave men met their fate, no desire to make the moment a dramatic one. As I spoke my dry mouth told me that fear had set in.

'I am.'

It was now up to my interrogator. For a brief, torturing moment he fixed me with a one-eyed, expressionless look.

'What'll you have?'

For the remainder of that morning the Worshipful Master – for my questioner was the Master of a Lodge – and his friends supplied me with liquid refreshments up to – indeed, possibly beyond – the limits of my needs. When I sought to return some of their hospitality, I was shouted down. As individual friendships blossomed, I was assured repeatedly that I would be a welcome guest at any time I chose to visit their Lodge in Ballymacarret. To ensure that I would feel completely at home in their company they joined in singing Republican songs which expressed the most treasonable intentions. And all the time the sounds from the pageantry outside were coming through the open windows.

As the morning wore on I was introduced to Orange wives, kissed Orange mothers-in-law, dangled Orange babies on my knee. Somewhere there is a photograph of me, wearing an Orange sash, a small girl on my lap, sitting in the midst of a party of smiling males and females like a newly-returned prodigal son.

When at last I decided that I must take my leave, for which the imminence of lunchtime seemed inadequate justification, it was necessary to make a round of farewells. Finally, in the middle of the room, I engaged in a protracted hand-shaking epilogue with my good friend the Worshipful Master. To put a seal on our friendship he summarised his thinking about local political stances.

'This is a damned funny country,' he observed. 'There's one crowd sings "Wrap the Green Flag Round Me" and another crowd sings "Rule Britannia" and there's a lot of bloody civil servants up there in Stormont drawing twenty pounds a week and laughing at the lot of us.'

I ran for my life.

Index